To the *Purchaser*

of this Book, from its Publisher:—

ALL PAPER, *including the paper on which books are printed, as well as the materials which go into the manufacture of paper, is absolutely essential to the prosecution of the war.*

§§ Because of this, book publishers are now seriously restricted in the amount of paper which is available for books. For 1944 my firm is allowed but three-quarters as many pounds of paper as we used in the calendar year of 1942.

§§ This means that unless we economize in the use of paper in every way possible, we shall not be able to print anything like all of the books readers will demand of us. This is particularly important because our list abounds in good books published as long as twenty years ago (the Borzoi was founded in 1915) for which there is still steady demand and which we do not wish to let go out of print.

§§ We are therefore reducing the size of our books and also their thickness, and have made an effort, without sacrificing readability, to reduce the number of pages by getting more printed matter on each page. For this we must beg your indulgence, though I think that in many ways the smaller and thinner books are more attractive to handle and to read than their larger and fatter fellows. On the other hand, despite the shortage of all materials that go into the making of books and the critical manpower shortage among all printers and binders, we intend in every way possible to preserve those physical qualities which have long made Borzoi Books outstanding. We will use cloths of as good quality as we can procure and will maintain the same high standards of typographical and binding design.

Books on the Theatre
by George Jean Nathan

Mr. Nathan, who is the authority on the American theatre and drama for the *Encyclopædia Britannica* and the *Britannica Book of the Year,* has published the following books on the subjects:

Testament of a Critic
Art of the Night
The House of Satan
The Autobiography of an Attitude
Since Ibsen
Land of the Pilgrims' Pride
Materia Critica
Comedians All
The Popular Theatre
The Critic and the Drama
The Theatre, the Drama, the Girls
The World in Falseface
Mr. George Jean Nathan Presents
Another Book on the Theatre
The Avon Flows
Passing Judgments
The Intimate Notebooks of George Jean Nathan
The Theatre of the Moment
The Morning after the First Night
Encyclopædia of the Theatre
The Entertainment of a Nation
The Theatre Book of the Year, 1942–43

Books on Mr. Nathan

The Dramatic Criticism of George Jean Nathan, by Constance Frick, M.A.

The Theatre of George Jean Nathan, by Professor Isaac Goldberg, Ph.D.

The Quintessence of Nathanism, by Vladimar Kozlenko.

The Theatre Book of the Year

1943 ❧ 1944

The THEATRE Book
OF THE YEAR

1943 ✧ 1944

A Record and an Interpretation

BY

GEORGE JEAN NATHAN

ALFRED  A. KNOPF

NEW YORK : 1944

Manufactured in the United States of America
Published simultaneously in Canada by The Ryerson Press

PUBLISHED OCTOBER 16, 1944
SECOND PRINTING, NOVEMBER 1944

Foreword

THE PURPOSE OF this volume is to provide a complete critical record of the plays produced during the year in the New York theatre. All professional presentations, as well as those of the leading experimental groups, are included. The emphasis is upon interpretation rather than statistics, although the latter, when critically appropriate to the immediate subjects, are not omitted. The result, it is hoped, may offer an analytical picture of the stage of the American theatrical capital in the season of 1943–1944.

That season was one of the most financially prosperous in local history. Plays that in other years would have been abrupt failures achieved long runs, since the city was full of visitors with war-time money to spend and not too particular as to how they spent it. Those exhibits that failed despite the boom were save in a few exceptional cases so disastrously poor and so violently condemned by the daily press that it was hopeless for them to try to contend further. Not only in the metropolis was business otherwise extraordinarily lush; the same held true in most of the outlying cities.

So far as genuine dramatic quality went, the year was on the indigent side. There were pleasant plays and amusing plays but drama of real worth was largely absent, as the record will attest. The stress was on "entertainment," and various plays and musical shows met fully the public's partiality for the lighter fare.

The war was instrumental in diminishing or withholding the activities of a number of the better known American playwrights. Although Eugene O'Neill, for example, had completed two new plays and although both were ready for production, he preferred to delay their presentation until a future day, allowing that the psychic restlessness of audiences in war-time might not be conducive to any sound reaction to them. Robert Sherwood, devoting himself still to the Office of War Information, declared that he would abandon playwriting until peace relieved him of his governmental duties. S. N. Behrman negotiated no independent effort and contented himself with the revision of a play by Franz Werfel. And so, in one way or another, with several others.

The established American playwrights who did present themselves came off variously. Lillian Hellman's *The Searching Wind* was a keen disappointment, and indicated that her increasing absorption in contemporary alarms was taking its toll of her as a dramatist of any artistic merit. Maxwell Anderson's *Storm Operation* detracted further from his old standing. Rose Franken earned critical respect for her *Outrageous Fortune,* a meritorious play, and lost it in the instance of her *Doctors Disagree,* a surprisingly inept performance. William Saroyan's *Get Away, Old Man,* written some time before he entered the Army, was so badly botched both by himself and his producer that it was impossible to realize that the manuscript originally had points of merit. Elmer Rice sank lower in critical esteem with his *A New Life,* a machine-made and bogus performance. Moss Hart, following Irving Berlin's fine lead for the Army, concocted a show for the Air Forces, *Winged Victory,* which was heavily on the juvenile side. John van Druten, now an American citizen, contrived in *The Voice of the Turtle* a remarkably skilful and delightful comedy. Zoë Akins reappeared after a long absence so far as original and not merely adapted work was concerned with an agreeable comedy, *Mrs. January and Mr. Ex,* but one considerably beneath her early best mark. And Paul Osborn rested with an engaging free dramatization of the Richard Hughes novel, *A High Wind In Jamaica.*

The newcomers, with one exception, offered little testimony to quality. In *Career Angel,* Gerard M. Murray had an available, if synthetic, dramatic idea but indicated too weak a hand at dramaturgy to do much with it. The same with Thomas McGlynn in the case of *Caukey*. Howard Rigsby and Dorothy Heyward, the latter with some previous experience, managed in *South Pacific* an intelligent melodrama for part of the distance but then went to pieces. The actress Ruth Gordon contrived in *Over 21* simply a box-office personal vehicle, although the actress Margaret Curtis, working to the same personal end, provided in *A Highland Fling* a fantasy of considerable merit. George Seaton's " — *But Not Goodbye*" was a feeble paraphrase of *The Return of Peter Grimm,* and of no least consequence. Aided by the experienced Reginald Denham, the actress Mary Orr delivered in *Wallflower* a periodically comical minor farce.

In the musical field, *Carmen Jones* stood head and shoulders above all the other entries.

In the foreign dramatic field, Russia was represented by a mildly diverting little comedy by Alexander Afinogenov, *Listen, Professor!,* and England by a dated sex comedy by Frederick Lonsdale, *Another Love Story;* one of W. S. Maugham's minor efforts, *Sheppey,* written twelve years ago; and such trashy specimens as Dodie Smith's *Lovers and Friends,* Patrick Hamilton's *The Duke In Darkness,* and J. Lee Thompson's *Murder Without Crime.*

The season, in short and in sum, was, to repeat, mainly on the light entertainment side and was intermittently in that direction satisfactory, but negligible in drama of any altitude and definite importance.

Contents

Foreword   **v**

Honor List   **1**

The Year's Productions   **3**

Especially Interesting Performances   **327**

Index: Plays   **i**

Index: Authors and Composers   **iii**

The Theatre Book of the Year

1943 ❧ 1944

For Eventually

Jus

1945

Honor List

THE BEST NEW DRAMATIC PLAY:
OUTRAGEOUS FORTUNE,
by Rose Franken

THE BEST NEW COMEDY:
THE VOICE OF THE TURTLE,
by John van Druten

THE BEST NEW FANTASY:
A HIGHLAND FLING, by Margaret Curtis

THE BEST NEW FARCE:
SUDS IN YOUR EYE, by Jack Kirkland

THE BEST NEW MUSICAL EXHIBIT:
CARMEN JONES, by Oscar Hammerstein II
and Robert Russell Bennett

THE BEST MALE ACTING PERFORMANCE:
JOSÉ FERRER, in *Othello*

THE BEST FEMALE ACTING PERFORMANCE:
ELSIE FERGUSON, in *Outrageous Fortune*

THE BEST STAGE DIRECTOR:
JOHN VAN DRUTEN, in *The Voice of the Turtle*

THE BEST SCENE DESIGNER:
STEWART CHANEY, in *Jacobowsky And The Colonel,* etc.

THE BEST COSTUME DESIGNER, DRAMATIC:
MOTLEY, in *The Cherry Orchard*

THE BEST COSTUME DESIGNER, MUSICAL:
RAOUL PENE DU BOIS, in *Carmen Jones*

THE BEST STAGE LIGHTING:
HASSARD SHORT, in *Carmen Jones*

The Year's Productions

THE STUDENT PRINCE. June 8, 1943

A revival of the musical version of Meyer-Förster's time-honored romantic reverie, Old Heidelberg; *book and lyrics by Dorothy Donnelly, score by Sigmund Romberg. Produced to satisfactory returns for 153 performances by the Messrs. Shubert in the Broadway Theatre.*

Program

Prime Minister Von Mark		Lutz	Detmar Poppen
	William Pringle	Hubert	Jesse M. Cimberg
Dr. Engel	Everett Marshall	Grand Duchess Anastasia	
Prince Karl Franz			Nine Varela
	Frank Hornaday	Princess Margaret	
Ruder	Walter Johnson		Helene Arthur
Gretchen	Ann Pennington	Captain Tarnitz	
Detlef	Roy Barnes		Charles Chesney
Von Asterberg	Lyndon Crews	Countess Leydon	
Lucas	Daniel De Paolo		Helena Le Berthon
Kathie	Barbara Scully	Rudolph	Herman Magidson

SYNOPSIS: Prologue. Act I. Scene 1. *Ante-chamber in the Palace at Karlsburg.* Scene 2. *Garden of the Inn of the Three Golden Apples.* Act II. *Sitting-room of Prince Karl Franz at the Inn.* (*Three months later.*) Act III. *A room of state in Royal Palace at Karlsburg.* (*Two years later.*) Act IV. *Same as Act I.* (*Garden of the inn. Next day.*)
Time. *Spring, 1830.*

P RODUCED ORIGINALLY in 1924 and revived in 1931, this latest resuscitation of the Kathie-Prince Karl sigh-pumper brought nothing new to the exhibit save a song called "I've Never Heard About Love," although it brought a great deal in the way of staging that was old at least a quarter of a century before the date of its first showing.

We thus had the leading lady, not to mention the maid, periodically hoisted atop a table by the student chorus, there gayly to execute her singing and dancing whilst the students cavorted around her. We thus were reminded of our boyhood's stage when the tall, fat comedian, momentarily distracted, olfactively mistook a feather duster for a bouquet of flowers and when the contrasting diminutive assistant comedian lost himself under the tall, fat one's protruding corporation. The grand duchess, after a period of proper elegance, as of yore suddenly emitted a shrill whistle through her teeth to a lackadaisical lackey and subsequently threatened to swoon three or four times, necessitating the frantic rushing of chairs and divans underneath her by the palace attendants. The singing of a sentimental song by the tenor or baritone was usually prefaced by someone depositing a rose in his hand, and the crystal chandelier in the room of state was large enough to illuminate the whole of the 1893 Chicago World's Columbian Exhibition. The little serving maid pertly flounced her skirts up over her subcheeks with her every other move; the young princess duly conducted herself with the hauteur of De Wolf Hopper spurning the Rajah's gold; and the roistering Heidelberg student corps bibulously raised aloft steins that could not have held more than six ounces of beer at most.

Romberg's score, with its familiar "Golden Days," "Deep In My Heart," etc., remains still in its suggestion of Emmerich Kalman holding hands with Victor Herbert, the while Franz Lehar winks critically at the audience, an effective instrument for the emotionalization of all such yesterdaydreamers as are distilled into a copious wistfulness on coming upon an old pressed flower in a forgotten book, a lock of some long past flame's hair, or a cigarette picture of Queenie Vassar in tights. Which is to say, about eight out of every ten persons in the average present-day audience.

THOSE ENDEARING YOUNG CHARMS
JUNE 16, 1943

A sex morsel by Edward Chodorov. Produced for 60 performances by Max Gordon in the Booth Theatre.

PROGRAM

MRS. BRANDT	*Blanche Sweet*	LIEUT. HANK TROSPER
HELEN	*Virginia Gilmore*	*Zachary Scott*
JERRY	*Dean Harens*	

SYNOPSIS: Act I. *Friday evening.* Scene 1. *The Brandt living-room.* Scene 2. *Later.* Act II. *Saturday evening.* Scene 1. *The Brandt living-room.* Scene 2. *The hotel room.* Scene 3. *The living-room.* Act III. *Sunday morning.* Scene 1. *The Brandt living-room.* Scene 2. *The hotel room.*

THIS WAS UNDOUBTEDLY a bad play before the author undertook to rewrite it following an unsatisfactory try-out in Philadelphia. It is in its final shape an even worse one. The reasons are four: Mr. Chodorov does not know what he is talking about; he is apparently unfamiliar with the drama of the past and hence imagines himself to be daring when he is only humorously passé; he believes that comedy relief may be achieved by an exuberant delivery of comatose material; and, above all, he has been willing to cheat what measure of probity his old sex theme has by toadying to the box-office with a cheap and fraudulent moral ending. Mr. Chodorov has been in Hollywood.

Consider the reasons in order. First, Mr. Chodorov argues that a typical young woman of the year 1917 and directly thereafter would under the morals obtaining at the time be given to a strict puritanism, in contrast to one of the present who would be sexually emancipated. In 1917, Mr. Chodorov, according to the vital statistics, was thirteen years old. Let us discreetly rest the case there. Secondly, suffering in an unbecoming manner of speaking from dramatic delusions of glandeur, he considers himself thematically revolutionary in his plot of a present day young woman who gives herself freely to a young aviator who has fascinated her and who is about to go overseas to probable death. If he knew the theatre he would appreciate that, far from being the sexual novelty he thinks it is, that plot in one form or another has been paraded on the stage for years and was already gathering dust when Stanley Houghton, the Chodorov of his day, almost three decades ago put it over on the more virginal English and American critics and audiences.

Thirdly, both in his capacity as playwright and director Mr. Chodorov persuades himself that humor may be extracted from the essentially unhumorous through extrinsic actor means. That it may be on isolated occasions is true; an accomplished actor is sometimes successful in making the unfunny seem funny by virtue of his own comedy technique; but it can not be done, however adroit the actor, throughout a whole evening, as blood said to the turnip. And, fourthly, when Mr. Chodorov completely violates his theme of sexual freedom by tacking a matrimonial finale onto it, he offers himself as a mountebank with one eye on Will Hays and a potential movie sale. (The sale subsequently and duly went through.)

In a sex play like the one under consideration, whether it be good or bad, much depends upon the acceptability of the actors as individuals apart from their acting. An audience must believe, wholly apart from the performances, that the girl in the case is the sort who would inflame the libido of the man in the case, and vice versa. (There is less difference of tastes in an audience in such directions than is commonly imagined.) Virginia Gilmore here met the demand fully, in addition to the attractiveness of her performance. But so miscast and unbelievable was Zachary Scott in the role of the adducent male that persuasion was wholly non-existent, and the girl's passion for him on the refractorily comical side.

EARLY TO BED. June 17, 1943

A musical show with book and lyrics by George Marion, Jr., and tunes by Thomas ("Fats") Waller. Produced for a run of 11 months by Richard Kollmar in the Broadhurst Theatre.

Program

Lily-Ann	Jeni Le Gon	Pooch	Bob Howard
Mayor	Ralph Bunker	Pablo	George Zoritch
Marcella	Louise Jarvis	El Magnifico	Richard Kollmar
Pauline	Choo Choo Johnson	Lois	Jane Deering
Interlude	Peggy Cordrey	Wilbur	Jimmy Gardiner
Jessica	Mary Small	Coach	George Baxter
Butch	Eleanor Boleyn	Eileen	Jane Kean
Duchess	Helen Bennett	Charlotte	Charlotte Maye
Minerva	Honey Murray	Burt	Burt Harger
Madame Rowena		Naomi	Evelyn Ward
	Muriel Angelus	Admiral Saint-Cassette	
Isabella	Angela Greene		Franklyn Fox

SYNOPSIS: Act I. Scene 1. *A bar in New York City.* Scene 2. *Villa of the Angry Pigeon, Martinique. Daybreak.* Scene 3. *A corridor. Later that morning.* Scene 4. *Bedroom of the royal suite.* Scene 5. *The Angry Pigeon. Still later that morning.* Act II. Scene 1. *Again the bar, in New York City.* Scene 2. *Corridor of the Angry Pigeon. That afternoon.* Scene 3. *The Angry Pigeon. That evening.* Scene 4. *Tradesmen's entrance to the Angry Pigeon. Later that night.* Scene 5. *The Angry Pigeon. Later that afternoon.*

THE FIRST MUSICAL SHOW of the previous season, *By Jupiter,* was sponsored in part by this same Mr. Kollmar, who seems to be of the conviction that all that is necessary for the book of any such pastime is one basic joke prolonged for two hours. In *By Jupiter* the joke consisted in aligning masculine women against effeminate men, with the obvious single facetious result. In the present instance it consists in causing several males to mistake a house of ill-fame for a girls' boarding school, with a similarly obvious single facetious result. In the second case as in the first, the wear and

tear on one's humorous reaction is readily to be anticipated.

The theme of a bordello mistaken for an innocent institution, or vice versa, is an even more familiar theatrical device than the just before noted one concerned with a young
woman's anatomical surrender to a young man bound for
a perilous mission from which he may never return. In the
one instance as in the other its later-day difficulty is that so
few changes remain to be rung on it that, once the idea is
stated, the rest of the evening most often takes on the complexion of a stalled automobile originally headed for a picnic. When, as in *Early To Bed,* the first male imagines he is
in a fashionable girls' school, some mild amusement, despite the antiquity of the idea, may be forthcoming. But
when a second male subsequently imagines it, and then a
third and even fourth, humor becomes as foreign to the situation as laughter to a funeral or British farce. In the present show, however, considerable realism was imparted to
the aforesaid male's imaginings by the girls hired by the
management. Most of them in looks and figure might have
deceived any man accustomed to the superior contours encountered in the better bordellos into confusing them with
girls in the average finishing school.

It was thus that the producer's failure to provide sufficient external distraction focused the attention altogether
too steadily on the book, and to the show's consequent critical undoing. Save for some striking costume color by the
talented Miles White and some romantic tropical settings
by George Jenkins, with an attractive colored miss named
Jeni Le Gon thrown in, there was little on the stage, including Waller's juke tunes, to divert the notice from that depressing, heavily repeated, initial plot whimsy.

Which brings us to an element in our contemporary musical shows that for some time now has impressed itself upon
the Athenians amongst us. I refer, obviously and once
again, to the girls. And what is there about the girls that
has brought the aforesaid purists to ponder? It is this: that
for all the splendor of the shows in other directions they
are in the overwhelming main devoid of the kind of young

women who in the yesterdays lent to them that air of romance, that flavor of midnight champagne and that fillip to
the imagination without which they aren't all they should
be, save possibly in the appetite of a bourgeois box-office.

I am not speaking particularly of the ladies of the chorus,
since every few years some show up who may compare fa-
vorably with ensemble belles of other days, although even
in this direction considerable debate money might be won
by anyone who ventured in rebuttal such memorable con-
gresses of ticklers as composed the choruses of old shows
like *The Wild Rose, The Belle of New York, The Casino
Girl, Havana* and, of course the Ziegfeld *Follies*. If per-
chance some upstart challengingly offers to lay his cash on
the line, paternally counsel him to recall, for instance, the
names of some of the girls who figured at one time or another in the chorus of the first-mentioned feast, generally
agreed by historians to be the all-time high in the field of
American beauty. The names: Lotta Faust, embalmed for
posterity in the Malcolm Strauss portraits; Evelyn Nesbit,
whose youthful loveliness is still preserved in the celebrated Sarony photograph showing her curled up on a
white bearskin rug; little Marguerite Clark, destined for
future stage and screen acclaim, with eyes like wondering
chestnuts and hair like a shower of Coca-Cola; and Elsie
Ferguson, who was to become a dramatic star, looking for
all the world like a kid Clare Boothe Luce, minus politics.

More: Marie George, who made the college boys of the
period sigh so loudly that football cheer-leaders thought for
a time of substituting the sighs for the college yells; Madge
Marston, with the surprised look of always just having had
her feelings pleasantly hurt; Nina Randall and Viola Carl-
sted, who had the beaux of the town, including Stanford
White, Jimmy Breese and Freddie Gebhard, dispatching
them roses and caviar in beer-wagon loads; and Irene
Bishop, with eyes like sunshine after rain and a figure like
a cobra about to strike. And more still: Teddie Du Coe,
who, if Ziegfeld had then been around, would have had the
future master screaming for joy; Belva Don Kersley, one of
whose cigarette pictures was worth six Pauline Halls and

all of fourteen Pattis on the swap bourse; Neva Aymar, with
a face like a Corot twilight and such a shape as caused Jim
Huneker, Vance Thompson, Percy Pollard and even Henry
Krehbiel to form a quartet on the spot and rattle the glasses
behind Luchow's bar with renditions of "Ave Neva!"; and
tantalizing Hazel Manchester, to whom four members of
Teddy Roosevelt's cabinet sent hopefully autographed photographs, unsolicited.

And that, though tops, was still a chorus line not alone.
Among others, let the aforesaid upstart be apprised, were
lines offering such rapturous souvenirs as those that composed the "Hello, People, Hello" squad in the later *Havana,* including Erminie Clarke of the peculiarly impressive
drooped shoulders; Dorothy Sayce, with the soft smile of a
Partenkirchen awakening to a Spring morning, whom the
gallants of the town were even willing to ferry back to her
Hoboken fireside in return for a mere mutual midnight
glass at the marble bar of the Beaux Arts; and half a dozen
other such visions. And as those in the earlier *The Casino
Girl, A Dangerous Maid, The Princess Chic, San Toy, The
Geisha, The Telephone Girl, In Gay New York,* and *The
Whirl of the Town.* Let comparison be as odious as is its
wont, yet where among the current crop of sabbatical Powers models and the like, even those from Texas, will you
find the equivalents of, for example, Vashti Earle, probably
the most beautiful girl ever to adorn an American chorus;
or Diamond Donner, who looked as if Tommy Lyman had
sung her; or Geraldine Fair, of the mouth like a Clover
Club cocktail; or Theresa Vaughn, with legs that only Ar-
chie Gunn could draw and a profile that only Penrhyn Stan-
laws later could dream up? And where the present equals
of other such poppers as golden Pauline Chase, later to become London's pet Peter Pan; or Gladys Wallis, who looked
like all the theoretical wonderful little girls who lived next
door in boyhood; or Camille Clifford, who moved like the
fingers of de Pachmann over Chopin; or Clara Selton, Ethel
Elverton, Edna McClure, Edna Hunter, Vonnie Hoyt, May
Naudain, Minnie Ashley, Nellie Follis, Edna Dodsworth,
Ruby Reid, and all that fragrant and memorable bouquet?

It is perfectly true that not all the girls of those days were like these; very far from it. A liberal measure of them, despite the auld-lang-syners, were substantial clock-stoppers. The much touted original *Florodora* sextette, for just one example, offered only one girl out of the whole six with anything in the way of looks above the modest average. But nevertheless, best for best, the girls you get today are with small exception relative selling-platers. The discovery of even one in the line whom you can look at with a feeling worthy of Michelangelo or a Colony headwaiter is a rarity.

Since, however, it is the principals, not the chorus maidens, who are supposed to occupy our thesis attention, let us to the main business. It is not, be reminded, that it is talent of which we speak but, solely and sheerly, looks. And what do we find? What we find is all kinds of talent but, when it comes to those looks, little or nothing. Consider in this regard some of the principals in the musical shows of the last few years, along with some of those in the season under consideration, and compare them with various women of the past:

Ethel Merman, in *Something For The Boys,* an otherwise admirable performer whom even her most enthusiastic admirers wouldn't think of comparing with Irene Bentley (who that ever saw her can forget that face which looked as if the angels had cooked it up out of apricots and honey and Leslie Stuart?) , or with Paula Edwards, whose long brown hair shadowing musing eyes gave her the appearance of a gentle Autumn evening, or with Mabelle Gilman, the gayer type of horticulture whose amused smile took her attraction lightly in its stride.

Muriel Angelus in this *Early To Bed* and, on the other hand, dark, lovely May De Sousa; or Virginia Earle of the hair like a rippling sunlit stream and the carriage of one who had suppered on sleigh-bells; or Helen Hale, the Jenny Wren of *Woodland,* who for all of Wellesley still suggested a bright amber Chinese lantern blown by the evening winds.

Mary Martin in *One Touch of Venus* and, in other days and not so far back, Jessie Matthews (the toast of New York and Long Island when Charlie Cochran first bequeathed her to America), or Marilyn Miller (no footnote necessary), or Kathleen Martyn, whose English loveliness floored even Ziegfeld's surfeited connoisseurs.

Joan Roberts in *Oklahoma!* and such tours de force as Edna May, whose "Follow Me" in *The Belle of New York* was sheer redundance, or that other Edna, the cute Wallace, whose saucy dazzle is still vividly remembered by men who can't for the life of them recall who played the lead in even last season's *Count Me In* and *Once Over Lightly*, or Sandol Milliken, above all Sandol Milliken, who always suggested a Cinderella democratically turning her coach back into a pumpkin and who seemed to have been born in the window of a wedding-cake shop.

Marta Eggerth in the latest revival of *The Merry Widow*, Jarmila Novotna in *Helen Goes To Troy*, Rosemary Lane in *Best Foot Forward*, Marie Nash in *Viva O'Brien*, Mary Jane Walsh in *Let's Face It* and *Allah Be Praised!*, Helen Gleason in *Night of Love*, Gertrude Niesen in *Follow The Girls*, Mitzi Green and Sue Ryan in this and that — and then yesterday's Eleanor Mayo (recall *Miss Bob White*), and Camille D'Arville (a Lillian Russell from Holland), and that dancing combination of willow and Moselle named Frances Pritchard, and Mabel Carrier, and surely, surely, the matchless, peerless Marie Doro of *The Circus Girl, The Billionaire* and *The Girl From Kay's*, and Adele Astaire, who could laugh beauty into a face that was not particularly beautiful and dance beauty into a figure that was.

And any of the other present-day musical show principals you happen to think of — compare them, if you will, with Pauline Frederick, one of the legendary lilies of the American theatre, and Phyllis Rankin, who vied with Edna May for honors when, in *The Belle of New York*, she set the last hold-out's heart a-flutter with "When We Are Married," and Edna Goodrich (often wrongly nominated as having started in the original *Florodora* sextette; she was in one of the subsequent sextettes and outlooked the girls in the original by some ten thousand points), and the so pretty Julia Sanderson. And, if you need a couple of additional irresistible statistics, Violet McMillen, the blonde flowerlet whose looks alone guaranteed the original Chicago run of 465 performances for the same *The Time, The Place and The Girl* that last year, with Irene Hilda in the role, ran only a few nights in New York; and Christie MacDonald, who resembled a pint of champagne in a Delft vase.

But all, nevertheless, is not lost, which admission, it is to be hoped, will reassure skeptics who may by now conceivably have dismissed the present chronicler as an old fogy. For in the musical shows' greenhouses there are some fair blossoms that, as yet awaiting their full day in court, may at least in a measure help to balance the scales. Marcy Wescott, for example, who disappeared after *Too Many Girls,* may push plump, blonde, little Della Fox, that favorite pin-up girl of the De Wolf Hopper era, completely out of memory with her slender, blonde, mischievous appeal. Nanette Fabray, who succeeded Constance Moore in *By Jupiter* late last season and has this season reappeared in *My Dear Public* and *Jackpot,* with her dark, shining beauty and figure like a warm Katharine Hepburn may exile from sentimental recollection not only the dark delight of Eva Fallon that illuminated Herald Square in the early 1900's but also to a degree the dark delight of Gertrude Bryan that shone on Times Square some years later.

Lotus Robb, who adorned the stage all too briefly fifteen or so years ago, isn't easy to forget when the wine is waltzing, nor is Mollie King, who all in soft pink danced her fairness into men's reveries at about the same time. But Mary Roche and Pat Marshall, seen briefly in *What's Up,* have looks enough to satisfy anyone for, anyway, a couple of hours; and Evelyn Wyckoff, who was sacrificed to the overnight failure, *The Lady Comes Across,* and who has been on the road with *Oklahoma!,* has enough for a couple of hours extra. Louise Brown, whose gentle bloom warmed the musical stage eighteen years ago; Constance Carpenter, who ornamented the original production of *A Connecticut Yankee;* and Irene Delroy, who brought to the old *Greenwich Village Follies* their single touch of feminine radiance — they ornament memorabilia still. But Milada Mladova,

who has come to view this season in *The Merry Widow* and
Allah Be Praised!, is slipper-drinking material; Lucille
Norman, who was introduced to us last season in *Show
Time*, isn't half-bad; Vera-Ellen of *A Connecticut Yankee*
in revival is summa cum; and Jeni Le Gon, the hereinbefore noted dusky nosegay in this *Early To Bed*, while maybe
no Evelyn Laye or even Jacqueline Hunter, is a spangle
hardly to be sniffed at.

STARS ON ICE. June 24, 1943

A soi-disant second edition of last season's skating spectacle of the same name, which negotiated 427 performances. Produced with equal success by Sonja Henie and Arthur M. Wirtz in the Center Theatre.

PRINCIPALS

Freddie Trenkler, Carol Lynne, Mary Jane Yeo, Paul Duke, May Judels, Twinkle Watts, Muriel Pack, James Wright, Geoffe Stevens, et al.

SINCE THE SHOW consisted for the greater part in a repetition of the antecedent show's numbers, the ethics of the management in implying that it contained a majority of new features were open to criticism, though apparently not on the part of addicts to these ice skating exhibits who seem to rejoice in laying out their money for much the same old thing year after year. This notation is therefore simply for the record. The appraisal of the previous show, in *The Theatre Book Of The Year, 1942–1943*, sufficiently covers the present offering. Save for some performing newcomers who repeated under different program titles the glides and twirls of the performers they supplanted, a spectacle or two that seemed to have been borrowed from the *It Happens On Ice* shows of two and three seasons before, and a few new costumes, the two exhibits were as alike, and in their likeness as monotonous and unstimulating, as a pair of metronomes timing the brewing of a vat of iced tea. At least in the impression of any spectator who is unable to see anything remarkably different in fifty skaters clad in white and programmed as a "Jack Frost Ballet," and the identical fifty clad in brown, executing the same tricks, and programmed as an "Autumn Leaves Ballet."

THE VAGABOND KING. June 29, 1943

A failure revival of the musical play based upon Justin Huntly McCarthy's If I Were King. *Book and lyrics by Brian Hooker and Russell Janney; music by Rudolf Friml. Produced for a brief run by Russell Janney in the Shubert Theatre.*

Program

Rene De Montigny		François Villon	John Brownlee
	Artells Dickson	Katherine De Vaucelles	
Casin Cholet	Bert Stanley		Frances McCann
Jehan Le Loup	George Karle	Thibaut D'Aussigny	Ben Roberts
Margot	Jann Moore	Lady Mary	Teri Keane
Isabeau	Evelyn Wick	Noel of Anjou	Dan Gallagher
Jehanneton	Rosalind Madison	Oliver Le Dain	Curtis Cooksey
Huguette Du Hamel		Herald of Burgundy	
	Arline Thomson		Earl Ashcroft
Guy Tabarie	Will H. Philbrick	The Queen	Betty Berry
Tristan L'Hermite		The Hangman	Craig Newton
	Douglas Gilmore	The Cardinal	Vincent Henry
Louis XI	José Ruben		

SYNOPSIS: Part I. *The Fir Cone Tavern.* Part II. (a) *The court: that night.* (b) *The court: next morning.* Part III. *The court garden. The masque.* Part IV. (a) *A gate of old Paris.* (b) *The place de Greve.*

The entire action takes place in old Paris in the period of Louis XI.

First produced in 1926 and achieving a New York run of 511 performances this purple mash of Villon made king of France for a day by Louis XI calls for something of the grand stage manner if it is to get by. In its initial presentation it got it, at least to a sufficient degree. In this revival the manner suggested a fancy dress party of haberdashery clerks and their ladies. It was pretty disturbing to hear a Villon who articulated some such line as "Would it not be a pity, sweet lady?" as "Would ut nut be a pity, sweat lady?" Nor was it less disconcerting to hear a stately Katherine de Vaucelles exude such Brooklyn titbits as "wuz" and "becuz." Add to this comportment on the part of all the royalty save Louis (played by José Ruben) which was more aptly suited to something like *Three Men On a Horse,* some dreadful 52nd Street night-club clowning on the part an even more dreadful comedian named Philbrick, tights that mistook themselves for accordions and played wayward duets with the actors' knees, and stage lighting so inappropriately bright that you could have read a time capsule reduction of *The Forsyte Saga* in the back row of the theatre, and you have an idea of the romantic flavor of the occasion. And add further a corps de ballet with legs the size of wine casks and whose combined virtuosity seemed to consist solely in standing on its big toe, grinning, and turning slowly around four times, and you have an idea plus.

Friml's score remained the evening's one asset. *Song Of The Vagabonds, Only A Rose, Love Me Tonight,* the *Huguette* waltz, and the rest retained much of their old sentimental sauce, even though the voices to which some of them were entrusted appeared to confuse certain of their measures with college yells. Perhaps the program notes hinted at the reason. Mr. Brownlee, the Villon of the occasion, they informed us, "was from childhood a splendid cricketer, swimmer, golfer and all-around athlete," and Miss McCann, the Lady Katherine, "aspired to rival Annette Kellermann as a swimmer and diver, securing many trophies, medals and diplomas; she was chosen as one of the team to represent the Golden State at the Olympic games in Berlin in 1936 . . ."

THE ARMY PLAY–BY–PLAY. August 2, 1943

Five short plays selected by a prize jury composed of Elmer Rice, Kenyon Nicholson, Russel Crouse, Frederick Lonsdale and John Golden, written, acted, directed and designed by enlisted men from various military posts. Produced for a limited engagement by John Golden and the Special Service Branch, Headquarters of the Second Service Command, in the Martin Beck Theatre.

PROGRAM

Where E'er We Go, by Private John B. O'Dea
First Cousins, by Corporal Kurt S. Kasznar
Button Your Lip, by Private Irving G. Neiman
Mail Call, by Air Cadet Ralph Nelson
Pack Up Your Troubles, by Private Alfred D. Geto

ALL THE AUTHORS save one, Neiman, had theatrical experience before they donned uniforms. The prevailing impression that the plays sprang full-fledged from the heels of soldiers who before they entered the service had had no slightest connection with the stage was thus ill-founded, but most of the reviewers, by way of promoting patriotism into' chauvinism, did little to discourage it. Nelson was an actor who had appeared with Lunt and Fontanne in *Idiot's Delight, There Shall Be No Night,* and other plays. O'Dea had played on European and Australian stages as well as on the stages of New York and California. Kasznar had been associated with Max Reinhardt in the Salzburg festivals and had produced and directed *Crazy With the Heat* on Broadway. And Geto had been associated with stock companies as a writer, actor and director.

The plays are of varying quality. O'Dea's *Where E'er We Go* shows a group of soldiers about to leave for an unknown destination, wildly guessing where they are headed, and exchanging articles of apparel with one another best suited to the climate they think they are going to encounter. Some of the incidental humor, particularly that involving the kind of girls they may find when they get there, is natural and amusing. Some of it, on the other hand, like selling a heavy overcoat in anticipation of the tropics and collapsing when the destination is announced to be Alaska, is less successful.

Kasznar's *First Cousins* is a minor Grand Guignol melodrama laid in a German submarine. One of a group of captured American seamen is of German descent, pretends to be a traitor, persuades the German commander that he is his cousin, gains his confidence, kills him, achieves control of the submarine, and delivers his American brothers to safety. Pretty bad.

Neiman's *Button Your Lip,* laid in the washroom of a barracks at Camp Downey, is comical low stuff retained by an ear that has caught nicely the idiosyncrasies of soldiers' talk. Around the anticipated visit to the barracks of a well-known female screen star, the author has sketched a picture of imbecility that has a deal of freshness and hilarity.

Nelson's *Mail Call* — the scene is a shelter in an almost destroyed village behind the lines — is sentimentality plus. One of the men, an overly sensitive fellow, has proved cowardly in action. His buddies comprehend his fear in the face of fire and, when he is killed, plan to apprise his family that he died the death of a hero. Only one man objects. The dead soldier was a coward, he proclaims, and that is that. The enemy again attacks, and the objector in turn proves himself a coward, whereupon the buddies force him to sign the letter to the other man's family. Pretty bad.

Geto's *Pack Up Your Troubles* is a comedy-melodrama about Nazi spies laid in a warehouse at a receiving station. The comedy consists in a soldier's efforts to make a long distance telephone call to the hospital where his wife is giving birth to a baby and is based primarily on his inability to find the right change to put into the slot and the constant getting of wrong numbers. The melodrama consists in trapping the Nazi spies who are intent upon blowing up a troop train. The comedy is furthered by the spectacle of the soldier-papa in his underwear; the melodrama by the hiding of the eavesdroppers under the table around which the spies are doing their plotting. No.

Several of the performances in the various plays were uncommonly good, although it was difficult, in view of the complexity of the playbill, to apportion credit where credit was due. It is easy enough, in the case of the usual program, to pick out the actor you want merely by reading from the left (Sir Montague Titt) to the right (John P. Jones). But it is far from easy when the program is loaded with, on the left, a multiplicity of Joes, Texs, Sams, Elmers, Eddies, Captains, Sergeants, Privates, etc., and, on the right, registry numerals running into eight figures, ranks, companies, branches of service, and what not else.

TRY AND GET IT. August 2, 1943

A farce by Sheldon Davis, previously titled The Key To
Vivy's Room, Sex Takes A Holiday, Cinderella Goes To
Town, *and* Goodbye To Love. *Produced for immediate fail-
ure by A. H. Woods in the Cort Theatre.*

Program

Mignonette	*Hattie Noel*	Barry Pickens	*Donald Murphy*
Evelyn La Rue	*Virginia Smith*	Mickey O'Toole	*Raymond Rand*
Vivienne Gordon	*Iris Hall*	Simon Beazle	*Charles Knight*
Thomas Barton	*Albert Bergh*	Grace Barton	*Claire Meade*
Sarah Smith	*Margaret Early*		

SYNOPSIS: Act I. *A morning in January, 1942.* Act II. Scene 1.
Late that night. Scene 2. *Eleven o'clock the next morning.* Act III. *Late
the same day.*

*The entire action takes place in Vivienne Gordon's apartment in
New York City.*

THE PRODUCER of *Up In Mabel's Room, Getting Gertie's
Garter, Parlor, Bedroom and Bath, The Demi-Virgin,* and
Ladies' Night In A Turkish Bath has never been distin-
guished for subtlety and his reputation remains unblemished with the production of *Try And Get It.* Like its pred-
ecessors, it takes over the elements of the poorer old French
farce and makes them tenfold more elementary, italicizing
the dirt, vulgarizing the vulgar to the n-th, and substituting
five-cent smut for ten-cent innuendo. The tone of the whole
is registered within three seconds after the first curtain rises.
A fat Negro maid waddles to the door of the bedroom in the
kept blonde's apartment and shouts to her mistress, "Drag
your fanny outa bed, Miss Vivienne; it's ten o'clock!"

What follows for the rest of the evening is of a piece.
Evelyn La Rue, Vivienne's friend, who confesses to being
such a pushover that her tail needs only a bit of chalk to
blend its red and blue with the national flag and whose comedy consists mainly in wriggling the aforesaid anatomical

section and ejaculating "Pu-lease!," follows on the maid's
heels and urges Vivienne to can the old goat who is putting
up the dough for her and join her in a week-end with a
coupla muscular football players from Yale. Vivienne says
O.K., as she needs the exercise she has been missing, but
that she will have to find someone to take her place, since
the old goat has insisted she entertain, so to speak, an old
goat friend of his who is coming to town and since he himself can't be around for certain reasons, meaning a wife.

As luck would have it, there then instantaneously happens into the apartment a young miss named Sarah Smith,
who is brought on the scene by the playwright under the
pretext of being a home cookie-baker. Sarah wears horn-
rimmed glasses, a pork-pie hat and a Klein's dress, but when
she feels at one of Vivienne's silk gowns lying on the sofa
both Vivienne and Evelyn La Rue get an inspiration. "Put
it on!" they command, and Sarah strips down to her old-
fashioned long white muslin slip, dons the gown, turns her
back to the audience, is hair-dressed, rouged and mascara'd
by Evelyn, turns around again, and makes the audience
aghast at her lovely metamorphosis, although, except for
the horn-rimmed glasses and pork-pie hat, she doesn't look
materially different to the skeptics than she looked before.

Vivienne and Evelyn now instal Sarah in the apartment
and rush forth to join the coupla football players, pausing
only long enough, for twenty minutes or so, to roll on their
tongues the amatory delights that are to be theirs. Rings
the door-bell. It is Vivienne's old goat's old goat friend
whom she is supposed to make up to. But no! Who should
enter but the handsome young son of the old goat's old
goat friend! Little Sarah, having been told to expect an oc-
togenarian and frightened for the safety of her virtue, collapses.

Barry — that is the handsome one's name — naturally
thinks Sarah is Vivienne and, knowing all about Viv, proceeds forthwith to go to work on her. He plies the little one
with alcoholic liquor; he seeks subtly to reduce her to his
will by undressing and donning beautiful silk polka-dotted
pajamas; he cleverly suggests that they begin telling each

other dirty stories. But Sarah, when the awful moment threatens, persuades Mignonette, the Negro maid, to sleep at the foot of her bed and thus foil the wolf.

This obviously makes the wolf very angry indeed and, after another vain half hour of trying to make the little one, he wrathfully puts on his clothes and starts to depart. Enter Vivienne. "Who's that?," she demands of the little one. "Who's that wonderful man?" The little one tells her. "Those goddam football players!" moans Vivy. Curtain.

Follows an hour more, with the old goat's wife showing up, getting drunk, and consoling Vivy for the time she has had to spend in her impotent husband's company; with Evelyn La Rue shaking her rear at all and sundry; with the Negro maid ambling on and off remarking on her own happy promiscuity; with little Sarah turning out to be a gold-digging bitch of the first water; and with the final sop of holy matrimony. It's all there, save for the open articulation of the four-letter word for sexual intercourse and the sight of a confined-to-the-wings active watercloset.

It was the management's intuition, by way of publicity, to present keys to every male buying a ticket and to reward the one with the right key to Vivy's bedroom with a $25 war bond. The authorities quashed the idea on the ground that it was in the nature of a lottery. The management might have got around the ban and taken the words right out of the audience's mouth by rewarding the possessor of the door-opening key with a jug of disinfectant. (Less than a week's supply of jugs would have appeared on its expense account.)

THE TWO MRS. CARROLLS. August 3, 1943

A play by Martin Vale, nom de plume of the widow of play-wright Bayard Veiller. Produced with inexplicable success by Robert Reud and Paul Czinner in the Booth Theatre.

Program

Geoffrey	*Victor Jory*	Mrs. Latham	*Margery Maude*
Clemence	*Michelette Burani*	Cecily Harden	*Irene Worth*
Pennington	*Stiano Braggiotti*	Dr. Tuttle	*Philip Tonge*
Sally	*Elisabeth Bergner*	Harriet	*Vera Allen*

SYNOPSIS: Act I. Scene 1. Living-room. May afternoon. Scene 2. The same. Three months later. Scene 3. The same. That afternoon. Act II. Scene 1. The same. That evening, after dinner. Scene 2. Sally's bedroom. A moment later.

The action takes place in the Villa La Vista in the south of France.

This is what is known in intellectual Broadway circles as a "psychological" murder play, which is to say a sub-melo-drama in which the actors depict their soul struggles by making worried faces, walking hesitantly around the stage, and speaking their lines as if the playwright had left out every other word, which would have been an improvement.

The plot, which in one form or another has done valiant service over a period of a quarter of a century, on the present occasion concerns an artist who resorts to poisoning his successive wives when they get in the way of a new romance and who, when he isn't furtively doping their food and drink, is given to extended meditations on the spiritual beauty of death. In this instance, the business is orchestrated to one of those theatrical tropical winds — the scene is the French Riviera — which exercise a peculiar effect upon people and which conveniently, when the action demands, alternately blow window blinds open and shut with a terrifying bang, cause the members of the cast nervously to peer into space, and make the hands of the household maid so tremble that she almost drops whatever she may be serving. If, furthermore, you have been wondering whatever became of that old Pinero scene wherein a suspicious husband cross-examines his wife by way of dragging the truth from her, wonder no longer; it is here. As is the bedroom scene from the same period of French drama wherein the husband and wife, following the cross-examination scene, have it out to the bitter end. And as is also the incidental old Riviera-play badinage about the peccadillos of royalty. And as are still further the characters of the wife's highminded and devoted ex-fiancé; the fashionable, blasé medico who deplores that the bottle of champagne hurled across the gambling casino at Monte Carlo by an indignant husband at his errant wife was Pol Roger '21; the siren in the body-clinging gown who seductively puffs at a cigarette in a six-inch holder and galvanizes the libido of the artist; the latter who, when he first beholds her draped against the fireplace, raptly cries out, "Don't move; stay exactly where you are! Wonderful! You are the epitome of all I have been seeking! Will you be my model? I shall paint you for my masterpiece!"; etc.

The general devices are not less neighborly. The husband-poisoner pulls out the desk drawers, upsets the furniture and breaks a window pane to make it appear that a burglar has been responsible for the contemplated murder. The wires of the telephone over which the terrified wife seeks aid are announced by the husband to have been cut. A carelessly dropped corsage informs the wife that, despite denials, her rival has had a rendezvous with her husband. Doors are frantically pounded on; the bell cord is ripped from the wall to forestall the maid's inconvenient intrusion; the villain horrifies the heroine, who has locked the door against him, by suddenly appearing at the French window; the wife, suspecting her husband's evil intent, pretends accidentally to have spilled the poisoned drink on the floor; and the poison itself, which is supposed to take two or three weeks to work in the case of the undesired wives, obligingly contrives at the final curtain to kill the husband in two seconds flat.

Elisabeth Bergner, the celebrated German actress who

engaged the star role, once again brought American critics to ponder on the high estate she occupied in her native land in the pre-Hitler period. Although she indicated some improvement over her absurdly artificial performance of eight years ago in *Escape Me Never,* she still failed to suggest that, direction or not, she understands in the least how to incorporate her own histrionism into the compositional flow of a play and not allow it to become mere extrinsic solo exhibitionism. In addition, she still persistently and continuously so screws up her features into various exaggerated patterns that the effect is of two hours' D. W. Griffith old closeups of a cross between Blanche Sweet and Ben Turpin.

There is no doubt that Miss Bergner is an accomplished technician. But there is similarly no doubt that she is ignorant of the means wherewith to conceal it in a semblance of normal human conduct. Viewing her performance, one was cruelly reminded of the one merchanted several years ago in another "psychological" murder drama, *They Walk Alone,* by her English sister artist Elsa Lanchester who, while assuredly not comparable to Miss Bergner in the craft of acting, still shares many of her idiosyncrasies. Both can act more in one short evening than all the ladies in the Actors' Equity Association in combination have acted in the last ten years. Here, for example, is a picture of Miss Lanchester's projection methods, to which Miss Bergner's bear a considerable measure of resemblance:

Coquetry. Sly gargling of an imaginary quart of Listerine accompanied by eye blinking of sufficient velocity to dislodge 318 cinders, along with a shoulder shimmy dance and gestures more usually reserved for washing the back of the neck and behind the ears.

Terror. Eyes popped out of the sockets like copious soap bubbles, features wrinkled into a pattern resembling slept-in corduroy, little throat noises suggestive of half-swallowed fish-bones, and staccato dashes hither and yon about the room further suggestive of the first lesson in an Arthur Murray dancing class.

Insanity. A rigid pose with gaze fixed straight ahead and abruptly resolved into a mild form of epilepsy (interpreted by swallowing a pint of imaginary vinegar and giving evidence that it was not too appetizing), issuing a hollow laugh after the manner of Gaspard in *The Chimes of Normandy*, vibrating the torso as if to ease a severe itching of the back, and thereupon suddenly turning sidewise and giggling.

Ferocity. Standing grimly immobile for a moment and then rushing frantically to the window and ravenously gazing out of it as if beholding ten acres of hamburgers with onions, the meanwhile allowing the body to jiggle back and forth as if to the tune of "Yes, We Have No Bananas."

Amorous Impulse. A cat-like approach to the object of desire with waist bent in as if from a severe abdominal pain, with posterior projected rearward like a football center in the act of snapping back the pigskin, and with a series of gurglings suggestive of water running out of a tin bidet.

Unconcern. Head thrown back and hair tossed after the manner of a Katharine Hepburn loftily saying no to an invitation to take a ride in a second-hand Ford and have a beer.

Contrition. Dejection of head and intense scrutiny of the floor as if looking for a four-leaf clover, shoulders huddled like Quasimodo, and with sniffles and gulps indicative of an imminent seizure of hay fever.

Panic. Rapid looks to left and right, nervous paddling of thighs, wild brushing of hair up from ears, more rapid looks from right to left, execution of a few steps of the rhumba, and rapid inhalations and exhalations as if uncomfortably anticipating the imminent approach of a glue factory.

Gaiety. Wide dental display accompanied by chuckles siphoned through the nose, sudden revolutions and skirt swishings, gestures suggestive of playing an extra-large harp, and a culminating laugh of the species usually described by critics with a mash on an actress as "musical."

Modify all this but slightly and add a liberal dash of soubrette coyness and I fear you have a description of the technique of what the program handsomely described as "the idol of the European theatre, supreme in Berlin's theatre, beloved la Bergner of Paris, and the recipient of the most rapturous praise London had bestowed on an actress since Duse came that way."

THE MERRY WIDOW. August 4, 1943

A revival of the Franz Lehar operetta, with the Leo Stein-Victor Leon book revised by Sidney Sheldon and Ben Roberts. Produced for a record 321 performances by Yolanda Mero-Irion for the New Opera Company in the Majestic Theatre.

Program

The King	Karl Farkas	Sonia Sadoya	Marta Eggerth
Popoff	Melville Cooper	Prince Danilo	Jan Kiepura
Jolodon	Robert Field	Clo-Clo	Lisette Verea
Natalie	Ruth Matteson	Lo-Lo	Wana Allison
Olga Bardini	Etheleyne Holt	Frou-Frou	Bobbie Howell
General Bardini	Ralph Dumke	Do-Do	Babs Heath
Novakovich	Gene Barry	Premiere Danseuses	
Cascada	Alex Alexander		Lubow Roudenko
Khadja	Arnold Spector		Milada Mladova
Nish	David Wayne	Premier Dancer	Chris Volkoff
		Headwaiter	Karl Farkas

SYNOPSIS: Act I. 1. *Prologue.* 2. *The Marsovian embassy in Paris. A summer evening in the year 1906.* Act II. *Grounds of Sonia's house, near Paris: the following evening.* Act III. *Maxim's restaurant, Paris, later that same evening.*

The best answer to those younger critics who deride any faintest testimonial to the romantic stage of the past is to be found in the circumstance that when the contemporary theatre seeks to adopt a romantic air it has to borrow it from that very bygone stage. Lacking such romance on its own, it is forced to dig up those musical shows and operettas which induced in the audiences of other days that purple mood which remains ever one of the theatre's most welcome narcotics. It thus is compelled to fall back upon revivals of *Die Fledermaus* or *Rosalinda,* with its old Strauss waltzes to soothe anew the fancies of later-day audiences; *The Merry Widow,* with Danilo again to sing his Leharian way into the hearts of the vicarious Sonias up in the bal-

cony; *The Vagabond King,* with its consoling tale of a poor
poet made proud monarch of France for a day; *The Student
Prince,* with its royalty melting before the charm of a little
Heidelberg waitress and its melodic tributes to a time that
even then had already passed into the recesses of fond recollection; *The Chocolate Soldier,* with its Oscar Straus souvenirs of a jazzless era; and the mythology sung by Offenbach and the blossom-time love sung by Schubert.

While in the way of dramatic quality our theatre indicates a great improvement over the one that our fathers
knew and peculiarly relished, it just as certainly in its other
branches of entertainment lacks the romantic flavor that our
fathers knew and far less peculiarly revelled in. Save alone
for the two Jerome Kern exhibits, *Show Boat* and *Music
In the Air,* presented respectively in 1929 and 1932, the
stage, though it has offered a number of very worthy musical
shows, has not provided any which have permeated their
auditors with that half-sad, half-smiling, boozy feeling which
so often was their grant in a remoter day. An *Oklahoma!*
may induce a transitory such feeling when one looks at
Lemuel Ayres' Grant Wood-Thomas Benton scenic paraphrases of the sweeping South West countryside and when
one hums along with its "People Will Say" tune, which at
that brings up visions not of wondrous Ruritania princesses or the moonlit winding Nile but of hand-holding with
a cutie in the Savoy-Plaza Lounge. And now and then something equally exceptional may for a moment or two cause
the mind pleasurably to wander afield from the prosaic
immediateness and pick clover in the imagination's happy
hunting grounds. But for the overwhelming part the mood
inspired in one is as removed from the starlit and cloud-
woven as that inspired by J. K. Lasser's *Your Income Tax,*
even in its 1937 edition.

Where romance is attempted today, the results, to say the
least, are slightly confusing. For few will deny that it isn't
easy to sink oneself in the warm stream of reverie while
contemplating, as in *Early To Bed,* young love blossoming
in a bawdy house; or, as in *Something For The Boys,* a more
adult love involving a lady who at one point in the pro-

ceedings gets herself up as a low-comedy cigar-store Indian;
or, as in many another melody show, a grand passion expressed in lyrics dealing with Mrs. Vanderbilt, Mr. Ickes,
Toots Shor, and Jack and Charlie's.

The current frequent tendency to laugh off anything
that may be regarded as romantic, customarily praised by
amateur intelligences as being a sign of health, is rather a
sign of emotional deficiency. Incapable of deep feeling and
of sentiment without sentimentality, and devoid of that experience of the world which leaves ever in its wake, however sprayful, a trace of sadness and regret, the purveyors
to our musical stage simply conceal in a sissy derision the
qualities and attributes they lack. It takes a shameless emotional bravery to write a forthright romantic musical play.
It requires only a shameless confession of emotional cow-
ardice, or impotence, to write a romantic spoof, that is, save
wit be its portion, which it presently isn't. Only a man contemptuously independent in Æolian emotion can have the
nerve to write a song called "The Stars of Egypt Are In
Your Eyes, My Darling." It is the drugstore Romeo or the
emotional weakling who in the general run of things writes
the one called "I'll Love You, Baby, By the Gowanus
Canal."

It is all very well to curl a corner of the mouth over some
of the romantic business of yesterday's stage. Some of it,
God knows, was pretty innocent and not a little out of keeping with discomfiting truth. Certainly the real Maxim's
never in the least resembled the transcendent Everleigh
Club of *The Merry Widow's* stage. Certainly anyone who
had ever been in the Balkans and had gone bathless for a
week had considerable trouble reconciling his recollections
with the immaculate splendors of *The Balkan Princess.*
And equally certainly the Japan of *The Geisha,* with its
long, slim-legged English and American sing-song girls; or
the Spain of *Maritana,* with its ladies of the court mostly
looking like Maxine Elliott; or the Italy of *The Fencing
Master,* with its plazette in Venice smelling of delicate sa-
chets and its Milan as spick and span as Litchfield, Connecticut; or the Portugal of *The Queen's Lace Handkerchief,*

with its inn in the Sierras indistinguishable from the Paris
Ritz; or the Poland of *The Beggar Student,* with its peas-
ants conducting a continuous Elsa Maxwell party; or the
France of *Madeleine,* or *The Magic Kiss,* with its villagers
and courtiers cavorting hand in hand in the gardens of the
Château de Grimm; or the Africa of Von Suppe's *A Trip
To Africa,* with its Bedouin camp's close resemblance to old
Newport at the height of the season — certainly the realist,
contemplating such candied fact, was to be forgiven a way-
ward smile.

But no matter. Beneath and above it all, even for the recalcitrant realist, there was a genuine romantic cajolery.
The moonlight may have been a bit too purple; the stars
may have been as large as the argent mirrors over Denver's
old Silver Dollar saloon bar; the desert may have seemed to
have been laid out by Robert Moses; and none of the black
huzzars may have had knock-knees or bowlegs. Yet on those
stages, take it even from one still often given to deplorable
critical raillery, there persisted something that has largely
disappeared from our stages of today, and that something
was the brilliant fiction of undying love, the unabashed
song of hearts among the roses, the flowing plumes of
princes in armor, and all the throb and derring-do of men
and women above the clouds of our commonplace existence. And one gave in to it, one gave in to it irresistibly,
and came away, maybe foolishly but all the same unmistakably, with a grand feeling that just around the corner
lay a very beautiful world, and that in that very beautiful
world one must one day surely share.

And how, save something from those days is given revival, does one usually come away in this day? One comes
away from a *Something For The Boys* with the memory of
a plot about a house for aviation officers' wives mistaken
for a bordello; from an *Early To Bed* with the memory of
a plot about a bordello being mistaken for a girls' boarding
school; and from a *Let's Face It* with the memory of a plot
about a trio of silly, sexy old hags who take on three young
soldiers as gigolos. One comes away, further, from such and
other shows with ears still buzzing painfully from dialogic

barroom wit in which a male who means to say that he got back on his feet last night becomes confused and says to the blonde that he got his feet on her back last night. And one comes away in general with the memory of lyrics consecrated to the rhyming of Goering and herring and heart-of-my-life with something like tart-of-a-wife, of heroes who drolly slap women on the behind, of heroines who crack jokes about toilet rooms, and of love duets ending in passionate clog dances.

The answer that the younger critics make is that we live in a realistic age and that there is small place in our theatre today for the old romantic escape. The answer, I fear, is largely bosh. Otherwise how account for the enormous success of an *Oklahoma!* which in its timid way makes at least a gesture toward capturing the old trovatore mood and the titles of whose three most popular songs sufficiently indicate their content: *Oh, What a Beautiful Morning, The Surrey With the Fringe On Top,* and the before-mentioned *People Will Say We're In Love?* And how account for the great success of *Rosalinda,* the persistent road prosperity of such shows as *Blossom Time, The Student Prince, Countess Maritza* and the like, a Metropolitan Opera House packed to the doors, the City Center opera doing a land-office business, a Gallo troupe playing to overflowing houses, and the tremendous sheet-music sales of such songs as *As Time Goes By, You'll Never Know, In The Blue of the Evening,* and others of a similar nature?

The notion that the realistically minded audiences nowadays do not care for romance boils down to the simple fact that they do not care for it when it is presented to them in a shabby manner. Nor, for that matter, did they care for it even in the long past when it was presented to them in that manner. It is thus and accordingly that the younger critics argue their false general conclusion from the failure of something like *Night of Love,* which, taking a cue from Al Woods' old farce, *Ladies' Night In A Turkish Bath,* might better have called itself *Night of Love In A Shubert Storehouse;* or of something like the revived *The New Moon,* which seemed to have been hastily costumed in a couple of

hours' Bronx shopping tour and whose scenery looked as if
it had been painted by the artist responsible for the Sells-
Floto sideshow banners; or of periodic other such shoddy
presentations — *The Vagabond King* for just one — that
couldn't possibly succeed in any theatre that didn't serve
free beer and pretzels.

To return to an earlier motif, it isn't the simplest thing
in the world to inspire the romantic feeling in audiences,
where producers may hope to do so, with the kind of materials they presently often employ. Consider, for instance,
the stage settings. In the yesterdays, the scenes relied upon
to create that feeling were "The Marchesa's Villa near Venice," "The Court of Palms Outside Prince Guido Malespi-
no's Manor House at Cipriani," "The Governor's Palace
On the Island of Estrella," "Ruins of a Castle Near the
River Temes," "The Gypsy Encampment on the Road to
the Fair at Presburg," and "The Shore of the Mediterranean at Eventide." What, on the other hand, are the kind
of scenes intended to make us dream similar warm dreams
today? I select at random from among a half-dozen more
recent exhibits: "The Corridor of a Texas Hotel," "The
Smoke House on Laurey's Farm," "Skidmore's Kitchen
Porch," "Lawn of the Keely Cure," "The Boiler Room of
the Savoy-Perkins Hotel in Washington, D. C.," and "Erwin's Home, Jackson Heights."

Consider in turn, for another example, the mere names
of the characters. All other things being equal, it is nevertheless a bit harder, I believe you will agree, to think in
terms of moons and stars and tropical skies in the company
of such present nomenclatures as Muriel McGillicuddy,
Private Sweeney, Petunia Jackson, Hattie Maloney, Joey
Evans and Elmer Whipple — I again select at random from
the shows of the last three or four years — than in the company of such of yesterday's (we'll snobbishly leave out the
Princess Flavias and Duke Del Dragos) as Francesca Tor-
quato, Myles Na Coppaleen, Phoebe Fairleigh, Captain
De Merrimac of the man-o'-war *Cormorant,* Isabella Lot-
teringhi, and Raoul St. Courmandet, for all their affinity
to Laura Jean Libbey.

In conclusion, the younger critics' lofty contempt for the species of comedy relief in the stage valentines of another epoch. Without contravening them in the least, in point of fact applauding them, let them nevertheless be reminded that if that past comedy was sufficiently reflected in such fearful comedian character names as Bouillabaise (*Paul Jones*), Count Maladetto Spaghetti (*Sinbad*), Baron Grog (*The Grand Duchess*) and Popoff (*The Merry Widow*), the considerably later-day comedy is reflected in such as Mr. Rubbish (*Yokel Boy*), Woozy (*Panama Hattie*), Henry Clay Pigeon (*Let's Face It*) and Alexander Throttlebottom (*Of Thee I Sing*).

Presented in Budapest for the first time on the first night of the year 1906 and since played frequently throughout the western world, Lehar's famous operetta in this revival received a far better deal than locally has often been its portion. If Jan Kiepura, the Danilo of the evening, seemed to have mistaken the operetta for a murder play in the vein of the exhibit of the previous night and to have cast himself as the corpse, Marta Eggerth, except for a squeaky lapse in the lovely "Vilia" song, was one of the most acceptable Sonias I have encountered in a round of so many Sonias here and abroad that I can not remember their number. The usual Merry Widow, quality of singing voice aside, seeks to convey her convivial disposition through an Aunt Jemima set smile, her coquetry by rubbing the end of her nose with a fan, her physical allure by so adjusting herself to a sitting posture that her tight gown will give her the aspect of a languorous cervelatwurst, and her amorous nature by dreamily closing her eyes and inhaling a fanciful delicious pork chop. No such nonsense for Miss Eggerth. Her merriment is a sly inner merriment; her flirtation has in it a reasonable resemblance to what makes fools of men; and her anatomy has small need of Delsartian mummery.

The revival had many other points of merit, notably Balanchine's choreography; the direction of the delightful score by the same Robert Stolz who directed it at its first hearing in Vienna; one of the few ballet dancers in the person of a girl from Oklahoma who calls herself Milada

Mladova with calves one could look at without being reminded of a couple of Primo Carneras; settings by Howard Bay that suggested a past era without hitting one in the eye with it; and a comedian in Melville Cooper actually successful in making the deadly role of Popoff if not humorous at least not too objectionable.

CHAUVE–SOURIS 1943. AUGUST 12, 1943

A hypothetical new version of the Balieff Russian vaude-ville revue seen originally in New York in 1922. Music ar-ranged and composed by Gleb Yellin. Produced for speedy failure by Leon Greanin in the Royale Theatre.

PRINCIPALS

Marusia Sava, Zinaida Alvers, Vera Pavlovska, Tatiana Pobers, Zhenia Soudeikine, Dania Krupska, Norma Slavina, Georges Doubrovsky, Michael Dalmatoff, Simeon Karavaeff, Arkady Stoyanovsky, et al.

THE TRUTH WILL OUT. Those critics who for years have been urging that vaudeville elevate itself at least a little above the why-does-a-chicken-cross-the-road?, June-moon-spoon and acrobat-and-trick-dog level have been wrong, and freely admit it. This Chauve-Souris has convinced them. It began faintly to convince them when it was first shown locally twenty-odd years ago; it convinced them increasingly when new editions were imported at frequent intervals for the ten successive years; and upon this latest revealment it convinced them flatly, finally, and for once and all. If there still exists a critic who thinks vaudeville has been enormously improved by grim selections from Tchaikovsky, Moussorgsky and Shostakovitch played on an accordion, sung by fat male Russians in red blouses and danced by fat female Russians in white blouses, he was not to be seen the morning after its opening night.

Proceeding and speaking strictly for myself, the next time one of these Chauve-Souris vaudevilles again offers me that old *Parade of the Wooden Soldiers* number, I am going to make a scene. If the management succeeds in quieting me and thereupon again tries to entertain me with the number called *Harvest Festival* in which a group of Russians squat-dance as if the hay field were the Stork Club, the meanwhile yelling their heads off as if the Stork Club in turn were the Army-Navy football game, I am going to

make another and even louder scene. And if it manages to
subdue me a second time and then tries to gladden me with
the number called *The Nightingale* in which a female toe-
dancer with legs suffering from the mumps twirlingly con-
fuses a nightingale with a Ringling Brothers' performing
Shetland pony, not to mention the male choir number in
which a portly Slav excruciatingly pretends to pull the
tones out of the singers' mouths with his undulating fingers,
I am going home and get a gun.

The old, stale sit-down-and-kick dances; the conferencier,
or master of ceremonies, who speaks a halting and broken
English and glares with a whimsical fixity at the audience
by way of registering his supposedly comical delivery; the
quartet of adipose women in fancily colored shawls who
joyously shout songs that are essentially as merry as malaria;
the gypsy number; and the folk dance in which everybody is
so gayly and exuberantly folksy that you get the impression
every peasant in Russia has a million dollars, more girls
than he knows what to do with, and leads generally the life
of Reillyvitch — you can also have all those, if your taste
runs that way, in exchange for Lou Holtz's cane.

The present version of the show, which to boot didn't
overlook the old 1922 *Katinka* number, was further dead-
ened by the inclusion of several items hopefully intended
to give it a good-neighbor touch of Americanism. One of
these called *The Wac and the Sniper,* showing the affection
of a Ludmilla Pavlichenko for a Susie Smith in uniform,
was even more disconcerting than another in which the
quondam Cossack choir — the item was called *Hobo-Gen-
ius Chorus in 4F* — was dressed like Bowery gutter-bums,
with one of the number conducting himself like a fairy.

RUN, LITTLE CHILLUN. August 13, 1943

Revival of the Negro folk song play, shown originally in 1933, by Hall Johnson. Produced for 16 performances by Lew Cooper in association with Meyer Davis and George Jessel in the Hudson Theatre.

Program

Sister Mattie Fullilove	Ella Jones *Helen Dowdy*
Bessie Guy	Jeems Jackson *Edward Roche*
Sister Flossie Lou Little	Bessiola *Miriam Burton*
Bertha Powell	The Rev. Sister Luella Strong
Sister Mahalie Cockletree	*Olive Ball*
Rosalie King	Rev. Jones *Louis Sharp*
Sister Judy Ann Hicks	Jim *Caleb Petersen*
Maggie Carter	Charlie *Charles Holland*
Sister Lulu Jane Hunt	Sulamai *Edna Mae Harris*
Eloise Uggams	Mary Lou Mack
Sister Susie May Hunt	*Violet McDowell*
Eva Vaughan	Elder Tongola *Service Bell*
Brother Esau Redd	Brother Moses *P. Jay Sidney*
Robert Harvey	Mother Kanda *Maude Simmons*
Brother Bartholomew Little	Sister Mata *Fredye Marshall*
Wardell Saunders	Brother Jo-Ba *Walter Mosby*
Brother Goliath Simpson	Sue Scott *Lulu B. King*
William O. Davis	Sexton of the Hope Baptist
Brother Jeremiah Johnson	Church *Adolph Henderson*
Randall Steplight	Brother Absalom Brown
Brother George W. Jenkins	*Roger Alford*
Elijah Hodges	

SYNOPSIS: Act I. Scene 1. *The parlor of Rev. Jones's house.* Scene 2. *Fork of the road.* Scene 3. *The New Day Pilgrims' meeting.* Act II. Scene 1. *The back porch of Sulamai's house in Toomer's Bottom, three days later.* Scene 2. *Fork of the road.* Scene 3. *Interior of Hope Baptist Church, the same evening.*

Place. *Somewhere in the South.*

THE struggle between Good and Evil for the soul of man, a theme favorite of contemporary Negro drama and even musical comedy (*vide Cabin In The Sky*), provides the evening's sub-stratum, superimposed upon which is a folk song festival, choreography of a sexual pattern hardly exceeded by the late Nazi Strength Through Joy exercises even when under the supervision and encouragement of Julius Streicher, and a Baptist revival meeting so equally ecstatic that the difference between its religious fervor and the sexual fervor of the opposing pagan church is indeterminable. The fundamental dramatic passages, involving the temptation of the parson's son and his eventual redemption, are feeble. But the song and dance embroidery go to make Negro entertainment of a superior sort.

Any such presentation of ambitious aim provides a welcome relief from the more general Negro offering consisting for the major part of jokes about fried chicken, hoofers who patronize Fred Astaire's tailor, beaming ladies who sing mainly with their teeth, and skits in which a towering darky scares the hell out of a diminutive one until the peewee, unable to take any more of it, cries out that a ghost is creeping up behind the big boy, suddenly jumps with both feet on his trembling vis-à-vis' amplitudinous brogans, causing him to howl in anguish, and then, after lifting the gold watch which big boy has appropriated from him, nonchalantly walks off with the saucy soubrette who was standing where the feared ghost was supposed to be. Johnson's large choir is a stimulating body; its spirituals are admirably handled. And the Negro dancing is, literally, sensational.

MURDER WITHOUT CRIME. August 18, 1943

Another in the line of imported English spasms, this one known originally as To Fit The Crime, *by J. Lee Thompson. Produced for 37 performances by the Messrs. Del Bondio, Windust and Weatherly in the Cort Theatre.*

Program

Stephen	*Bretaigne Windust*	Matthew	*Henry Daniell*
Grena	*Frances Tannehill*	Jan	*Viola Keats*

SYNOPSIS: Act I. Scene 1. Evening. Scene 2. About one hour later. Act II. Scene 1. Next morning. Scene 2. Half an hour later. Act III. A few minutes later.

The action of the play takes place in Stephen's flat in Matthew's house in Mayfair.

THIS HAS BEEN wrongly designated as a four character play. What it is is merely a four actor play, since the author has neglected to convert them into characters save in the most superficial sense. He is, however, not alone in the oversight. Various other English concocters of such murder exhibits have been guilty of a similar lapse, and in a way intentionally. They write with specific actors in view and these actors, generally popular with London audiences when they appear in such pathological spectacles, are often themselves so heavily invested by nature with the appropriate credentials that the characters, so to speak, inevitably become of a realistic piece with them, thus making any playwriting attempt at genuine character drawing gratuitous and unnecessary.

The present specimen is a mediocre paraphrase of Patrick Hamilton's *Rope's End* which, shown locally some ten or more years ago, was a superior example in kind. The device of keeping the box containing the murdered party's body in view of the audience throughout the evening is again brought forth for shudder reaction. The sinister acquaintance of the murderer who haunts the premises and

slowly tortures the latter with his suspicions is similarly
once again in evidence. And the decadent flavor of the
whole provides still another echo.

The plot on this occasion, while departing the strict
Leopold-Loeb essence of Hamilton's play, retails a liberal
smell of it in the soi-disant character of the stygian friend.
A cowardly neurotic whose separated wife is about to return to him has a quarrel with his jealous mistress and, in a
scuffle, stabs her. Thinking her dead, he hides her body in
an ottoman. His landlord, a sadist who has long concealed
his envy of the fellow's sexual success with women, becomes
suspicious and cross-examines the young man into a tan-
trum. When the latter leaves, the landlord investigates and
discovers that the supposed corpse is not a corpse. (It was
only a wound and the mistress was only temporarily uncon-
scious.) Spiriting the woman away without the hypothetical murderer's knowledge, he thereupon subsequently enters into a prolonged, agonizing baiting of the former which
drives the accused to plan murder of him in turn in order
to cover up, as he thinks, the initial murder.

In the telling of the story the playwright falls back upon
most of the hackneyed tricks: the check with which the
young man tries to buy off his mistress ("You swine!" she
cries) ; the mortal dagger on the wall significantly illuminated by the library lamp; the William Gillette-*Secret Service* red ink covertly spilled on the hand to indicate blood;
the ledge beneath the window that might have served a possible intruder ("But the window was locked from the inside!") ; the lights suddenly snapped on and off; the suspicion that a drink has been poisoned, with the debonair
switching of the glasses only to take the one which actually
has the poison in it; the casually picked up book which
happens to deal with murder; the nervously broken-off telephone call for the police; the but partly burned incrimi-
nating evidence retrieved from the fire-place — all these
and others they readily suggest suffer a dramaturgical revival. And, throughout, that recorded leaven of perversion
which seems to be so largely the portion of these English
grandguignolisms.

Add, in conclusion, the species of playwriting which talks what might otherwise conceivably be tense scenes into drowsy interludes, along with an airy philosophical cynicism of the kind encountered among schoolboys who have come upon Huysmans or Wilde for the first time, and you have a fairly clear notion of the sickly claptrap.

THE SNARK WAS A BOOJUM
SEPTEMBER 1, 1943

Another one by Owen Davis, based on a novel of the same title by Mrs. Richard Shattuck. Produced as a box-office zero by Alex Yokel in association with Jay Faggen in the 48th Street Theatre.

PROGRAM

RODNEY SHILLY	*Frank Lovejoy*	MAYBELLE	*Florence McMichael*
MRS. WILSON WILSON		HENRY	*Fleming Ward*
	Catherine Willard	VIVIAN ·	*Phyllis Adams*
ELWOOD	*Dickie Van Patten*	WARD McKAY	*Francis Compton*
MILLIE SMITH	*Joan Banks*	AUNT ADELINE	*Ann Dere*
SIDNEY	*Ben Lackland*	DAYBREAK	*Harold Waldrige*
SANDY GATE	*Jane Huszagh*	DOCTOR MORTICE	*Frank Wilcox*
MARTIN	*Mervyn Nelson*	ROSIE	*Grania O'Malley*

SYNOPSIS: Act I. *Late afternoon.* Act II. *That night.* Act III. *Later the same night.*

The Scene. *The old Shilly homestead.*

THE AUTHOR is in percentage by volume the Lope de Vega of the American theatre. He has written to date close to three hundred plays, so small wonder they have not been much good. This one is no exception.

Our Lope started his dramaturgical career, back in the days when Al Woods was still rapturously dreaming of becoming one day as great a producer as Gus Hill, with something called *Through the Breakers,* a succotash of melodramatic corn and ham that ran on and off in the 10-20-30 parlors for all of seven years. With the monies thus handsomely acquired he bought several thousands of dollars' worth of carbon paper against the future. Soon, further such succotashes began to emanate from him in rapid succession, sometimes as many as five a month, and it wasn't long before the aforesaid Mr. Woods, in business collaboration with the Messrs. Sullivan and Harris and now his entrepreneur, attained to an eminence in the Bowery art world far surpassing that of the earlier envied Mr. Hill.

Among the works of that Davis period were such memorable mellers as *Nellie, the Beautiful Cloak Model, Bertha, the Sewing Machine Girl, Edna, the Pretty Typewriter, The Confessions of a Wife, Hounded To Hell, The Gambler of the West,* and four or five dozen similar masterpieces replete with blond nobility at stage right and brunet villainy at stage left and with appropriate backdrops showing the East River docks at midnight, the junction switch on the Altoona and Pottsville R. R., the chasm at Indian Falls, and the bridge over Devil's Gulch. The next period in the artistic career of our hero saw an abandonment of this species of melodrama in favor of melodrama of a somewhat higher tone, the higher tone being negotiated by moving the action indoors and shaving the villain.

Period No. 3 witnessed an even more ambitious step. Not only did our hero move his melodrama indoors and shave his villain but now he inserted several lines of dialogue of a profound mental cast, such, for example, as contending that a pure heart can not sin, that one misstep on a woman's part does not necessarily stamp her as a wanton, or that one should take stock of one's own shortcomings before seeking to pass judgment on one's fellow-man.

The subsequent period indicated still greater strides. It included not only a number of mystery operations in which the murder was found to have been committed either by a lunatic filled with a passion for revenge or by someone who bore a suspicious resemblance to the household's butler, but also a succession of dramas in which our Lope proved he had a social conscience. The proof took the form of arguing gravely that gangsters were a menace to decent society, that grafting politicians were a menace to a decent municipality, and that the gin-and-jazz age was corruptive of decent home life.

But Period No. 5 — I omit various dramatized drugstore novels and some pieces in which actors sat in rocking-chairs on porches, did nothing, and thus became lovable Yankee or Dixie characters — marked the real pinnacle of achievement. Contending that anyone could write the kind of plays Eugene O'Neill was writing, even with both hands tied behind one's ears, Mr. Davis dashed off a tragedy of Maine life and character called *The Detour,* which somehow nevertheless and disconcertingly left O'Neill just where he was before. Undeterred, however, our genius then dashed off another O'Neill tragedy called *Icebound,* which also dealt with Maine life and character, which was even worse than *The Detour,* and which accordingly was awarded the Pulitzer prize. Our man was now made. And going back to normal — he could now enjoy the comfortable luxury — he contented himself in his late sixties with the renewed confection of some thirty or so dramatizations of best-sellers, thrillers laid in haunted houses, comedies bearing such titles as *Beware of Widows* and *Gentle Grafters,* farces built upon the theme that automobiles always break down at embarrassing moments, and dramas in which hotheaded Southern belles plotted sinister revenges upon the men who had jilted them.

This latest contribution, an attempt at jabberwocky comedy, which was removed from view after five performances, is one of the worst of the lot. The title derives, obviously, from Lewis Carroll's *The Hunting of the Snark,* but the play, which aims to achieve an air of Carroll mad-hatterism, achieves only that silliness which is blood-sister to stupidity. Reared upon the ancient plot of a deceased eccentric who has willed his fortune to the first of his nephews or nieces to have a baby and involving some heavily incorporated mystery shenanigan, the evening is a compendium of characters, humors and melodramatic devices that were already hoary in the era of the before-mentioned Gus Hill. In the way of characters, Mr. Davis introduces the tough show-girl, the hard-boiled family lawyer, the comic servant girl, the butler who filches the liquor and gets drunk, the love-interest ingénue, the flinty maiden aunt, the overly sentimental husband, the bad little boy, et al. In the way of humor, he goes in for the jittery male whose wife is about to give birth to a baby; the joke about drinking hair tonic; the visibly inebriated man who solemnly confides to his wife that he has been drinking; the remark of a baldhead that he was so scared it raised the hair on his head, with the retort, "Which one?"; the Californian who allows that various phenomena of nature are "just like in the movies"; etc. And in the way of melodramatic devices, he harks back to the rattling chains, the sudden spectacle of a frightening face at the window, the pistol shot in the dark, the on-and-off electric switch, the falling of a body out of a suddenly pulled-open door, the shadows against the wall, the loud scream, the nervously secreted papers, the maniacal murderer at large reported by the radio, and so on.

It still takes O'Neill four or five years to write even one play.

FAMILIAR PATTERN. September 2, 1943

*A drama by David S. Lipson. Produced for a few perform-
ances by Modern Play Productions, Inc., in the Provincetown Playhouse.*

Program

Lou Zimmerman	*Herbert Giffin*	Boy	*Jerry Ohrbach*
Sam Miller	*Robert Feyti*	Rabbi	*Joseph Di Stefano*
Mrs. Miller	*Pauline Anton*	Sadie	*Mary Kleiman*
Mildred Silver	*Olga Novosei*	Mr. Silver	*Melvin Davis*
Doctor	*John Swier*	Mrs. Silver	*Anne King*
Woman	*Ona de Munoz*	Shirley Silver	*Florence Saks*
Nurse	*Miriam Hilsenroth*	Harry Stein	*Howard Bradler*
Daughter	*Marianne Gnann*	Girl	*Ona de Munoz*
Mother	*Mary Kleiman*	Detective	*Peter Zube*
Patient	*Gertrude Pastul*	Guard	*George Rae*
Client	*Mabel Nash*	Healy	*John Swier*

SYNOPSIS: Act I. Scene 1. *Mrs. Miller's Bronx apartment, November, 1935.* Scene 2. *The same. Half hour later.* Scene 3. *Doctor's office.
Next day.* Scene 4. *A street near Lou's home. That evening.* Scene 5. *The
Rabbi's home. Next day.* Scene 6. *The Silvers' home. Same evening.* Act II.
Scene 1. *Sam Miller's apartment. March, 1936.* Scene 2. *Hotel room. April,
1936.* Scene 3. *Visitors' room in the County Jail. July, 1936.* Act III. Scene
1. *The Silvers' home. November, 1937.* Scene 2. *The same. About a week
later.*

THE PERSISTENT, fond hope of the newspaper reviewers
that something in the way of drama to make the Broadway
species look especially childish in comparison will show up
one night in some remote little theatre up a dark alley —
duly remarked on in the previous edition of this yearly record — was once again, and for the fortieth or fiftieth time,
blasted by the candidate in point. Dealing with the long
dated theme of the idealistic and ambitious young man who
becomes sexually involved with a young woman, who is
forced to marry her, and who sees his career gradually ruined, Mr. Lipson's contribution to the elevation of the
drama took on the aspect of a cardboard jack. Not only was

his story culled from the stage's morgue and his manner of writing from the *Young's Magazine* which flourished esoterically at the turn of the century, but his imagination hewed steadfastly and undeviatingly to that of the trashier playwrights of the same period, if not a considerably earlier one. To quote the exasperated orchestra leader in *Music In The Air:* "God save us from amateurs!"

But maybe the reviewers are now at length beginning faintly to despair. "The tatterdemalion little band of the faithful wandered down to MacDougal Street last evening," gloomily wrote Mr. Nichols of the *Times,* "and gradually, by twos and threes, the tatterdemalion little band of the faithful went home again." "The new offering at the Provincetown Playhouse is off Broadway and off base," lugubriously observed Mr. Barnes of the *Herald Tribune;* "it is a very poor excuse for a trip to MacDougal Street, even on duty bound." "Perhaps on the whole the play might better have been produced in Yiddish at one of the East Side theatres where they enjoy doing these things at the top of their lungs, with gestures," wistfully allowed Miss Waldorf of the *Post.* "And when the spineless youngster is finally completely defeated by his tyrannical mother-in-law, his spoiled tart of a wife and his economic dependency, you are prompted to utter an irreverent So What?", morbidly shrugged Mr. Rascoe of the *World-Telegram.*

Further evidence of the increasing misgiving was to be had in the failure of most of the other reviewers to attend the performance.

BLOSSOM TIME. September 4, 1943

A limited revival of the veteran operetta, book and lyrics by Dorothy Donnelly adapted from the original by A. M. Willner and H. Reichert, music by Franz Schubert adapted and augmented by Sigmund Romberg. Produced previous to a road tour by the Messrs. Shubert in the Ambassador Theatre.

Program

Franz Schubert	*Alexander Gray*	Greta	*Jacqueline Suzanne*
Christian Kranz	*Doug Leavitt*	Rosie	*Helen LeBerthon*
Baron Schober	*Roy Cropper*	Mrs. Coburg	*Jane Spelvin*
Scharntoff	*Robert Chisholm*	Vogel	*Roy Barnes*
Mitzi	*Barbara Scully*	Von Schwindt	*George Beach*
Fritzi	*Monna Montes*	Kuppelweiser	*Nord Cornell*
Kitzi	*Loraine Manners*	Novotny	*Harry K. Morton*
Bella Bruna	*Helene Arthur*	Domeyer	*Walter Johnson*
Flower Girl	*Adelaide Bishop*	Erkman	*Willard Charles Fry*
Mrs. Kranz	*Zella Russell*	Binder	*John O'Neill*

SYNOPSIS: Act I. *Domeyer's restaurant in the Prater in Vienna. Twilight in May, 1826.* Act II. *Drawing-room in the house of Kranz. Three months later.* Act III. *Franz Schubert's lodgings. Two months later.*

SCHUBERT'S SCORE, despite the occasional gratuitous assistance of Mr. Romberg, remains the basic reason for the enormous success of this American adaptation of the operetta known in Europe as *Drei Mädel Haus*. Seen here first in 1921, it ran for all of 78 weeks on Broadway; subsequently, its popularity mounting by leaps and bounds, two companies were drafted to play it in New York simultaneously; and thereafter and since it has played repeatedly throughout the land.

Aside from the Schubert music, which is responsible for the pleasurable romantic air of the exhibit, there is critically little, although the polychromatic story of the young composer's love for the fair little Mitzi Kranz serves sufficiently to further the desired mood in that copious public which demands Technicolor prose as an accompaniment to music itself already drenched with color. To the more fastidious, the book, at least in its local overly popularized form, is an ineffable intrusion. It is, to such, something of an agony to listen, between the Schubert melodies, to wizened dialogic humors like the following:

"I am starved for a kiss" — "Then you will have to die of starvation."

"Marriage is an institution" — "But who wants to live in an institution?"

"There are a thousand reasons why I shouldn't take a drink, but I can't think of one of them."

"Is she married?" — "No; she's perfectly happy."

"I wrote it in a minor key" — "Why don't you write it for grown-ups?"

"I was thinking of nothing." — "When a woman says she's thinking of nothing, she's thinking of something!"

It is also hardly conducive to romantic surrender when the comedian to whom this lofty wit is entrusted embellishes it with such vaudeville antics as spitting into a vis-à-vis' eye; scratching a table leg under the impression that it is his own and, after a puzzled pause, exclaiming, "I'm dead!"; cupping up spilled liquor into his glass; and intermittently missing a resting-place for his elbow and precipitating himself on his ear.

And it is even less conducive when the evening is adorned additionally with off-stage laughter that sounds as if a stagehand were desperately tickling the revellers with a featherduster, with a Vienna Prater that looks as if it had been landscaped by a second-rate New York night club decorator, and with an elaborate Viennese drawing-room attended by a single maid-servant.

But the music still stubbornly dreams itself into a theatre, and the romantic audience mind suspends realistic judgment, and the angels are again in heaven, and all's right, for the moment, with the world.

TOBACCO ROAD. September 4, 1943

The record-breaker by Jack Kirkland, from the novel of the same name by Erskine Caldwell. Produced by Mr. Kirkland in the Ritz Theatre.

PROGRAM

DUDE LESTER	*Dan Denton*	HENRY PEABODY	*Fred Sutton*
ADA LESTER	*Sara Perry*	SISTER BESSIE RICE	
JEETER LESTER	*John Barton*		*Vinnie Phillips*
ELLIE MAY	*Barbara Joyce*	PEARL	*Luciel Richards*
GRANDMA LESTER	*Lillian Ardell*	CAPTAIN TIM	*Michael King*
LOV BENSEY	*Kim Spalding*	GEORGE PAYNE	*Edwin Walter*

SYNOPSIS: Act I. *Late afternoon.* Act II. *Next morning.* Act III. *Dawn — the following day.*

The entire action of the play takes place at the farm of Jeeter Lester, situated on a tobacco road in the back country of Georgia.

JUST TO KEEP the year's record complete, this listing of the 1943 reappearance of the modern theatre's phenomenon. First shown in New York on December 4, 1933, the play ran steadily until May 5, 1941, thus chalking up a world's championship in 3,149 performances. A year ago this September it returned for an additional 34. And on this re-return it ran for all of 66. Meanwhile, it has been showing with one troupe or another all over the country, playing as many as ten and twelve repeat engagements in various cities.

Incidental statistics: The play was at first thought to be a failure; only the confidence of the management, in the face of adverse newspaper reviews and many weeks of small box-office revenue, saved its life. At one time or another it was subsequently banned in Chicago after it had been shown there for almost two months, in Detroit after it had been played for a month, and in St. Paul and Raleigh, North Carolina. Produced in London, it promptly fell flat.

Otherwise, consult *The Theatre Book of the Year, 1942–43.*

LAUGH TIME. September 8, 1943

A vaudeville show. Produced for 126 performances by Paul Small and Fred Finklehoffe in the Shubert Theatre, with this pronouncement: "We have never conceded the corpus delicti. We have disbanded the pallbearers, halted the requiem, on the laudable suspicion that Laugh Time will demonstrate that the burial of vaudeville, circa 1932, was premature."

Principals

Frank Fay, Bert Wheeler, Ethel Waters, the Di Gatanos, Buck and Bubbles, Adriana and Charly, Lucienne and Ashour, Jerri Vance, Warren Jackson, and the Bricklayers.

THE SUSPICION of the producers, quoted above, aside from the question of its laudability, was only half true. The burial of any vaudeville that might contain Frank Fay, Ethel Waters, Bert Wheeler and perhaps even the Bricklayers was certainly premature. But I am not so sure of any that contained most of the other acts on the bill. If not exactly dead, vaudeville circa 1932 was dangerously sick from couples like Adriana and Charly in trampoline acrobatics, the Di Gatanos in ballroom dancing involving further acrobatics, Lucienne and Ashour in Apache dances involving still more acrobatics, Buck and Bubbles in labored comical dance steps involving yet further acrobatics, to say nothing of serio-comic piano playing, and Jerri Vance in contortions climaxed by bending a leg over the head and scratching the nose with the foot.

The delayed burial services were halted on this occasion rather by the performers earlier specified. Fay is an amiably droll comedian and Wheeler another. Singly or in joint operation they here kept vaudeville still out of the grave with their asides to the audience on the rascality of the producers of the show — Wheeler confided they had promised him ten percent of the intake above $32,000; with their cracks

about a member of the company who had been such a good
clothing salesman before he unwisely became an actor that
he had sold a suit to a widow, who was about to bury her
husband, with an extra pair of pants; with their additional
whimsicalities about Wheeler bragging that when he recently appeared in a Los Angeles theatre you could hear
them laughing across the street, and Fay's dry inquiry, "Who
was playing there?"; and with Wheeler's indignant denunciation of one of the producers who, while Wheeler was in
a telephone booth talking to his girl, peremptorily demanded the use of the phone, compelling Wheeler and his
girl to get out.

Ethel Waters, that warm dental personality, is a further
asset to any vaudeville with her "Taking a Chance On
Love," "Heat Wave," "Cabin In The Sky," "Stormy
Weather," and other such songs to which she gave vocal
birth. And the Bricklayers, even though by now pretty
stale, remain the best trained dog act in the business, for
those who admire trained dog acts.

The opening night performance was accompanied by the
following announcement on the part of the management:

"Our scenery, in case anyone cares, was last heard of
somewhere between Las Vegas, New Mexico, and LaPorte,
Indiana. En route from Los Angeles, we fear it has met
with foul play. Want to hear more about our scenery?
No? Well, you're going to. It was and is, for all we know,
a fusion of the best features of the Taj Mahal, the late
Josef Urban, the Grand Canyon and early Loew's State.
At a later date we may give a special showing of it to satisfy
non-believers. In our extremity we have whipped up such
velvet, velour and lumber as was available at the nearest
salvage piles. If it is a little on the ersatz side we know, in
your vast tolerance, you'll understand. The show, as some
dope once illogically remarked, must go on."

MY DEAR PUBLIC. September 9, 1943

Described as a "revusical story," with book by Irving Caesar assisted by Charles Gottesfeld and songs by Irving Caesar assisted by Sam Lerner and Gerald Marks. Produced for 44 performances at a loss of $180,000 by Mr. Caesar, who seemingly did almost everything but sew the costumes, in the 46th Street Theatre.

Program

Walters	Dave Burns	Byron Burns	Eric Brotherson
Tapps	Georgie Tapps	Lulu	Sherle North
Jean	Nanette Fabray	Gordon	Gordon Gifford
Daphne Drew	Ethel Shutta	Playwright	William Nunn
Barney Short	Willie Howard	Gus Wagner	Jesse White
Renee	Renee Russell	Kelly	Al Kelly
Louise	Louise Fiske	Rose Brown	Rose Brown
Mitzi	Mitzi Perry		

SYNOPSIS: Act I. Scene 1. *Backstage*. Scene 2. *Inside Barney Short's office*. Scene 3. *Private room in the Crystal Hill Hospital*. Scene 4. *Backstage*. Scene 5. *Private room in the Crystal Hill Hospital*. Scene 6. *Backstage*. Act II. Scene 1. *Pan American airport*. Scene 2. *Barney Short's office*. Scene 3. *Backstage*. Scene 4. *Jean's dressing room*. Scene 5. *Finale*.

FILE IT in the archives as one of the seediest musical shows of the last two decades. Plot for the first fifteen minutes: A zipper manufacturer whose ex-actress wife is still stagestruck is inveigled into backing a musical comedy for her. Plot for the rest of the two and one-quarter hours: None. Typical sample of humor, delivered by a character descending from an airplane: "From now on give me terra firma — the more firmer, the less terror." Typical lyric, sung by a Negro woman: "There ain't no color line around the rainbow (Ed. reflection: Since when?), there ain't no color line deep in the sea" (Ed. reflection: News to *Carcharodon carcharias*). Typical costuming: A Rumanian gypsy ballet with the gypsies dressed in duds apparently retrieved from the old Castle Square Opera Company's 1898 *Carmen*. Typ-

ical comic tune: "If You Want To Deal With Russia" derived from "If You Want To Deal With Sweeney," an olio
favorite of the early Nineties. Typical scenic ingenuity: A
backdrop with phonograph records painted on it. Other
items: Three female radio yodlers called The Harmoneers,
the comedian in grotesque pajamas, the song wittily titled
"Pipes of Pan-Americana," and the act finale, "May All Our
Children Have Rhythm," accompanied by a large metronome swinging back and forth behind the dancing chorus
line.

Relied upon to inspirit the mess with some gayety was
Mr. Willie Howard. Nobody can say that Willie doesn't
work hard. No one, in point of fact, has worked so hard
since the late Jimmie Powers. After looking at Jimmie for
two hours I used to be so exhausted that I always had to take
a week off and rest up in Atlantic City, where I would periodically run across Jess Dandy in some try-out or other and
get a relapse.

Willie does everything to make you laugh but jump down
into the auditorium and tickle you with a feather. (I'm
sorry I mentioned that one; he may regard it as a further
available idea and take it up.) He strides ferociously, makes
sudden violent revolutions, tosses his head from side to side
as if caught in a two-way hurricane, frantically moves his
shoulders up and down, gesticulates wildly, quivers at the
knees, howls like a coyote, collapses his body, and in his
avarice for laughter goes to every other length save the old
vaudeville one of pausing when a laugh is not forthcoming,
quizzically glaring at the audience, and demanding to know
if everyone out front is still there. I don't say it doesn't succeed with a lot of his customers, but somehow it doesn't
seem to work in my case, even when his material is fifty
times better than on the occasion in point.

The spectacle of a comedian pulling for laughter like the
stroke oar of a college crew and dripping gallons of perspiration is hardly conducive to humorous reaction on the part
of your recorder. It is true that Bobby Clark, that old and
beloved master, doesn't go about his business quite like
Virginia Harned languidly smelling at a rose in *Iris*. But

Bobby's activity is essentially part and parcel of his comedy; it isn't, as in Willie's case, visited upon it externally. And it is probably equally true that those two hot boys, Smith and Dale, or at least whichever is the more ebullient one, do not conduct themselves exactly like Sothern and Marlowe. But in their case once again the furor is an integral part of their humor and is not, as in Willie's case, mere appendage bait.

You will, I believe, if you think over the comedians who have made you laugh loudest, find that it has been the quieter ones who with small exception stand at the top of your list. W. C. Fields has surely loosened your midriff more salubriously than Leon Errol; Dan Daly and Raymond Hitchcock got you going more auspiciously than Gus Rogers and Joe Cawthorne; and George Bickel was twice as comical as his partner Harry Watson, who did everything but throw the bass-drummer at you. In the same way, old Pete Dailey made you laugh a great deal more than the before-noted Powers; George Jessel, Lou Holtz and Frank Fay are funnier than Pat Harrington, Frankie Hyers and Teddy Hart; and Victor Moore can make you forget Sam Bernard without half trying. Have I overlooked the big exception? I certainly have overlooked the big exception. Jimmy Durante. But Jimmy is a genius, and there's all the difference in the world between a genius and Willie Howard.

Howard's technique is a poor paraphrase of that of certain comedians of a past era. It is also a relatively outmoded one, since popular taste has materially changed. Compare, for example, the method of some such admired newcomer as Danny Kaye (who fertilizes me personally no more fruitfully than Howard) with that of the aforementioned B. Clark, that exceptional clown of another epoch who, to repeat, is paradoxically still going strong, and you get an idea of the difference between some of the old zanies and some of their successors.

Bobby, a graduate of the circus and the minstrel shows, achieved his early position chiefly through spectacles painted on his eyes, an uncontrollable bamboo cane, and a comical cigar butt. Danny comes on dressed much like you

or me and without a prop to his name. Bobby on his first
appearance strode brazenly down to the footlights, puffed
out his chest, glared audaciously at the audience, the meanwhile tripping over his cane and elaborately, upon regaining his equilibrium, flicking the ash off his stogie, and then
fell precipitantly on his face. Danny comes on quietly and,
much like any actor in a straight play, enters calmly into the
plot dialogue. A slight nance touch is his sole compromise
with the older order. (This is certainly meant to be no reflection on Bobby. He is still, regardless of everything, the
kingpin of them all. But the new boys derive their comedy
more often directly from the lines and business of the shows
they are in than from extrinsic and gratuitous antics.)

In the past days, a comedian had to have at least four or
five bits of comical business to supplement even a line of
dialogue sufficiently jocose on its own. Take this Bobby.
When his partner McCullough was still alive, the pair of
bums appeared in a skit laid in a war trench. A terrible battle was on. What to do? wailed the unwashed and filthy Mc-
Cullough as the enemy approached nearer. Whereupon
Bobby finally concluded: "I shall recommend to the captain that he send you over the top in lieu of a gas attack."

But was that enough for the audience? It was not. It was
thereupon incumbent upon Bobby to go into a little dance,
click his heels together in the air, fall on his ear, get up and
brush a half ton of dust off himself and onto his aggrieved
partner, fall on his other ear, arise as if he had while on the
ground contracted lumbago, blow a kiss to McCullough, allow his hat to drop over his eyes, execute another pas seul,
and maybe deject himself again on both ears.

Some such clown of today as Danny, cracking any such
wheeze as that cited, would no more think thereafter of entering upon any such repertoire than he would think of
asking a reduction in salary. Danny now and then may follow a gag by leaning drolly against a wall and grinning
sheepishly at himself or by wriggling a hip in a too-too manner, but his approach to and withdrawal from a line are otherwise generally unembellished with any antic parsley.

Even in the case of the new stage comedians drafted from burlesque, it is the reading of line that seems to count with the customers. Thus, when Jack Mann, with a face resembling a lascivious Halloween pumpkin, recites his ideas for naughty blackout sketches, the audience reaction is considerably more puissant than when he squirts water through his puckered lips halfway across the stage. Thus, when chubby little Joe Besser, standing in military line in an army camp and getting balled up in counting off the numbers, is indignantly challenged by the sergeant, "Are you *one*?" and archly grins, "No. Are you?", it is his manner of delivery and not his incidental elaborate knee collapse that evokes the laughter.

Another new comedian who, like Kaye, has won wide approval is Joe E. Lewis. Even less than Kaye does Joe depend upon external monkey-business to get his laughs. His lyrics, with maybe a small joke or two on the side, are his buffoon weapon. The two clowns differ markedly, however, in the way they sell their songs. Whereas Danny grimaces his, Joe delivers his in mock-undertaker fashion. And the only accessory business he indulges in is an occasional pretended shoulder pain. Give him a song like *The H. V. Kaltenborn Blues,* in which he lugubriously recounts the thrills that descend upon him when he listens to the outpourings of that great sage over the radio, and the audience is his.

Even when Joe, edging up to a cutie, cracks some such line as "Do I come over to sleep in your house, or do we sleep in the gutter?" there is no facial play or vocal trickery. He goes about his irresistible comic business as placidly as a man buttoning his shirt. I once observed him negotiating the old business of stepping off an imaginary stair, and he seemed to be so thoroughly ill at ease and downright embarrassed that I doubt he ever attempted it again. Nor is he by nature a man with a particularly comical face. His nose is a city block shorter than Jimmy Durante's; his eyes have nothing especially humorous about them, as, say, the late William Danforth's had; his hair is neither red nor bushy in the hokum tradition of Jimmie Powers' or even

Danny Kaye's. Yet there is an inner spirit of true comedy in him that pops merrily to the surface.

As for Willie Howard, remove his wig, take off his loud pajamas and sit him quietly in a chair, and the comic spirit remaining in him would be largely invisible.

PORGY AND BESS. September 13, 1943

Return of the George Gershwin, Du Bose Heyward and Ira Gershwin musical folk play. Produced for a limited engagement by Cheryl Crawford in the 44th Street Theatre.

Program

Maria	Georgette Harvey	Crown	Warren Coleman
Lily	Catherine Ayers	Bess	Etta Moten
Annie	Musa Williams	Policeman	Kenneth Konopka
Clara	Harriet Jackson	Detective	Richard Bowler
Jake	Edward Matthews	Undertaker	Coyal McMahan
Sportin' Life	Avon Long	Lawyer Frazier	Charles Welch
Mingo	Jerry Laws	Nelson	Charles Colman
Robbins	Henry Davis	Strawberry Woman	
Serena	Alma Hubbard		Catherine Ayers
Jim	William C. Smith	Crab Man	Edward Tyler
Peter	George Randol	Coroner	Don Darcy
Porgy	Todd Duncan		

SYNOPSIS: Act I. Scene 1. *Catfish Row. A summer evening.* Scene 2. *Serena's room. The following night.* Act II. Scene 1. *Catfish Row. A month later.* Scene 2. *A palmetto jungle. Evening of the same day.* Scene 3. *Catfish Row. Before dawn, a week later.* Scene 4. *Serena's room. Dawn of the following day.* Act III. Scene 1. *Catfish Row. The next night.* Scene 2. *Catfish Row. Early morning.* Scene 3. *Catfish Row. Five days later.*

WHEN FIRST PRESENTED in New York by the Theatre Guild, in 1935, the exhibit was what is known to the Broadway world as an artistic success, meaning that it pleased too few people to make a load of money, which load of money is held by the Broadway world to mean a genuine success, regardless of the success' quality. When revived by Miss Crawford in 1942, it ran for 281 performances, made a load of money, and was accordingly hailed by Broadway, in its own terminology, as a genuine artistic smash.

There were at the presentation's beginning, as there still remain, a quota of devotees who regard it as a work of genius, and one that lifts Gershwin into the ranks of the exalted composers. There were others, and these too remain,

who regard it rather as merely a better than usual gesture
toward folk operetta and its score a better than usual but
hardly important contribution to the tone art. Frequently
derivative and here and there compromising with popular
taste, that score contains, undeniably, some fetching melodies — indeed, one or two that are something superior to
simply that — but its ecstatic veneration as a signal feat
must be left to the round-table of the late Mr. Gershwin's
loving cheer-leaders and to others such whose enthusiasms
are predicated less on sound musical knowledge and criticism than on a patriotic desire to give an American aspirant
a front seat in the sun, on an admiration for a young man
who had successfully self-press-agented his great and laudable ambition to reach the musical heights into an already
fully achieved fact, and on an actual achievement of above
par Broadway musical stage compositions. For such songs
as "Summer Time," "Bess, You Is My Woman Now," "A
Woman Is a Sometime Thing," "I Got Plenty o' Nuttin',"
and "It Ain't Necessarily So," with their apt lyrics by Heyward and Ira Gershwin, are sufficient, understandably, to
overpower the critical faculties of persons who have hitherto subsisted on the regulation Broadway diet.

Rouben Mamoulian's original production was a highly
imaginative job, particularly in its details. When the production was brought back in 1942 and with Mamoulian no
longer in supervision, much of the imagination had vanished. And on this occasion it had vanished almost entirely.
The management's apology, in both instances, was that the
production had been "streamlined" to meet the current
popular prejudice. Streamlining, it seems to me, is somewhat more appropriate to bathrooms than to operettas,
whatever their quality.

There was a repeat engagement at the City Center, beginning on February 7, 1944, for a short run, and a double-
repeat, some weeks later, for a six weeks' run.

A NEW LIFE. September 15, 1943

A play by Elmer Rice. Produced for 69 performances by the Playwrights' Company in the Royale Theatre.

Program

Theodore Emery		Gustave Jensen	John Ireland
	Sanford McCauley	Dr. Lyman Acton	
Miss Hanson	Alice Thomson		Blaine Cordner
Miss Devore	Coleen Ward	Miss Kingsley	Frederica Going
Miss Murphy	Ann Driscoll	Samuel Cleghorne	
Miss Weatherby	Sara Peyton		Walter N. Greaza
George Sheridan		Isabelle Cleghorne	
	Kenneth Tobey		Merle Maddern
Lillian Sheridan	Timmie Hyler	Millicent Prince	Joan Wetmore
Esther Zuckerman		Grover C. Charles	
	Dorothy Darling		Arthur Griffin
Mollie Kleinberger		Miss Swift	Terry Harris
	Dora Weissman	Captain Cleghorne	
Edith Charles Cleghorne			George Lambert
	Betty Field	Ruth Emery	Helen Kingstead
Olive Rapallo	Ann Thomas	Miss Woolley	Shirley Gale

SYNOPSIS: Scene 1. *A foyer on the fifth floor. Afternoon.* Scene 2. *Edith's room. Immediately following.* Scene 3. *The foyer. The early hours of the next morning.* Scene 4. *The twilight zone. Two hours later.* Scene 5. *The foyer. An hour later.* (Intermission.) Scene 6. *Edith's room. Several days later.* Scene 7. *The foyer. A week later.* Scene 8. *Edith's room. Late afternoon of the same day.* Scene 9. *The foyer. Next morning.* Scene 10. *Edith's room. Immediately following.*

The action takes place in the East River Hospital in New York City.

Mr. Rice's grave condition is a case for the critical psychoanalyst. When he started out in the playwriting business, the patient was an incomplex personality perfectly happy to write simple melodrama like *On Trial, For the Defense,* and *It Is The Law.* It was not long thereafter, however, that the first symptoms of what may be termed dramaturgical schizophrenia were detectable in his desire, in *The Adding Machine,* to lend to his melodrama a somewhat deeper import. Conquering himself for a spell largely

through the kindly ministrations of collaborators, there en-
sued a brief period of comedy as simple as his initial melodrama and, solo, once again even melodrama (*Street Scene*)
that concealed the developing mental bacilli. But presently the patient was unable to control his older suppressed
desire, the desire to be not Elmer Rice but a cross between
Augustus Thomas and Samuel Grafton, and the result was
a synthesis of aphronia, mental narcissism, poriomania and
plain, everyday katzenjammer which produced a succession of plays whose possibly valid melodramatic and comedy elements have been vitiated by injecting into them political, economic, theological and sociological dicta that may
best professionally be described under the cross-file head-
ings of dramatic algolagnia and Westbrook Pegler cathar-
sis.

This latest demonstration by the patient further substantiates the findings. What might conceivably have been an
affecting play about bringing a child into the world and
planning its future well-being has been botched by the patient's complexes. His cosmic cure-alls and soap-box ideolo-
gies invade the properly innocent dramaturgic organism —
and the consequence is theatrical astasia.

Against their considered judgment people nevertheless
somehow generally admire the man who in the face of criticism, however sound, persists resolutely in continuing on
his own independent course, however in turn unsound. It
is, perhaps, the same impulse which induces them to side
with the underdog, even when the underdog is something
of a sonofa, or to feel sympathy for a man whose wife has
treated him badly, however much the jerk deserved it.

It is thus that Mr. Rice seems to enjoy the left-handed esteem of folk who should know better but who perversely
appreciate the spectacle of a playwright bravely, if rather
foolishly, constituting himself a martyr to criticism. For
some years now the critics have been generously telling Mr.
Rice that his excessive immersion in social significance and
the like is ruining his plays, and that the plays would be a
lot more acceptable if he forgot for a moment his passion to
be a crusader and devoted himself to drama as uncorrupted

by editorial indignation as were some of his earlier efforts. But he has been as loftily disdainful of their solicitude as a Skippy Homeier; he has stuck resolutely to his guns; and the guns have duly gone pop.

It isn't that a dramatist must arbitrarily under all circumstances avoid social significance or anything else of the kind in his work. That would be the rankest critical nonsense. It is simply that it takes a considerably more gifted and considerably more cerebrally puissant playwright than Mr. Rice, first, to weld the element with his other dramatic materials so as to make it seem naturally part and parcel of them and not a Dr. Munyon index finger poking its way out of the play's flow and, secondly, to invest it, even if it be on the fundamentally obvious side, with at least the gilt veneer of a sprightly viewpoint.

In this his latest play Mr. Rice again succeeds in doing neither of these things. And, as a result and as before intimated, a play that in less ostentatious hands might have amounted to something is sacrificed to the shelf next to the collected speeches of Henry Wallace.

The apology that his admirers and his less forthright critics make for Mr. Rice is that he is at least trying to do something better for the drama, whatever his actual achievement, than the general run of our playwrights. This, I have the presumption to believe, is the purest blabber. The notion that most of our playwrights, even some of the very poorest of them, do not in their hearts believe that what they write is grand stuff and a credit to the drama is pretty far-fetched. The trouble with the majority of them is certainly not lack of honesty and sincerity and hard striving but simply of reputable talent. The writers of the profound junk shown down in the Provincetown Playhouse in the last several years have tried to do something better for the drama just as his friends assert Rice has. But in the one case as in the other it all comes sadly to little or nothing.

What people mean when they indulge in such rhetoric is that a playwright who talks about something like economic determinism, religious freedom, the Bill of Rights or the evils of Fascism is ipso facto, whether he knows what he is talking about or not, superior to one who writes instead about such things as sequestered loafers like Strindberg and Rostand have written. What they further mean, and honestly believe, is that a bad play treating of important matters is more highly to be venerated than a good one dealing with matters of relatively little importance.

Not only does Rice present himself increasingly as trying to fly to the dramatic heights with one wing, and that a left one, but his take-off is more and more from long-plowed ground. His social thinking amounts to little more than old carbon copies of stuff from Mike Gold's *New Masses;* his characters in the present play are such stock figures as the Plutocrat, the Plutocrat's Haughty Wife, the Rebellious Son of the Plutocrat, the Young Radical In Sweater, the Wisecracking Comedy Relief Chorus Girl, the Golden Hearted If Humorous Old Jewish Woman, et al.; his "sensational" stage business of the delivery of a child (with appropriate verbal sound effects) is familiar from Gustav Eckstein's *Christmas Eve,* to say nothing of from the Continental drama of twenty and more years ago; his hospital setting, tone of newborn life, and struggle of mother for child are reminiscent of Mary Macdougal Axelson's *Life Begins;* and his mental processes which bring him thematically to view a rich and comfortable home for a baby as being certain to pollute its mind, whereas a cheap three-room flat is certain to guarantee the unimpeachable integrity of its future political, economic and sociological philosophy, are those of a Theodore Burt Sayre with a Ph.D. from the College of the City of New York.

BRIGHT LIGHTS OF 1944. September 16, 1943

Billed as an "intimate musical revue," with dialogue by Norman Anthony and Charles Sherman, lyrics by Mack David, music by Jerry Livingston. Produced in the Forrest Theatre by Alexander H. Cohen, in association with the Messrs. Poll and Kipness, and withdrawn after three nights.

Principals

James Barton, Smith and Dale, Frances Williams, Buddy Clark, Jayne Manners, Billie Worth, Jere McMahon, Renée Carroll, the Royal Guards, and John Kirby and his orchestra.

THE MAJORITY of the reviewers became very waxy at the presentation and mercilessly excoriated it because the management announced it as a musical revue whereas it was revealed to be simply a vaudeville show. If *Laugh Time* had been billed in the same manner, they doubtless would similarly have denounced it but, since it was frankly designated a vaudeville show, they warmed to it enthusiastically. Although the management was clearly at fault in the billing, I can't see why indignation over a mere label should have operated to condemn outright a show that, had it been labeled otherwise, would have been reviewed with some favor, since it was no better or no worse than the aforesaid *Laugh Time*.

It did, true enough, get off to a misbegotten start in a scene laid in Sardi's theatrical restaurant wherein a pair of potential producers planned the show that was to follow. The dialogue fashioned for the scene deserved all the contumely the reviewers heaped upon the evening as a whole. "Who's your backer?," inquired one producer of another. "The Angel Gabriel," was the reply. "Oh, a trumpet player!," wittily retorted the first gentleman. Subsequently, one waiter, glowering at another, exclaimed, "Don't you know you mustn't insult the customers until they have paid the check!," and followed it up by sampling a glass of champagne, remarking "It's vintage" — "What vintage?" — "Vintage of 1943," making a wry face, and spitting it out into his vis-à-vis' eye. "What is that fellow's name?," he then inquired, indicating a man seated in a corner of the restaurant. "Mr. Potts," was the answer. "Where does he come from?" he further inquired. "Pottstown," was the information. "Oh, I know, that's in Pottsylvania." Pausing for the non-existent roar of laughter to subside, he thereupon excruciatingly observed, "I knew him when he didn't have a pot." Going over to one of the customers, the other waiter asked him what he would have to drink. "Scotch," said the customer. "How will you have it?," bade the waiter. "With Scotch," screamingly answered the customer. "Is he a legitimate actor?," asked one of the producers, pointing to the customer. "No, he's an illegitimate one," came back another. And so on.

Once this euthanasia was over, however, and the evening got down to straight vaudeville turns, it frequently offered some very fair, albeit familiar, entertainment. Smith and Dale came along with their famous Dr. Kronkite act, which still remains the funniest sketch, after all these years, in the theatre, although I could wish they had left it in its pristine form and had not sought to bring it up-to-date with such gags as the doctor's "If you don't keep quiet, I'll give you gas" and the patient's "All right, I'll take six gallons." Nevertheless, the old howls were still there, including the bland observation of the patient, his eyes rivetted on the posterior of the exiting nurse, that she has an honest face; his remark on the whoopsy doctor that he can't tell whether he is Dr. Jekyll or Oscar Wilde; and when the doctor examining him idiotically puts the stethoscope in his, the patient's, ears, he listens gravely for a spell and warns the doc that he had better take care of himself. As for the rest, consult *The Theatre Book of the Year, 1942–1943,* and let yourself go all over again.

James Barton's fabulous drunk act, *The Pest,* continues also to be serviceable for laughs; Kirby's is a superior swing band with a sense of critical humor; Barton's act in conjunction with it, wherein a great itching and scratching is indulged in by the ensemble as an obbligato to the hideous musical rhythms, is amusing low clowning; at least one of the girls in the chorus was pinchable; and a "Frankie and Johnny" number wasn't half-bad. On the other hand, I could sympathize fully with the reviewers when it came to Frances Williams yelling ditties like "That's Broadway!," a white male quartet known as The Royal Guards vocalizing an alleged Negro song in the dark and accompanying it with gesticulations with hands fitted with phosphorescent gloves, a pair of smirking young hoofers named McMahon and Worth, a *Tobacco Road* parody song by Barton (who had played Jeeter Lester in that play on Broadway all of 1899 times), a radio crooner named Clark who moaned a blues song called "Thoughtless" ("Although I was thoughtless, it didn't mean I thought less of you"), and one or two other such death-rattles.

LAND OF FAME. September 21, 1943

A war drama by Albert and Mary Bein, based on a story by Mr. Bein and Charles Paver. Produced in the Belasco Theatre by Mr. Bein and Frederick Fox, who also did the scenery, it ran for only six performances to a loss of more than $30,000.

PROGRAM

STEVE	Kenneth Le Roy	SENTRY	George Dice
ANGELA	Beatrice Straight	VILLAGE ELDER	Lester Alden
SERGEANT HAUPTMANN		GEORGIUS	Royal Dana Tracy
	Richard Basehart	THANOS	John Buckwalter
COLONEL REINICKE		JOHN	Harron Gordon
	Hunter Gardner	HELEN	Naya Grecia
KYRA MARIA		MICHAEL	Jack W. Bittner
	Beatrice de Neergaard	PETER MELINAS	Norman Rose
LIEUTENANT WERNER		SCHOOLTEACHER	Charles Kuhn
	Stefan Schnabel	WAGON-MAKER OF MANDRA	
GENERAL VON OBERMANN			Whitford Kane
	Ed. Begley	LAMBROS	Karl Weber
MAJOR KRANZ	Theo Goetz	OLD VILLAGER	Harron Gordon
CAPTAIN RICHTER			
	Peter von Zerneck		

VILLAGERS, GUERRILLAS AND SOLDIERS

SYNOPSIS: Act I. Scene 1. *The Shepherd's Stone.* Scene 2. *German Staff Headquarters in the village of Talom. Half an hour later.* Scene 3. *A clearing in the forest. That night.* Act II. Scene 1. *Staff Headquarters. The following day.* Scene 2. *At Shepherd's Stone. That night.* Scene 3. *Staff Headquarters. Fifteen minutes later.* Scene 4. *The guerrilla camp. Daybreak.* Act III. Scene 1. *Staff Headquarters. That same day.* Scene 2. *Shepherd's Stone. Twilight.* Scene 3. *Staff Headquarters. Dawn.*
Action takes place in Greece, summer of 1942.

Mr. BEIN, as his previous plays like *Little Ol' Boy* and *Let Freedom Ring* have indicated, is a passionately sincere fellow and Mr. Fox, as his previous productions have indicated, is a gifted scene designer. But their collaborative efforts on this occasion got them nowhere. Passionate sincerity often has a way of abandoning drama in favor of ringing

speeches, and gifted scene designers, when they find themselves in a position of independent authority, often have a
way of not only going the whole hog but of putting sleigh-
bells around its neck. In this case there were accordingly
so many and such fancy stage elevations that the actors were
forced frequently to substitute athletics for histrionics, and
the play haplessly took on the aspect less of drama than of
an Olympic games contest between the Germans on one
side and the Greeks on the other.

It was the Germans and the Greeks that the drama sought
somewhat otherwise to concern itself with. A paraphrase of
Steinbeck's *The Moon Is Down* with the scene transferred
from Norway to Greece, the intention of the authors was to
present in similarly heroic terms the dégringolade of the
Nazi forces of occupation under the indomitable guerilla
will of a conquered people. The intention, however, while
laudable, was reduced by overwriting to something that approached the dimensions of a Pain's Fireworks show presided over by Dorothy Thompson. The indignant rhetorical sky-rockets, the purple wraths shooting off in all
directions, the patriotic roman candles exploded against
the Nazis' seats, and the general pyrotechnic hot-foots, along
with the contrasting chromatic testimonials to the spirit of
Thermopylæ, the valor of Marathon and the glories of
Greek architecture, literature, poetry, and so on, buried the
simple theme in the multi-colored garrulity and, before the
evening was over, lent to the play the refractorily ridiculous
air of a circus act in which Byron was shot out of a cannon
into a net filled with Gerhart Hauptmanns, dejecting the
latter en masse onto the lions and tigers in the ring below.

At least one of the characters, a Gestapo officer attached
to the German command, was similarly ridiculous, what
with his constant badgering of Nazi generals and colonels
with derisory nose-thumbings at Hitler, loudly expressed
admiration of everything Greek from the Acropolis to Katina Paxinou, and confidential betrayals of his army's military plans roared at the top of his voice, in a room just off
one occupied by members of the Nazi staff, to a leader of the
Greek rebels. The general quality of the writing was suffi-

ciently to be suggested by some such speech, addressed to
the aforesaid Gestapoist, as "Then maybe you are ashamed
to be here right now — to rape and plunder the country
that showed you such hospitality!" And the theatrical effect
of the whole was hardly helped by casting in the role of the
Greek hero an actor who bore a frightening resemblance to
Jed Harris, by employing an actor for the role of the ferocious Nazi general who looked like a fat Jimmy Durante,
and by presenting the Irish Whitford Kane, rich brogue
and all, as a Greek wagon-maker of Mandra.

The best play about guerilla warfare in any of the occupied countries thus far shown remains *Winter Soldiers* of
the antecedent theatrical year. A play dealing specifically
with the Greeks under Nazi domination, also of that year
and tried out briefly in a sidestreet theatre — its title, *God
Strikes Back;* its author, Paul Nord — was considerably
worse than this *Land of Fame*. But *Land of Fame* remains
secure in second place.

The defect in all the various anti-Nazi plays is that the
villains are naturally set-ups and that an audience's emotional reaction is automatically supplied to it before the
curtain goes up. That way lies bad drama, and good cinema.
One of the reasons for the superior quality and success of
What Price Glory? — immediacy of war or not — perhaps
rested in the fact that the German villain was kept in the
wings.

ALL FOR ALL. September 29, 1943

A comedy by Norman Bruce, derived to a wholesale degree from Aaron Hoffman's Give and Take, *presented in 1923. Produced for a forced 85 performances by A. L. Berman in the Bijou Theatre.*

Program

Marion Kruger	*Flora Campbell*	John Bauer, Sr.	*Jack Pearl*
John Bauer, Jr.	*Lyle Bettger*	Daniel Drum	*Wyrley Birch*
Albert Kruger	*Harry Green*	Thomas W. Craig	*Loring Smith*

SYNOPSIS: Act I. A morning in June. Act II. Several weeks later. Act III. Two weeks later. Evening.

All the action takes place in the executive office of Bauer's K. O. Brand, Bauerville, California.

O NE MIGHT have thought that the comedy wrought for the purposes of a pair of friendly but explosively argumentative German comedians (in times of the habitual wars with the Germans for greater acceptability's sake given a Jewish veneer) had passed into the discard, even in the estimation of actors whose talents were appropriately vested in the ability to suggest that they subsisted on a diet of spitballs. But the Messrs. Pearl and Green (a sometimes gifted clown) thought otherwise, at least until the public instructed them differently. We consequently here received again, and after these many years, another of the bygone exhibits involving a duo of brotherly business partners who consume two hours in vociferously and damply insulting each other and who wind up with their arms once more affectionately around each other.

As their vehicle, the two comedians in point offered Hoffman's old elaborated vaudeville sketch about a canning factory which one of them wishes to convert into a cooperative plant. The revised, up-to-date version consisted chiefly in the insertion into the original dialogue of references to the draft, rationing, the *March of Time* movie, and President

Roosevelt. For the rest, the fabric was much as it was twenty years ago, although some of the incorporated jocosities were evidently culled from a period rather before Hoffman's, say Fibber McGee's. Samples: 1. "I haven't got no use for Democracy; I'm a Republican." 2. "When the whale swallowed Jonah, he musta felt down in the mouth."

As for the stage comic business, these samples will suffice: 1. One of the comedians suddenly let out a yell, grabbed at his stomach, and howled that he had swallowed his cigar. The other indicated that he had it clutched in his hand. 2. After an abusive telephone conversation, one of the comedians irately slammed down the receiver and, after a moment, seized it up again to shout Goodbye. 3. The scheming banker, who had in his pocket the document that would ruin the partners, was challenged by one of them to fight. Both threw off their coats and, when they put them on again, the partner gleefully found that the coats had been exchanged and that the document was in his possession.

Sample of the stage direction: When one of the characters exited, two or three of the others invariably saw him out of the door.

The Rogers brothers, Weber and Fields, Kolb and Dill, Louis Mann and Sam Bernard, and the various Potash and Perlmutters were on the occasion mercifully in their graves.

HAIRPIN HARMONY. September 30, 1943

A musical farce written and composed by Harold Orlob, with additional dialogue by Don Witty, a misnomer. Produced for instantaneous failure by Mr. Orlob in the National Theatre.

PROGRAM

BILL HELLER	Lennie Kent	COBALT	Smiles & Smiles
HOWARD SWIFT	Carlyle Blackwell	LOOSEKNIT	
CHET WARREN	Gil Johnson	RACEY CORDAY	Fanette Stalle
REENIE FRANTON		REV. DR. BROWN	Don Valentine
	Maureen Cannon	CAPTAIN ROC	Ving Merlin
JACKIE STEVENS	Teri Keane	MRS. WARREN	Jean Moore
EVELYN	Karen Conrad	KEEPER	Scott Moore
BETTY	Gay Gaynor	STATE TROOPER	Clair Kramer
JUNE			
RUTH	Clawson Triplets		
SUE			

Scene. *Lucy Warren's California home.*
Time. *Summer afternoon and evening.*

FROM TIME TO TIME during the last five or six seasons various producers have toyed with the idea of a musical show dealing with the trials and tribulations of a band, an idea that the movies, which generally cabbage anything that is in the Broadway air, promptly upon getting wind of put into production. Mr. Orlob's exhibit was, after the delay on the part of his fellow-producers, the first of the exercises of the theme to reach the stage. The movies are welcome to it.

The movies, indeed, are welcome not only to the theme but to everything else connected with *Hairpin Harmony* which, beyond any possible doubt, was one of the worst musical shows ever to have been shown in the whole history of the American theatre. Beside it even *The London Follies* of a quarter-century ago, the *You'll See Stars* of the 1942–1943 season, and the *My Dear Public* of this do not seem to have been so dreadful as they unquestionably were. The

female band around which the plot revolved was not only
made up of some of the most hideous mammals observed
on the stage in its time, but when already hideous women
blow trumpets, saxophones and trombones out of their faces
the picture is too painful to contemplate. The plot, having
to do with the band's efforts to land a radio contract, involved as its first act dramatic climax the attempted passing
off of a man in a baby-carriage as a child prodigy and was
topped by the immemorial exclamation, "But that baby
needs a shave!" The humor fore and aft was directed mostly
toward reflections on the virginity of the women members
of the cast and included at least four items of an indelicacy
seldom encountered in the theatre, even on the old burlesque show stages at their dirtiest. One of the aforesaid
items concerned with sitting on soldiers' laps and with
loaded guns caused numerous ladies in the audience to
scurry to the exits. The scenery was borrowed from a failure of two seasons before; the costumes were even more
hideous than the females they covered; the actors were
drafted largely from night club floor shows, Grade-F movies and the soap opera radio; and the music and lyrics
would not have been tolerated by a small-time juke box.

The catastrophe was withdrawn after three performances.

ONE TOUCH OF VENUS. OCTOBER 7, 1943

A musical comedy by S. J. Perelman and Ogden Nash, with music by Kurt Weill and lyrics by Nash. Produced for a season's run by Cheryl Crawford in the Imperial Theatre.

PROGRAM

WHITELAW SAVORY	*John Boles*	MRS. KRAMER	*Helen Raymond*
MOLLY GRANT	*Paula Laurence*	GLORIA KRAMER	*Ruth Bond*
TAXI BLACK	*Teddy Hart*	POLICE LIEUTENANT	*Bert Freed*
STANLEY	*Harry Clark*	ROSE	*Jane Hoffman*
RODNEY HATCH	*Kenny Baker*	ZUVELTI	*Harold Stone*
VENUS	*Mary Martin*	DR. ROOK	*Johnny Stearns*
MRS. MOATS	*Florence Dunlap*	ANATOLIANS	
STORE MANAGER	*Sam Bonnell*	*Sam Bonnell, Matthew Farrar*	
BUS STARTER	*Lou Wills, Jr.*	PREMIERE DANSEUSE	*Sono Osato*
SAM	*Zachary A. Charles*		

SYNOPSIS: Act I. Scene 1. *Main gallery of the Whitelaw Savory Foundation of Modern Art.* Scene 2. *Rodney's room.* Scene 3. *Arcade of N. B. C. Building, Radio City.* Scene 4. *Waiting room of Mid-City Bus Terminal.* Scene 5. *The roof of the museum.* Scene 6. *Rodney's barber shop.* Scene 7. *The roof of the museum.* Act II. Scene I. *Savory's bedroom.* Scene 2. *The Tombs.* Scene 3. *A hotel room.* Scene 4. *Main gallery of the Foundation.*

WHEN THE FIRST CURTAIN went up and disclosed a modern art gallery I said to myself that, since both Perelman and Nash had proved themselves highly amusing fellows in the past, here would doubtless result some fine satirical fooling in the manner of Rip's memorable fooling with a similar scene in one of his gay Paris revues. But disappointment was not long in coming. Not only in this scene but in those that followed the erstwhile witty twain produced next to nothing in the way of humor to justify their reputations. Worse, they saw fit frequently to resort to smoking-car whimsicalities to coax the laughter which failed to ensue from other portions of their dialogue, and the smoking-car was of the fifty-year-old Wagner period.

The book, suggested by F. Anstey's story, *The Tinted Venus,* was, further, hardly on the inspired side, dealing as it did with the familiar fancy about the statue of a woman that comes to life, finds itself in a world it can not understand and, after the customary amorous contretemps, returns to its original marble. The authors' idea was obviously to fashion another *I Married An Angel* out of the material, but they got within hailing distance of that diverting fable only in a five-minute episode in the second act wherein the come-alive Venus goddess paradoxically breathes earthiness into her cold lover. Nash's lyrics, here and there fair enough, were more often of a routine Broadway essence, including even such jocosities as the squirting proclivities of grapefruit. Weill's score, however, though at almost all times teatable and derivative, contained a number of pleasant melodies, notably "West Wind," "Speak Low," "That's Him," and "Foolish Heart."

While, like the next one, I feel it a relief occasionally to get away from the standardized lines of chorus girls, I nevertheless feel that the recent substitutions of ballets, as in this show and several antecedent others, may be carried too far. It is an unfortunate circumstance that ballet dancers do not seem always to have been overly blessed by nature in the matter of looks and it is an even more unfortunate circumstance that even the two or three who may have been given a better deal by Providence have, as a result of long and strenuous training, developed calf muscles of such size as suggest that the ladies' bosoms have slipped down into their stockings. The consequence is that, while the artistic side of their activities may pass muster, the visual side violates cruelly the romantic aspect of the shows they are in and makes the spectator pine again for the good, old chorus girls who, even though they may not be able to dance, are at least in comparison a faint satisfaction to the eye.

The deterioration of the American musical show, once the pride and glory of our theatre, is a matter for some critical pondering. Where any longer are there any counterparts not only of the old George Lederer shows and the great Ziegfeld shows and the George White shows and those smaller but delightful Princess Theatre shows and such wonderful shows as *Show Boat* and *Music In the Air,* but counterparts even of the considerably less wonderful shows of six and seven years ago? Certainly a *Something For the Boys* does not compare with an *I Married an Angel,* or an *Early To Bed* with a *Leave It To Me,* or a *Follow the Girls* with a *Du Barry Was a Lady,* or a contemporary de-Ziegfelded *Follies* with a *Cabin In the Sky,* or a show like this *One Touch of Venus* with a *Louisiana Purchase.* And even more certainly these shows of today are not in the running with the shows that still earlier made our stage the leader in the field and the envy of producers the wide world 'round.

It would obviously not be fair to bring into the question of comparison such of this season's turtles as *What's Up, Jackpot, Allah Be Praised!,* and the like, since it would not be difficult to find their equivalents in other and more remote seasons. But all the same they indicate, at least to a degree, the way the wind is blowing. The old lustre, the old excitement, the old quality and the old almost everything else, save only now and then in the case of some attractive settings and costumes, seem to be disappearing. Against one *Oklahoma!* or one *Mexican Hayride* (*Carmen Jones* is obviously in a separate category) you will have to search hard for a single new show that gives you even an ounce of the one-time big kick.

It isn't a matter of economy, for producers are often spending quite as much if not more money on the shows than producers spent in the past. Nor is it lack of trying, since there is every indication that they exert themselves to do the best they can. They get the best performers they are able to, and the best designers, and the best directors, and the best orchestra leaders, and even go to the extent of washing the lemonade glasses in the foyer at least once a week. Then what is the trouble?

The trouble, I think, is the 10-cent point of view behind even the $125,000 shows. This 10-cent point of view may be divided into three $3\frac{1}{3}$ cent sections. The first is the cheapness in book taste; the second, the cheapness in humor taste; and the third, the vulgarity of taste in relation to the women performers.

The first thing the average music show producer seems to do these days is to make certain that the theme of his projected exhibit will be sufficiently smutty, at least in part, to embarrass any well-bred, educated theatregoers and to appeal rather to that metropolitan element whose early schooling in belles-lettres was confined to the literature of the lavatory wall and to out-of-towners, otherwise as respectable as so many golf club presidents, who come to New York as similarly reputable New Yorkers once came to Paris or St. Louis. It is thus that in the last few seasons we have been tendered shows laid in brothels, other shows with scenes laid in proximity to men's toilets, still others concerned with the anatomical peccadillos of dizzy married females, yet others involving as their climactic business the forcible disrobing of women, still yet others having to do with intruders into the marriage bed, yet others still that have dealt with homosexuality, and so on. In some cases, it has got to be so that, as you recall, even the morality cops have seen fit to heave themselves into action.

Secondly, the average producer's taste in humor appears to run in a collateral direction. That, as a critic, I have no more moral indignation than an Italian operatic baritone is, I hope, sufficiently well-known. That, further, I now and then relish a bit of ribaldry no less than did and do Abe Lincoln, Chauncey Depew and President Roosevelt is, I hope, also sufficiently recognized. But, when in the course of duty I listen to some of the witless and wormy dirt peddled in some of the musicals, I long again even for the dreary but decent wastes of such home-made road turkeys of an earlier day as dealt endlessly and at third-hand with princesses exchanged at childbirth with the offspring of gypsies, gay young dukes and village stableboys who looked so much alike that the latter were able to take their places in the ducal mansions when the dukes wished to hit it up at the Chat Noir with Fifi, and captains of smuggler bands who fell in love with the daughters of Spanish mayors and were disclosed in the last act to be not the scoundrels the girls' papas wrathfully imagined but, one and all of them, Henri de Lantiponnage, son of the richest banker in Lan-gouste-sur-mer.

Thirdly, the vulgarity in connection with the female performers. It is a rare contemporary show that offers in its principal woman's role an actress who, however otherwise she may naturally be, has not been converted into a creature with the demeanor of a washerwoman and the vocal delicacy of an auctioneer, it being the producers' belief that such a conversion is necessary to what they call "pep" and to "getting the show across." It is thus that the rendition of a simple, sentimental love song frequently takes on the air of a drowning woman screaming for help, and the singer herself the aspect of a combination Emma Goldman and Billy Sunday. And it is also thus that the heroine whom we are asked sentimentally to admire is made to present herself physically as a montage advertisement of bust developers, electric vigor belts, aerial iron-jaw acts, and Old Dr. Doodle's Magic Youth Restorer.

If you were to invite the producers to go around, take another look at *Oklahoma!* and observe what a quieter approach can do for a show and the box-office, the answer would probably be that *Oklahoma!* was an exception to the general rule and just a lucky break. And if you were to smile at the answer and further recall to the gentlemen a dozen or more other such quieter successes of the happy past as the before-mentioned *I Married an Angel, Music In the Air* and *Show Boat,* along with *The Cat and the Fiddle, The Band Wagon, Sweet Adeline, Bitter-Sweet,* etc., what their reply would be, I do not know, save that, whatever it was, it would be senseless.

It seems that you can't teach new dogs old tricks. And the consequence is that certain shows that might otherwise have a doubled critical appeal are sacrificed not only to Pinero's absurd old theory that you have to tell an audience a thing seven times in order that it may be sure to get it, but that in telling the audience you have to proclaim it so at the top of the lungs that, by the time it is finally gotten, the audience has split eardrums and is exhausted to the point of a wholesale faint.

Searching my memory, it is all I can do to remember more than three shows in the last four or five seasons, of which *One Touch of Venus,* whatever its other manifold aches, is one, whose leading women have been permitted to comport themselves in a manner conducive to inspiring one with the notion that it would be very pleasant to take them out to supper. And if the heroine of a show doesn't induce such a notion, the show in most cases may be put down as lacking something. In the instance of many of the shows it is next to impossible to surrender one's imagination to the point where it can accept the idea that the hero could conceivably fall in love with the star noisebox and that he isn't a damned fool for not chucking her on the spot and giving his whole heart to one of the chorus girls who hasn't a line to speak and can't sing.

I can only hope that the future will give us back female principals who will hit their producers and directors over the head with shillelahs if the latter order them to forget that they are ladies and seek to transform them instead into so many barkers for boiler-works.

Incidental box-office report on *One Touch of Venus:* a mint.

ANOTHER LOVE STORY. October 12, 1943

A comedy by Frederick Lonsdale. Produced with small results for a few months' forced run in the Fulton Theatre.

Program

George Wayne	*Roland Young*	John Asprey	*Arthur Margetson*
Mortimer	*Henry Mowbray*	Michael Foxx	*Philip Ober*
Elsie Williams Browne		Molly Asprey	*Augusta Dabney*
	Doris Dalton	Celia Hale	*Fay Baker*
Robert Crayle	*Richard Barbee*	Diana Flynn	*Margaret Lindsay*
Reginald Williams Browne		Maggie Sykes	*Jayne Cotter*
	Fred Irving Lewis		

SYNOPSIS: *Act I. The home of Mrs. Williams Browne. A sitting-room. Morning. Act II. Scene 1. The same. A weekend a fortnight later — after dinner. Scene 2. A charmingly appointed bedroom. That same evening. Scene 3. The living-room. The following morning.*

WHATEVER ELSE the English theatre was deficient in, we could usually in the past look to it for amusing polite comedy. Pinero, Wilde, Henry Arthur Jones and even on stray occasion Alfred Sutro might be relied upon in the far days to animate us uncouth Yankees with fables of the high-toned British drawing-rooms. Following them came H. V. Esmond, Hubert Henry Davies, Haddon Chambers, R. C. Carton and several others such to pleasure us with the species of theatrical fare that only Clyde Fitch and Langdon Mitchell seemed able at odd times to negotiate on the home coast. In their wake appeared W. S. Maugham and, a little later, Frederick Lonsdale and Ashley Dukes. And in their wake in turn, a coterie of younger men led by Noel Coward, none of whom was their equal but one or two of whom seemed to be successful in catering to the local dramatic appetite for inferior mortals in superior surroundings.

The last decade or so, however, has witnessed an almost total collapse of such English benefactions. Maugham, the best of the later lot, has given up playwriting save for a revision of a minor comedy, *Sheppey*, written some years ago.

Lonsdale, as this, his newest effort, all too regrettably indicates, has lost the ground that first began to quake badly in
his directly antecedent *Foreigners* and *Once Is Enough.*
Dukes has not been heard from in years. Coward, although
showing some remaining popular wind in *Blithe Spirit,* has
fallen off markedly since *Private Lives.* And none of the
Rattigans, Savorys, Novellos and the other juniors has done
anything to make the native Behrmans blush even faintly
with envy.

What, specifically, are the reasons for this latest and further Lonsdale decline as evidenced by a play that is a pitiably far cry from his early *Aren't We All?, Spring Cleaning,*
and *The Last of Mrs. Cheyney?* The first seems to be that he
is living so far in the theatrical past that he can almost
reach out and touch Sydney Grundy. His present characters, for all his hope that they may appear otherwise, are
ghosts of those who long ago paraded the fashionable London stages at which Bernard Shaw, then a drama critic,
blew his memorable derisive bean-shooter. Though they
try desperately to speak another and more modern language, their intrinsic processes of thought betray them and
one momentarily expects them to indulge in asides confid-
ing to us that *The Second Mrs. Tanqueray* is selling out at
the St. James's, that Clement Scott, who is sitting in the
third row, has had that same evening shirt on since the first
night of *The Pirates of Penzance,* and that considerable
gossip has been going on in the Albany about Lily Langtry
and the Prince of Wales. They seem to be blissfully unaware of the fact, for all their 1943 apparel and periodic allusions to contemporary life, that they one and all are on
the passenger list of the Sutton Vane liner *Outward Bound,*
and with the bar long since closed.

A second reflection brings us to the conclusion that, despite the circumstance that Mr. Lonsdale has been visiting
in America these last four or five years, he has learned very
little about Americans and that, as a result, the soi-disant
American characters in *Another Love Story* remain fundamentally English. Having occupied himself while here almost entirely with the New York society life, he seems to

have achieved the notion that all Americans are divided into two classes: those who live like Mrs. Cornelius Vanderbilt and those, on the other hand, who live in slums like the Ritz and the Sherry-Netherland. The term Okies, he has been persuaded by the swank and aloof existence he has led, probably refers to persons who hang around the Oak Room at the Plaza, and mugs are those things behind the bars in the West Side restaurants. Long Island, where he has spent many a jolly week-end, has just five localities in its entire length: Old Westbury, Roslyn, Port Washington, Oyster Bay, and Southampton. Bayside is doubtless in Arkansas, Flushing somewhere in Wyoming, and Patchogue, Yaphank, Riverhead and Far Rockaway are God knows where. The capital of the United States is El Morocco; Congress meets in the Union Club, when and if it is allowed in; and New York west of Fifth Avenue is an unexplored wasteland, inhabited chiefly by the very poor, with an annual pittance of twenty or twenty-five thousand. The majority of Americans, accordingly, are largely indistinguishable from the upper-crust British, save perhaps alone for better dinner tables and a propensity for denouncing President Roosevelt.

It is generally dangerous for a playwright of one nation to write of people of another nation. However observant at his best he may be, there will inevitably be numerous things in his play that will give him away. Even the shrewd and lately Americanized John van Druten several times in the past thus tripped up, despite the fact that in one instance he had the acumen to gather unto himself a checking American collaborator. Mr. Lonsdale, working solo, has found himself even more frequently with his braces down and his pantaloons slipping. His characters may be American in designation but the curtain has not been up ten minutes before they are discerned to be as essentially English as John Gielgud, fish and chips, and loose garters.

A third reflection has to do with humor. That the English conception of what is comical differs considerably from our own is, I take it, sufficiently well appreciated. It isn't that the English idea is wrong and that ours is right; it is simply that the two nations are often at striking variance as to what constitutes the prime materials for laughter. In an effort to bridge the gap, Mr. Lonsdale, who evidently while over here has not patronized the right saloons or engaged the society of the more experienced raconteurs, has unwittingly had recourse to some of the hoariest jocosities of the McKinley era. He has, true enough, dressed them up to look like Michael Arlen, but there they are in all their peg-topped trousers none the less. We can't be fooled that way. Maybe Mr. Lonsdale never heard them before but, since nothing travels faster in this country than bad news and bad jokes, we heard them when we were still riding Peer-less bicycles, wearing "Oh, You Kid!" buttons in our lapels, and drinking Moxie. So be yourself soon again, old boy, and give us back instead the entertaining English wit and humor of the plays you wrote while still in England, and leave your idea of American humor to the English movie directors in Hollywood, which will be a sufficiently venge-ful, if superfluous, legacy.

We now reflect on the matter of theme. I will not, of course, be so foolish as to argue that marital infidelity and miscellaneous sex should at last find a permanent place on the index of polite comedy expurgations; it is entirely pos-sible, as we shall subsequently see, that some turns may still be called upon them that will reconstitute them lively entertainment. But the turns they take in *Another Love Story* are the venerable pirouettes, and we have been all too familiar with them these countless years.

Observing the amorous gyrations of Mr. Lonsdale's char-acters, I seemed to see passing as an endless pageant before my half-closed eyes the comedies of several generations. Here again were the same old tired bodies simulating a celery-tonic vigor and putting it into words that needed a shot of strychnine to make them believable. Here once more was the old Parisian give-and-take filtered through the greater London punctilio. Here were the tomcats again mewing Chopin, and the anatomy charts hung alongside the pictures of Henry Guy Carleton, and the Palais Royal turned Episcopalian. And, observing, I seemed to be say-

ing to myself that surely the Lonsdale who personally is a
fellow of wit and wisdom and a large natural sagacity
should have known as well as the rest of us that such damp
spats dramaturgy was not only as outmoded as Hannen
Swaffer's hat but no more critically suited to a New York
stage, even at its current feeblest, than gas footlights or the
plays of Gilbert Lennox.

The play was staged by author, whose idea of direction
is apparently to have the actors regard their exits either as
whippets or as tortoises, causing them in the first case to
dart off like lightning or in the second to conduct themselves like persons who suffer paralytic strokes, accompanied by an epigrammatic rash, at the mere sight of a
door or French window.

THE FAMILY CARNOVSKY. OCTOBER 18, 1943

A Yiddish drama by I. J. Singer. Produced briefly by Maurice Schwartz in the Adelphi Theatre, for the occasion rechristened the Yiddish Art Theatre.

PROGRAM

THE NARRATOR		LIPPMAN	Michael Goldstein
	Anatole Winogradov	DR. COHEN	Anatole Winogradov
DAVID CARNOVSKY	Isidore Casher	DR. KIRCHENMEYER	
LEAH CARNOVSKY			Abraham Teitelbaum
	Rebecca Weintraub	KOMMERZRAT MOSER	
GEORG CARNOVSKY			Morris Feder
	Maurice Schwartz	FRAU KOMMERZRAT MOSER	
THERESA HOLBECK	Muriel Gruber		Seesel Pearson
JEGOR CARNOVSKY	Paul Levitt	SAMUEL LEVI	Meyer Scherr
MRS. HOLBECK	Lisa Silbert	STORM TROOPER	Morris Krohner
HOGO HOLBECK	Mario Gang	DEAF PATIENT	Jenny Casher
SOLOMON BURAK	Yudel Dubinsky	GRETA	Rosetta Cohen
YETTA	Rose Greenfield	SCHOOL SUPERINTENDENT	
RUTH	Zelda Gould		Frank Kressman
RABBI DR. SPEIER	Leon Gold	KARL	Benedict Stein
EFRAIM WALDER	Boris Auerbach	HERMAN	Solomon Krause

The action, in seven scenes, passes in Berlin and in New York.

THE PRODUCTION, which was the 125th by Mr. Schwartz and his company, marked the twenty-fifth season in the organization's life. Beginning on Second Avenue, the Yiddish Art Theatre in 1919 found a stage farther uptown in the old Irving Place Theatre and now moved up even farther to the Broadway theatrical district, for a short spell. This anniversary presentation, by the author of *The Brothers Ashkenazi* and *Yoshe Kalb,* deals mainly with the effect of Hitler's advent upon the Jews of Berlin. Tracing the history of a German-Jewish family through two decades and three generations, it treats of the effect of eventual Nazi rule upon a Jewish physician who marries a Gentile and of the effect of that rule upon the family in general. Although, as observed in the *Theatre Book of the Year, 1942–1943,* I understand no word of the language in which the play is written and acted, a detailed synopsis printed in the program, together with almost equally detailed incidental pantomime on the part of the players, seemed to indicate that the playwright is no man for half-measures and that, given a dramatic situation, he does not let go of it until every last bit of melodramatic juice has been squeezed out of it.

Being thus suspect as an entirely reliable critic, I simply make this note of the production for the record.

Further notes. Other Yiddish exhibits shown in the same week were, on October 15, *Lucky Days,* an operetta by Sholem Secunda with a libretto partly in English by William Siegel, produced by Menasha Skulnik in the Second Avenue Theatre, and, on October 17, *The Golden Land,* a musical play by Julie Berns, produced by Judah Bleich in the Public Theatre. Skulnik is a favorite comedian on the East Side and *Lucky Days* was apparently tailored to his measure, including (somewhat eccentrically for an operetta) a zoot-suit number in which he rendered that hardly Yiddish ditty, "Pistol Packin' Mama." *The Golden Land,* with a cast headed by another prime favorite, Ludwig Satz, dealt, according to the printed synopsis, with an East Side song writer who meets a celebrated actress at Coney Island, marries her, and learns to his agony that she will not forsake her career for home life, whereupon he leaves her and goes back to the East Side to write the great music born of his heartache.

In February, Mr. Skulnik produced another musical comedy as a personal vehicle, *My Friend Yossel.* Those who understood it seemed to enjoy it no end.

OTHELLO. OCTOBER 19, 1943

The tragedy by William Shakespeare. Produced success-
fully by the Theatre Guild in the Shubert Theatre.

PROGRAM

RODERIGO	Jack Manning	DESDEMONA	Uta Hagen
IAGO	José Ferrer	MONTANO	William Woodson
BRABANTIO	Averell Harris	FIRST SOLDIER AT CYPRUS	
OTHELLO	Paul Robeson		Sam Banham
CASSIO	James Monks	SECOND SOLDIER AT CYPRUS	
DUKE	Robert E. Perry		Eugene Stuckmann
LODOVICO	Philip Huston	THIRD SOLDIER AT CYPRUS	
A MESSENGER	Henry Barnard		Bruce Brighton
FIRST SENATOR	Jack De Shay	EMILIA	Margaret Webster
SECOND SENATOR	Graham Velsey	BIANCA	Edith King
THIRD SENATOR	John Ireys	GRATIANO	Robert E. Perry

SYNOPSIS: Act I. Scene 1. A street scene in Venice. Scene 2. The
council chamber. Scene 3. A seaport in Cyprus. Scene 4. The castle in
Cyprus. Act II. Scene 1. The castle in Cyprus. Scene 2. A room in the
castle. Scene 3. A street in Cyprus. Scene 4. A bedroom in the castle.

THE APPEARANCE OF Paul Robeson as the Moor was accompanied by the anticipated polemics on the appropriate-
ness of casting a Negro in the role. Margaret Webster, the
director, spread herself in scholarly testimony to the justification of such casting and found plenty of support from
critics and school children, who had known it all along.
Others issued forth in anthropological and racial rebuttal,
also in portentously scholarly accents equally familiar to
critics and school children. And all to small purpose. What,
may one ask, does it matter? Black or white, the whole
question rests in whether the actor can act the role. Robeson
acts it poorly.

If a Negro can act there is no more reason why he
shouldn't play Othello than there is why a good white
actor shouldn't, since even if Othello was not a Negro he
certainly was not an American, Englishman, German or

Russian, some of whom have been wholly and perfectly satisfactory as the character. We have had whites as everything black from Uncle Tom to the Sultan of Sulu and blacks as everything white from Macbeth (*vide* the Federal Theatre Project production) to George Kelly's Show-off, and no one has gone in for racial disputations the one way or the other. Whether Othello was or was not a Negro is thus purely an academic question, of interest only to academicians who have little else to do but bother their brains with such matters. It is of no interest to the theatre. The theatre has not stopped for a split-second to reflect that the Mikado, Simon Legree and the Lord God Almighty may not have been or are not Negroes, yet it has joyfully accepted them as Negroes on the stage.

It is surely no more out of place for a Negro to depict the Moor than it is for, say, a Canadian like Walter Huston. The Negro, as a matter of fact, enjoys at least one advantage, since his complexion already has the dark coloring necessary to the visual depiction and since he does not have to smear up his face with the load of black and tan makeup that usually makes the white actor look considerably less like a noble Moorish general in the Venetian service than a candy factory foreman who has fallen into a vat of licorice fudge. Mr. Robeson has the physical exterior for the role; it is the artistic interior that is lacking; and that alone is what counts.

Even such pundits as debated the propriety of Negro casting nevertheless concurred in this opinion that, whatever his other shortcomings, Robeson looked the part. And that, to repeat, seems to me to be something, since no small part of the critical skepticism over a certain production of *Hamlet* was predicated on the fact that John Gielgud suggested the physical picture of the heroic Dane considerably less than he did that of Osric, and over a certain production of this same *Othello* on the circumstance that Philip Merivale presented the aspect of a Moor much less than he did that of Anthony Eden with a barber-shop sun-tan.

The only difficulty with Robeson's looking like a Moor was that the other actors in the drama looked no more like authentic Venetians and Cyprians than James Monks, Averell Harris and Margaret Webster, and accordingly threw the whole picture out of visual focus. If none of the players looks really like what he or she is supposed to look like, an audience is generally willing to remit its judgment to the extent of accepting the cast as a unit for what it is programmed to be. But when so much as even one member of the troupe meets exactly and faithfully the pictorial demand, the general picture is thrown out of joint and the other actors seem just a bit ridiculous. Thus, if we are going to have a Negro in the Othello role, perhaps it would be better after all to have Negroes in all the other roles, or else engage a quadroon.

So far as the acting phase is concerned, Robeson's performance suggests mainly a Walter Hampden in blackface, overly rhetorical, monotonous, rigid, and given to a barely concealed consciousness of its vocal organ tones. Physically and pictorially perfect, it seems seldom able to step out of its handsome frame and take on other than purely photographic life. It becomes in the aggregate a recitative, and as such commendable, but rarely, if ever, does it generate within itself the vitality of dramatic histrionism.

The best performance is that of José Ferrer as Iago, which has been directed by Margaret Webster with considerable intelligence. As usually acted, Iago would no more deceive Othello, however at times thick-headed the latter unquestionably is, than a 5-and-10-store shoplifter would deceive the FBI. The Iago we commonly get performs his machinations hardly less subtly than the villains in the old saw-mill and railroad-switch melodramas. He sneaks around the stage like a one-ring circus panther, leers so leerishly that if Othello were just once to glance out of the corner of his eye he would burlesque the whole business by thereafter alluding to him as Sir Francis Levison, and comports himself generally so much like a whisper affianced to a loudspeaker that the only leading Shakespearean character he could fool for a moment would be Falstaff, and then only if Falstaff were more than usually drunk.

Some of the local Iagos we have seen have accordingly

belonged less in *Othello* than in *A Midsummer Night's Dream* with Quince, Snug, Bottom and Snout. Some, like Brian Aherne, have even gone to the extent of making out Othello a bigger blockhead than usual by pointing up their satanic prospecti with acrobatics, much after the manner of Lew Morrison's Mephistopheles in his spectacular version of *Faust*. Others like Kenneth McKenna have couched their villainy in terms of small town hotel house-detectives snooping the credentials of a colored guest whose suit-case betrays the presence of a brick. And the Iagos of still others have lacked only black mustaches, riding boots and crops to constitute them blood-brothers to Desperate Desmond. Miss Webster has gratefully so directed the Iago of Mr. Ferrer that he seems to Othello at least moderately believable and to the rest of us, if not that, at least occasionally distinguishable from the low scoundrel who used to lure little Nellie into the opium den.

The Desdemona of Miss Hagen has a single vocal tone, and that situated in the nose. The Cassio of James Monks evidently once rowed on the crew in *Brown of Harvard*. The Brabantio of Averell Harris seems more in the Denman Thompson line than the Shakespearean. Miss Webster's Emilia is altogether too shrewd and crisp for the role's intrinsic foggy mentality. And the Bianca of Edith King is strictly Earl Carroll.

The play is presented in two acts and eight scenes, and with a single intermission. The arrangement makes for some weariness. *Othello* profits theatrically, I believe, from two intermissions.

However and none the less, the production in its entirety was rapturously received by a majority of the reviewers and audiences, and managed a record run.

THE NAKED GENIUS. October 21, 1943

A comedy by Gypsy Rose Lee, eminent ex-exponent of the art of the strip-tease. Produced, statistics below, by Michael Todd in the Plymouth Theatre.

Program

Honey Bee Carroll		Mrs. Thompson	Emily Ross
	Joan Blondell	Miss Holmes	Edmonia Nolley
Angela	Pauline Myers	Emily	Rosemary Rice
Stuart Tracy	Millard Mitchell	Gladys	Mary Ashworth
Williams	Byron Russell	Teddy Martin	Gil Maison
Fred-Eric	Rex O'Malley	Sally Martin	Bernice Maison
Alonzo	Marcel Rousseau	First Judge	James Moore
Drunk	Anton McQuade	Second Judge	William Torpey
Pansy	Phyllis Povah	Judge Taylor	John Souther
Lollie Adams	Bertha Belmore	Mr. Goodwin	Judson Langill
Alibassi	Georgia Sothern	Mrs. Goodwin	
Sam Hinkle	Lewis Charles		Marie Louise Dana
Charles Goodwin		A Moving Man	George Cotton
	Donald Randolph	Life Man	Tom Daly
Myrtle McGuire	Doro Merande	A. P. Man	Ralph Lewis
Mrs. Davis	Frieda Altman	State Trooper	Robert Downing

SYNOPSIS: Act I. *Honey Bee Carroll's New York apartment. September.* Act II. *Honey Bee Carroll's house in the country. Eight days later.* Scene 1. *Saturday afternoon.* Scene 2. *Midnight.*

THERE IS NO GOOD REASON why it should be so, but whenever you look at a program and see, down at the bottom of the cast of characters, a State Trooper you may generally prepare yourself for the worst. Being down at the bottom of the program, you know that, since the characters are listed in the order of their appearance, the fellow will duly show up late in the evening just as the proceedings conventionally get rough, that his role will consist of several ferocious growls culminating either in the warning that if everyone doesn't pipe down he will collar the whole caboodle or in the actual arrest of someone (often the wrong person), and that the play in its entirety will be something of a stinker. *The Naked Genius* ran true to form.

Miss Lee, whose leading previous adventure into beautiful letters resolved itself into a mystery novel called *The G-String Murders,* sought on this, her first excursion into dramatic art, to confect a semi-autobiographical study of a strip-tease lady who publishes a novel which has been ghosted by a gangster who goes in for subsequent blackmail. The devices which she elected to further her comedy were as embarrassing as her initial idea that a gangster who was clearly illiterate could conceivably have ghosted a bestseller novel in the first place. The strain for humor centered largely on remarks about water-closets merchanted by a female character who presided over ladies' washrooms, and involved generally an effeminate milliner who groaned My God! every other minute, the meantime clasping his hand to his brow; a horsey, red-haired burlesque queen who held a fringed G-string to her green satin covered equator and bumped it violently at the audience; a fat woman who burst periodically into arias; and the laborious introduction of dogs, roosters and a monkey, not to mention a cuckoo clock that weeweed, whenever the actors had nothing to go on with. The incandescent story implicated a fashionable publisher who loved the strip-teaser whose book he had published and who deserted her at the altar when he learned from the gangster that the lady of his heart was a literary cheat.

In the play there was no faintest trace of the amusing burlesque lingo which enlivened the author's aforesaid mystery novel; only a pervasive vulgarity that hung over the play like a yellow fog. It was to the credit of both the author and her stage director, George S. Kaufman, that they exhorted the producer not to bring the mess into New York after its comprehensive critical slaying in the several tryout cities. It was to the producer's discredit that he refused to listen to them and, hoping for additional money, infected the metropolitan stage with an exhibition that should have been confined to a drain.

The acting, save for Doro Merande as the lavatory chatelaine and Phyllis Povah as the strip-teaser's grafting mother, was on a par with the choice elegance of the script. The uncommon talent of Mr. Kaufman as a director makes one regret that every once in a while he sees fit to waste it on things like this. No man in our theatre is more gifted in obtaining a sense of alive movement with a minimum of transparent device. Whereas a director like George Abbott, seeking animation and speed, causes the very gizzards of his actors to drip perspiration and makes his audience frequently wonder whether it is a play or an epileptic ward it is looking at, Kaufman seems to be able to get the desired effect without any such identification of his players with the cast of a roller skating show. It is only when he mixes himself up with an intrinsically static play like the one here considered that dull obviousness creeps into his work.

Again, as in the case of the Bergner play, the public shrugged its shoulders at criticism and rushed to the garbage in droves. Nevertheless, although it was playing to more than 17,000 dollars a week, or a net profit of 2,900 dollars, Mr. Todd, in a miraculously sudden seizure of repentance, closed it after thirty-six performances. Announced Mr. Todd, his face lighted with an angelic, aye holy, glow: "In show business you can't please everyone, but I believe pleasing less than half is not a good percentage. Therefore, in my eagerness to keep faith with the public, I am closing the show despite the fact that it is earning a very substantial profit. I believe the money I might be losing as a result is not as important as the loss of good-will of the people who might not like *The Naked Genius*. In this game, you're as good as your last show."

The angelic Mr. Todd somehow did not confide that, even so, he had, through big previous road business and the sale of the play to the Twentieth Century-Fox moving picture interests, already put something like 75,000 dollars into his pocket.

SLIGHTLY MARRIED. October 25, 1943

A comedy originally called Mother's Day, *by Aleen Leslie.
Produced as a casualty by Melville Burke in the Cort Theatre.*

Program

Brian Quin	Leon Ames	Lisa Ward	Kathryn Keys
Stanley Quin	Scotty Beckett	Grandma Jamison	
Audrey Quin	Leona Maricle		Isabel O'Madigan
Margaret Quin	Patty Pope	Bella	Teddi Sherman
Terry Jamison	Tom Seidel	Hortense	Kate Harrington
Josie Dowling	Mona Barrie	Dr. Obenhauer	Boyd Agin
Keith Morehouse	Jimmie Smith	Ambulance Driver	Bert Horton

SYNOPSIS: Act I. Scene 1. *Seven o'clock on a May evening.* Scene
2. *The next morning.* Act II. Scene 1. *Ten days later. Evening.* Scene 2.
Five months later. A November afternoon. Act III. Scene 1. *An evening
two weeks later.* Scene 2. *An afternoon one week later.*

The entire action takes place in the living-room of the Quin home
in Erie, Pennsylvania.

THIS WAS STILL ANOTHER in the series of obstetrical comedies, and the most painful of the lot. It gave evidence that the author knew considerable about plays, if nothing about playwriting. Her seventeen-year-old miss who shocks the family with news that she is with child was the seventeen-year-old miss who shocks the family with news that she is with child out of *Kiss and Tell.* The younger little brother given to a polysyllabic worldly philosophy in the matter was the younger little brother given to a polysyllabic worldly philosophy in the matter out of the same play. The low-comedy servant girl who amorously ogles the master of the house was the low-comedy servant girl who amorously ogles the master of the house out of the May Vokes plays of several decades ago. The exasperated father was the exasperated father out of *Three's A Family,* as the old maid busybody was the old maid busybody out of the same play. The

young man who experiences the jitters when his mate is
giving birth to a baby was the same character out of not
only *Three's A Family, The Snark Was A Boojum* and *A
New Life* but out of several dozen other previous comedies.
The maid who loftily declines to serve the family and packs
off in a huff was out of a gross of plays since the era of *My
Friend From India*. The situation in which the mistress of
the house mistakes her young brother's fiancée for a maid
applying for a job was out of an old vaudeville playlet of
the 1890's called *A Family Mix-Up*. The idea of the en-
ceinte young girl's formal innocence was out of *Kiss and
Tell*, as the idea of the youngster brother's sexual sophistication was out of *All In Favor*. The "my condition" humor
was out of *Boy Meets Girl*. The idea of the young woman
who doesn't want to give birth to a baby and tie herself
down to a humdrum life but who, once the baby is born,
is enraptured by it and wouldn't give it or her husband up
for anything in the world has been part and parcel of the
popular drama for at least half a century. The comical shifting of maternity blame from one woman to another was
out of *Baby Mine*. In short, about the only original thing
Miss Leslie contributed to her exhibit was the lovely bel-
letristic expression, "This is the ultimate end." As for her
dramaturgy in general, it would seem that she derived her
technique from some not too experienced steam-fitter.

The acting company and its director contributed to the
stuffing of the turkey with such chestnuts as violent pull-
ings at a pipe to register exasperation, mad slidings across
the floor to execute frantic telephone calls, pillows strapped
under blouses to indicate pregnancy, comical faintings and
dejections onto the floor to register overwhelming surprise,
furious dashes up and down a staircase to suggest dramatic
life, wild mussings of hair to depict perplexity and exacer-
bation, the sudden ejaculation on the part of a sedate grandmother of "Well, I'll be God damned!", open mouth and
pop eyes on the part of a young man to indicate mental vacuity, and a persistently intense frown on the part of a
young woman to register inner perturbation. The only

lagniappe was provided in the casting of a very pretty girl named Patty Pope as the frownee in question.

The play and company were brought on from San Francisco, where both scored a sterling success. The New York run lasted a week.

MANHATTAN NOCTURNE. OCTOBER 26, 1943

A melodrama by Roy Walling. Produced for failure by Walter Drey and George W. Brandt in the Forrest Theatre.

PROGRAM

EDDIE TALMO	*Dehl Berti*	GIMBEL	*Tom McElhany*
PETER WADE	*Eddie Dowling*	HELEN	*Julann Caffrey*
ANN STEVENS	*Terry Holmes*	DOLAN	*Wendell Corey*
GRACE WADE		MAHONEY	*John Farrell*
	Lorraine MacMartin	JUDGE PETRIE	*Howard Smith*
MONROE LESSING	*Donald Keyes*	CAREW	*Robert Toms*

SYNOPSIS: Time. *The present.* Act I. *A room in a hotel — about 10 o'clock at night.* Act II. *Same — the next morning.* Act III. *A magistrate's chamber in Felony Court later the same day.*

UNLIKE THE AUTHOR of the previous night's malfeasance, the author of this one apparently had not been in a theatre since the days of the Civil War and hence esteemed as something powerfully new the theme of a prostitute's redemption and regeneration under the influence of a pure love. We accordingly once again, and for perhaps the hundredth time, beheld the hard, brassy and bitter strumpet of Act 1 gradually mellowing into gentleness and spirituality in Act 2 and eventually converted in Act 3 into a creature beside whom Little Eva would take on the color of a gashouse moll. And we also duly beheld her noble Pygmalion, who as usual had lost all faith in women, regaining it in counterpoint to her beatification.

Written largely in terms of the Theodore Kremer school of drama, the peanut-gallery heritage missed none of the standard ingredients: the sleek, brunet knave who would win the prostitute back to a life of sin; the curt, hardboiled, crooked detective who mercilessly hounds her after her reformation; the comedy-relief waiter whose suspicious eye wanders around the hotel room in sly search of the suspected hiding female; the scene in the magistrate's court;

the comedy Irish attendant; the judge brusque on the surface but kind of heart; the mean, metallic and philandering wife of the hero who calls the heroine a prostitute and is called it back by the latter in turn; and the little farm upstate to which the redeemed heroine and the reinspirited hero ultimately hie themselves, there again to sniff God's clean air and begin life together anew.

Final horrible detail. The hero is a defeated novelist who under the encouragement of the prostitute begins to write his masterpiece inspired by her; title "Another Mary."

The highly proficient performances of Mr. Dowling and young Miss Holmes in the leading roles succeeded occasionally in rubbing a bit of the makeup off the script, but the foundation cream stuck. And the play closed after a forced run of three weeks.

VICTORY BELLES. October 26, 1943

A farce-comedy by Alice Gerstenberg. Produced by Henry Adrian in the Mansfield Theatre and desperately backed at a loss of $95,000 for a bogus run of 12 weeks.

Program

Miss Ann Stewart	*Ellen Merrill*	Private Eric Stanley	
Miss Kathlene Stirling			*Stanley Phillips*
	Sally Gracie	Sergeant Joe Collier	
Miss Mary Breton	*Marie Gale*		*Walter Appler*
Mrs. Grace Stewart		Colonel Edward Horton	
	Mabel Taliaferro		*Raymond Van Sickle*
Geejan	*Addison Randall*	Donald Bacchus	*Philip Denman*
Mrs. Mildred Stirling		Thomas Richardson	
	Jessie Miller		*Robert Ober*
Miss Flo Hilliard		Mr. Popa	*Burton Mallory*
	Barbara Bennett	Two Policemen	
Lieutenant James Richardson			*William Paul, Oscar Miller*
	Ralph Clanton	June Winkle	*Margaret Eckman*

SYNOPSIS: Act I. *Late afternoon in September, 1943.* Act II. *The same evening after dinner.* Act III. *The following morning.*

The entire action of the play takes place in the living-room of the Stewart home at Tarrytown, N. Y.

Thinking back over more than thirty-five years of professional playgoing, I can, as a student of the bishop's-nose drama, recall few plays as odorous as this. As a top-notch, incontrovertible, authentic garlic it takes its pungent place among the heavy-weight champions of the American theatre.

With a completely rewritten last act given to the actors half an hour before the curtain rose on the opening night, the fowl opened up with the reading aloud by a dimwit widow of a magazine article stating that after the war there will be left only four and one-half men for every seven women. This news so upsets the old girl that she determines to get her daughters married instanter to any of the boys in a nearby army camp. To that end, she gives a party for the boys and not only she and her daughter but all the other many itching females in the neighborhood go after them, and hot. It seems, however, that the women haven't the right technique and a family friend just back from Reno is hustled into the breach to provide instruction. It is at this point that the turkey begins really to spread its wings.

For the two succeeding hours the women now gurgle, purr, archly display their legs, make googoo eyes, temptingly slip off their shoulder straps, talk baby-talk, make naughty cracks, trip coyly hither and thither, and comport themselves generally like cute rabbits, the while a scowling butler sneaks grimly and furtively in and out of the scene. Presently the women get onto the laps of the boys and when the boys get rough let out howls of indignation because, it appears, the ones whose laps they are on are the laps of the ones their insides tell them they shouldn't be on. Still the scowling butler weaves his way ominously amongst them. Then, just as it looks as if the minks are at last about to find themselves on the right laps, ups the butler and wallops a Colonel, who has conveniently happened by and who has had nothing to do with the play before, on the head with a blackjack. "Who are you?" irately demands the mistress of the house of the butler. "I am an agent of the FBI!" proclaims the butler. "And why, pray, did you assault the Colonel, a grand gentleman?" further demands the lady. "He is a spy!" shouts the butler. Curtain.

Add to all this some of the worst actors ever seen in the worst turkeys, many of whom could not correctly pronounce the simplest English words; humor that took such contours as a man-chasing old maid's warning to a young girl that, when it comes to sex, "Don't you go and get it in the Black Market"; and stage direction that had the actors constantly falling over one another in an effort to get laughs; and you will understand why that portion of the first-night audience that didn't leave after the first act left after the second, and why the third act was played to about thirteen people, four of them helpless play reviewers, the press-agent and five of the ushers having already long vanished into a nearby saloon.

The history of the prime turkeys in our theatre embraces only three or four others that can compete with this
Victory Belles. There was, for example, a rare number labeled *Love's Call,* the chef d'œuvre of one Joe Byron Tot-
ten, which greeted the New York elite in September 1925
and which no one who saw it in its few days' run will ever
forget. Played in front of scenery described as Guadalharra,
Mexico, but evidently retrieved from an earlier play whose
locale was Fairbanks, Alaska, its hero was programmed as
"a handsome American" (impersonated by a very fat actor
in white skin-tights and a ten-gallon white sombrero) named
Clyde Wilson Harrison. This Clyde Wilson Harrison (he
was thus in full addressed throughout the evening by everyone who spoke of or to him) met up with a saucy package hight Piquita, impersonated by an actress with a thick
Polish accent, while promenading the Guadalharra-Fair-
banks boulevards, and gave her the high sign. "Me love
handsome American Clyde Wilson Harrison," allowed Piquita, coyly eating a rose. "Me love beautiful Piquita, ma
cherie, too," allowed Clyde Wilson Harrison; "but me engaged to Sue Gertrude Madison too."

Time passed, and again the juicy twain met, now in what
was designated "The Devil's Pass." Here Clyde Wilson
Harrison and his fiancée, Sue Gertrude Madison, were being held captive by the villainous Don Pedro De Scarillo,
fifteen-inch mustachios and all, who proclaimed, "Me love
Piquita too; me shoot handsome American Clyde Wilson
Harrison!" To save her handsome American hero, Piquita
thereupon threw herself in front of Clyde Wilson Harrison
and received the mortal bullet. Whereupon a quartet of extras named Juanita, Sancho, Francesco and Pasquale in the
costumes of Comanche Indians piously crossed themselves;
Sue Gertrude Madison deposited a bloom on the heaving
stomach of the prostrate Piquita; dawn (represented by
such a scarlet conflagration as hadn't been seen on a stage
since *The Still Alarm*) sprang up like a jack-in-the-box on
the backdrop; and handsome American Clyde Wilson Harrison removed his ten-gallon sombrero, tenderly deposited

it in turn upon Piquita's still heaving stomach, and — rising to embrace Sue Gertrude Madison — lifted his face to the flies and intoned climactically, "Love's call has been answered! Love conquers life and death! Clyde Wilson Harrison speaks to God!"

But, in Al Jolson's phrase, wait a minute; you ain't heard nothin' yet. In the general period came along another terrible turk, *The House of Doom,* by one whose name mercifully escapes me. This *The House of Doom* vies with *Love's Call* and *Victory Belles* for all-time top honors, although something named *Flesh,* news of which anon, is a gobbler you will have to keep firmly in mind. The curtain went up on an eerily lighted chamber decorated with skulls, daggers, scalping knives, shotguns, poisoned arrows, bottles marked *Poison,* a small guillotine, and what looked like an electric chair. "This room has a peculiar atmosphere," observed an elderly gentleman as he entered. "I think, however, I shall repose here for a spell and rest." No sooner had he reposed than up from behind the big electric chair oozed a ferocious, bewhiskered face with a green spotlight playing upon it. "Grrrr" grrrrd the face, which was the property of the man to whom, it seemed, the reposeful gentleman had once handed the dirty end of the stick.

That the owner of the face was bent on revenge began slowly to dawn upon the more sapient members of the audience. Every time the elderly gentleman, his wife, daughter or anyone else connected with his family reposed, up from behind whatever they were reposing on sprang the bewhiskered, toothless, green, grinning phiz, and with louder and louder grrrs. A succession of murders naturally followed, all accompanied by the hoots of owls and the mysterious openings and closings of secret panels and trapdoors which the playwright and director had somehow seemingly forgotten in any way to relate to the foul work in hand. It was grand! But not so grand as the big climax scene which, at least on the opening night, showed the hero's anaesthetized daughter being rolled by the villain on a table toward a fiery furnace and at the critical moment not only being

saved by her fiancé but being saved so ferociously that she
fell off the table on her behind and let out the loudest shriek
of the shriekful evening.

Flesh, which was practically hooted off the stage by ten
o'clock, was a serious sex drama. Its heroine was an amplitudinous actress with breasts the size of conga drums who,
clad in a series of gauzy gowns, languished passionately on
chairs, sofas, beds and the floor in her determination to
drive the male characters crazy with lust. I forget exactly
what it was that made her so determined but I seem to remember it had something to do with getting even with the
sex for having once done her wrong. Anyway, one by one
she drove the boys to distraction, the distraction being interpreted by hoarse breathings, trembling grasps at the
whiskey decanter, lush suckings of the heroine's ear, agonized gulps, vigorous scalp massagings and divers other reactions more generally associated with a morning-after
stomach than a night-before heart.

There was apparently no resisting the siren. Let her so
much as cross her legs and reveal an inch of ankle and
one or another of the males fell on his face in a paroxysm
of desire. Let her so much as elegantly extend her hand for
labial homage and one or another instantly confused it with
a lamb chop and started voraciously to eat it up. And let
her wriggle a mere miniature hinterwriggle and all hell
broke loose. What finally broke up the show on the first
night was the prehensile damsel's remark (not knowing
that her dress had split in the rear) "I wonder what it is
that keeps men following me? Can it be — can . . ." and,
as she hesitated, the contribution from a member of the audience: "You said it, babe!"

While this quartet of turkeys probably stands pre-emi-
nent in our modern theatre, there are a few others that his-
torically are not to be too airily waved aside. For example,
The Love City, hatched by a Mr. Hans Bachwitz and unloaded on the gourmets some eighteen years ago. Laid in
what is unarchitecturally generally described as a "house,"
this particular one situated on "The Hill of Delight in
China," it edified its two dozen or so customers with the tale

of little Tze-shi, acted by a tall blonde from Louisville, Kentucky. This little five-foot-eleven Tze-shi was sic'd by Chang Lo, the male madam of the house, on an English customer named Richard Cavendish whom Chang had foresightedly put under the influence of drugs. But Chang (not very clever, these Chinese) had given Richard an overdose which put him to sleep, thus ruining business.

Since you have to have such business in such a play or lose it at the box-office and since the business with Richard asleep stopped right then and there, Mr. Bachwitz had to do something. So in desperation he caused Richard to dream a dream, acted out on the stage, in which Richard saw little five-foot-eleven Tze-shi as his own wife and Chang as her lover, thus working in the necessary hot stuff. But wait for the climax! Richard, suddenly awaking from his Al Woods dream, pulled out a pistol and Chang, hanging around to eavesdrop the dream, followed suit for no reason anyone save maybe Mr. Bachwitz could figure out. "You have deceived me!" cried Richard and "You have violated the sacred code!" cried Chang, both also for no reason that made any sense. Bang, bang, and both Richard and Chang bit the dust, the while Tze-shi, who during the excitement had precipitantly rushed upstairs and changed into another and more elaborate evening kimono, peered derisively over the balustrade and softly hummed something that sounded very much like "A Bicycle Built For Two."

Right down the same cultural alley was a dish of collateral cranberry sauce called *Spellbound,* by Walter Elwood, produced about a year later. Lasting for just three performances and played by some of the damnedest actors seen on the local stage since the fire department eliminated nets, it had to do with a mother who had read that if you drop a certain kind of pill in a man's breakfast coffee you can not only cure him of his taste for alcoholic liquor but, even if he has never had a drink of it, prevent any possible future taste for it. Having two young sons, both strict teetotalers, she nevertheless and accordingly put the pills in their morning beverage and sat back and waited. She didn't have to wait long. One of the sons presently let out a yell, grabbed at the air, and tumbled to the floor. When they picked him up, it was found that the pill had paralyzed him below the waist. No sooner was the lad deposited on a divan than the second son let out an even more terrific yell, grabbed at the air, and started mumbling like an idiot. When they in turn got around to investigating him, it was found that the pill had rendered him dumb.

Naturally, the mother was rather upset, the ribald laughter of the audience not helping materially to quiet her nerves. Not knowing how otherwise to make amends, she announced to the two boys — the one tottering pitiably around the stage like Leon Errol in a bent-knee comedy act and the other making inarticulate sounds like Nat Goodwin — that she would leave the country, go to some far-off cannibal island and, as a missionary, devote herself by way of consolation to saving the cannibals' souls. Years passed. And after almost two decades she returned, partly insane, and the boys at length learned that it was their own dear mother who was responsible for their wrecked lives.

But again wait! If you think that ended the turkey you don't know a real turk when you see one. No sooner was the confession out of mama's lips than the first son let out a yell of slightly different timbre, grabbed joyously at the air, proudly assumed a ramrod position, and proclaimed, "Look, look, I am well again; I am cured!" And no sooner had the first son spoken than the second let out a yell of similar nuance, joyously grabbed at the air, proclaimed, "Look, look, me too; I am cured!", and launched further into quondam muted speech, unfortunately. And with the boys' arms enfolding their repentant mama the curtain fell on the happiest ending beheld on an American stage since, in an earlier turkey (the brainchild of one Helen Broun, called *Clouds*), a devoted mother suddenly restored her blind son's sight by shocking him with the lies that she had gone crazy, that his fiancée had secretly married his rival and that his pet dog had been run over by a street-car, thus bringing down the curtain on the rapturous spectacle of his triplicate embrace of mother, best girl, and Poochie.

Coming to more recent seasons (and by no means overlooking such birds as *Roman Servant, Arms For Venus, Popsy,* and *Boudoir*) , the vote for the choicest turkey after *Victory Belles* goes enthusiastically to *Reprise,* by W. D. Bristol, produced at 8:40 p.m. of May 1, 1935, and withdrawn at 10:55 on the same night. Presented as a serious problem drama, the honey opened with a young man about to throw himself out of the fifteenth story window of an apartment house, but who was restrained by a friend who screamed, "Halt! Desist! Life is worth living! I shall prove it to you by making you so happy in one short month's time that you shall be regretful that you ever cogitated such a sin!" The man thereupon crawled down from the window ledge and his happiness, sure enough, began forthwith in his falling in love with his rescuer's millionaire sister. So happy indeed was he that, needing funds to make his fiancée still happier, he swindled his benefactor, which made the latter's old grandmother so unhappy that she began making him doubt his own happiness and succeeded in goading him to climb up on the window ledge again and this time really jump off. As I recall the final curtain, Grandma was taking a hard look out of the window, shaking her head and musing, in view of the facts it seemed somewhat egotistically: "God's will be done."

CAREER. October 28, 1943

An item by Nan Kirby. Produced to no end by Modern Play Productions, Inc., in the Provincetown Playhouse.

PROGRAM

Edith Fray	Melanie Hilden	Madame de Savognia	Anne King
Maestro Tramavista		Rosa Carnella	
	John Francis		Josephine Lombardo
Anthony Malcolm	Robert Feyti	Miss Timms	Mary Kliman
Pietro	Joseph DiStefano	Martha	Lucille Grayson
Muriel Compton	Genie Conrad	Alice	Adeline Bitters
Edgar Knoll	Peter Zube	Ethel Terriss	Onda de Munoz
Valentine Herman		Harry Jones	Louis Carmole
	Maurice Vankin	Miss Carr	Mabel Nash

SYNOPSIS: Act I. Scene 1. *Maestro Tramavista's penthouse apartment: March.* Act II. Scene 2. *The same. The following September.* Scene 1. *Same as Act I. One month later.* Scene 2. *Rosa Carnella's dressing room. That evening.* Scene 3. *On stage at the Opera House.* Scene 4. *Same as Scene 2. Same as Act I. The following morning.*

———

An EXPERIMENTAL THEATRE is commonly supposed to be devoted to staging plays of an unusual nature. In this instance, the experimental theatre as represented by Modern Play Productions, Inc. in the little Provincetown Playhouse handsomely performed the expected task. It produced a play so unusual in badness that it almost equalled some of the plays lately produced in the so-called professional, or non-experimental, theatres of Broadway.

The unusual work in question had to do with the graft that goes on in the operatic world, consisted for the most part in heated animadversions on leeches who collect forty percent of the salaries of beginners, and was interrupted at intervals by two of the latter who unrestrainedly let go their vocal cords in selections from *Aïda, Cavalleria Rusticana* and *Traviata,* proving to the audience that the aforesaid leeches would have been justified in collecting at least eighty percent. While, despite the treatment they received, it was evident that Verdi and Mascagni knew their business, any evidence that Miss Kirby knew hers was unfortunately lacking.

The item was kept on the stage for one week.

THE PETRIFIED FOREST. November 1, 1943

Robert E. Sherwood's melodrama, originally produced in 1935. Revived by the Mary Elizabeth Sherwood stock company (vide *statistics below*) *in the New Amsterdam Roof Theatre.*

Program

Gramp Maple	E. G. Marshall	Mr. Chisholm	Robert J. Lance
Boze Hertzingler		Mrs. Chisholm	Natalie Benisch
	William Forester	Joseph	H. Randolph Nash
A Telegraph Linesman		Jackie	Jack Bittner
	William Marceau	Duke Mantee	John McQuade
Another Linesman		Ruby	William Toubin
	Frederic Cornell	Pyles	Slim Thompson
Jason Maple	Grover Burgess	Legion Commander	
Gabby Maple	Barbara Joyce		George Spelvin
Paula	Charlotte Rogers	Another Legionnaire	
Alan Squire	Wendell K. Phillips		Fred Spelvin
Herb	Clark Poth		

This was the second attempt within a year to launch a stock company on Broadway and, like the first, a quick failure. Such recent ventures seem to have been predicated on the theory that New York would welcome a company made up of inferior actors in dated old Broadway plays if only the box-office charge were less than that for superior actors in new Broadway plays. It didn't work, naturally. Not because most of the new plays were better than the old ones, not because the current professional actors in many cases were anything exceptional, and not because the low admission prices were not desirable but because, all this granted, a stock company that hopes to succeed has to be built around personalities and because such personalities were lacking.

It would have been shrewder, of course, had Miss Sherwood elected to open her season with a play less familiar and more stimulating than the embossed pasteboard melodrama of 1935 which she selected. Even so, pretentious and hollow though it is, it was considerably above the mark of then current Broadway plays like *Another Love Story, The Two Mrs. Carrolls,* et al. What is more, Miss Sherwood's elastic company, although second-rate, wasn't any poorer than certain companies playing around town to nice box-office returns. But something important was absent and that something, as noted, was actors who, whatever their degree of competence, constituted audience magnets.

If a stock company is an all-around efficient one, it doesn't matter. But where such a company is of no particular general lustre, good hard theatrical sense dictates that it offer at least one actor or actress with the kind of presence that attracts customers. The actor or actress in question does not, to repeat, necessarily have to have any especial histrionic talent, but he or she must have that personal pull that captivates the trade. It has always been so.

I am not speaking of the famous old stock companies, although the contention also holds true in those cases. I am speaking rather of the lesser companies. It was thus that Vaughan Glaser, a mediocre actor but one possessed of the look and manner to enchant the servant girls and their equally impressionable mistresses, made such a company a success in the Middle West. It was thus that Jessie Bonstelle, no shakes as an actress but with a personality that fetched them in, made another a success in the same part of the country. And it was thus that Priscilla Knowles, a minor actress but one who apparently had what it takes, put over the company at the old Academy of Music in Fourteenth Street.

There are all kinds of other similarly piquant examples. For one, Eugenie Blair, who was a marked-down combination of Mrs. Leslie Carter and Virginia Harned, converted a third-rate stock company into a money-maker through sheer force of her prehensile person. For another, Eva Le Gallienne who, though her Civic Repertory Theatre lost money in the long run, drew a lot of people downtown who wouldn't have made the trip had some less emphatic personality headed the troupe. For still another, and in an earlier day, Amelia Bingham who, though surely not much of an actress, had something that attracted customers, at least for a spell. And for others still, George Fawcett, whose company was a great draw in Baltimore; John W. Albaugh, Jr., a stock company juvenile who always packed them in; Robert Edeson, a ghastly ham, in the successful old Madison Square Theatre Company; Adelaide Keim of F. F. Proctor's Fifth Avenue Theatre company who played to large business in half a hundred different roles though her acting art was to be described by an unrefined word; and, above all, the one and only Corse Payton of Brooklyn stock fame, an actor beside whom even the Edeson aforesaid was a handbrother to Salvini but who nevertheless enjoyed that peculiar whateveritis which cajoled his public's susceptibilities. And not forgetting Corse's municipal histrionic sister, Cecil Spooner, who pulled in the stock crowds for years at the old Metropolis and Cecil Spooner Theatre.

It was Miss Sherwood's bad luck that her flexible company had in it no actor or actress with any perceptible such attribute. That the most of them were relative strangers to the local stage had nothing to do with the matter. Newcomers sometimes give evidence of possession of the hellish gift. Katharine Hepburn, Tallulah Bankhead, Katharine Cornell, Helen Hayes, Alfred Lunt and numerous others popped an audience's curiosity the very first time they showed themselves. Indeed, if you will go back into your memory you will find that most of the present eminentos on their initial appearances gave you that squirt of electricity, however slight, that marked them apart from the general.

Following *The Petrified Forest* came *Goodbye Again,* the Scott-Haight comedy of twelve years ago. Following *Goodbye Again* came the end of the venture.

OUTRAGEOUS FORTUNE. November 3, 1943

A play by Rose Franken. Produced for 77 performances and to no commercial profit by William Brown Meloney in the 48th Street Theatre.

Program

Mrs. Harris	*Maria Ouspenskaya*	Julian Harris	*Brent Sargent*
Dr. Andrew Goldsmith		Kitty	*Adele Longmire*
	Eduard Franz	Barry Hamilton	*Dean Norton*
Madeleine Harris		Crystal Grainger	
	Margalo Gillmore		*Elsie Ferguson*
Mary	*Mabel Taylor*	Cynthia	*Margaret Williams*
Bert Harris	*Frederic Tozere*	Gertrude	*Margaret Hamilton*

SYNOPSIS: Act I. *A Friday evening in the summer of 1941. Act II. The same evening. Act III. The following evening.*

The action takes place in the living-room of the Harris' shore home near New York.

This was the first new play of the season that called upon the attention of criticism rather than that of mere reviewing. In her initial attempt at serious drama the author of those two successful comedies, *Another Language* and *Claudia,* has come off with considerable honor. Up to this point in the year her play proved to be the only new one with the glimmer of a mind in it, the only one of even relative size, the only one of any critical merit.

Setting herself the difficult task of combining in a single dramaturgical pattern the problems of race, religion, homosexuality, psychotherapy, morality and, faintly, even metaphysics, Miss Franken has not been altogether prosperous in surmounting it. But out of the tangled web there emerges nonetheless what amounts to a drama, albeit fitful, that touches with liberal understanding and with high dignity upon the complex facets of the life and lives of the characters it deals with. Nor is sound and searching humor lacking.

The characters embrace a Jewish banker orthodox in his

view of life and morals and overproud of his race, his wife
become a neurotic under the pressure of his unyielding or-
thodoxy in the marital relation, his homosexual younger
brother and the young girl in love with him who is driven
to a try at suicide because of her unrequited passion, his
aged mother baffled by what is going on around her, the
defeated Jewish family physician and his Irish wife, a Gentile woman of the world who comes to spend a weekend,
her young protégé who is a borderline sexual case, and her
devoted Negro maid. What direct plot there is proceeds
from the wise and gentle and liberal philosophy of the visitor and its impact upon the befuddled and distraught members of the family. The orthodox husband feels his prejudices gradually yielding; the neurotic wife, taking a cue
from the wisdom of the experienced visitor, finds in the
healthy physical wish for another man the means to a re-
birth of love for her husband; the borderline young man,
taken under the sexual wing of the visitor, finds his way
also back to normality; the racial nervousness of the family
is dissipated; etc.

But if one gets the idea that Miss Franken has, in the
dramatic manipulation, resorted simply to the device of
such older tournaments in innocently affecting drama as
The Passing Of The Third Floor Back and *The Servant In
The House,* one is mistaken. Only superficially does the
catalytic character resemble the characters in those plays
and the several others like them. If there is any similarity at
all it is to the central character in William Hurlbut's play
of a quarter-century ago, *A Strange Woman,* which was
acted by the same Elsie Ferguson who acted the present role.
Unlike The Stranger or Manson of the Jerome and Kennedy plays, the character in both the Hurlbut and Franken
plays is one whose emotions are filtered through the in-
tellect.

The play, in sum, is a drama of misfits in the present
world and of the manner in which they habitually are not
but may possibly and conceivably one day be made less misfits. Therein lies its virtue, since the author offers no facile
cure-all as other playwrights with similar themes often

have but merely hints and suggestions, and always with a semi-skeptical smile.

If there is one signal fault with the play it rests paradoxically in its author's somewhat too determined intelligence. She is periodically so doggedly intellectual about so many things at one and the same time that her play occasionally and refractorily takes on the flavor of a dinner table disquisition by Dorothy Thompson. One theme crowds another theme so closely that a third, already hard pressed for breathing room, cries loudly for air and drowns out the voices of the other two. For no sooner does the racial and religious question take the floor than the question of homosexuality and original sin raises its hand to be heard and unwittingly gets its thumb in the eye of some other question that tries to attract the notice of the chair. It is all sometimes a bit confusing but nevertheless, despite the confusion, so immensely more interesting than anything else we had thus far in the season been inflicted with that the play came as a panacea to such audiences as had been thinking of deserting the theatre for the greater intelligence of the bowling alley or grand opera.

All save three of the daily reviewers, however, denounced the play out of hand as dull and worthless. It was argued by them, among other things, that — and this is something they apparently can not tolerate — "it unfortunately deals almost entirely with unpleasant and unlikeable people." So equally for that matter do some of the classical and modern masterpieces of drama: *Oedipus,* Gorki's *Night Refuge,* Wedekind's *Earth Spirit* and *Pandora's Box,* et al. It was also argued by them that "the drama is inconclusive." So equally for that matter are some of the finest modern plays (not to mention the older ones) like *The Weavers, Juno and the Paycock, The Plough and the Stars,* et al. It was further argued that the sexual element was "revolting." The same criticism might be directed against the Sophocles and Wedekind dramas aforesaid, *Mourning Becomes Electra, The Captive,* and a dozen other such excellent plays both classical and modern. Miss Franken's play may have its defects but these are not among them. What she has accomplished is a sometimes ill-joined mosaic but nevertheless a play whose delicate imagination and inner wisdom bulk above its defects and constitute it on the whole a credit to the American drama. And the acting company from Miss Ferguson down, together with the author's stage direction, was admirable.

ARTISTS AND MODELS. NOVEMBER 5, 1943

A revue by Lou Walters, Don Ross and Frank Luther with music and lyrics by Dan Shapiro, Milton Pascal and Phil Charig. Produced as a $225,000 failure by Lou Walters and Don Ross in the Broadway Theatre.

PRINCIPALS

Jane Froman, Frances Faye, Jackie Gleason, Marty May, Collette Lyons, Radio Aces, Nick Long, Carol King, Harold and Lola, Ben Yost, Billy Newell, the Worth Sisters, Don Saxon, and the Peters Sisters.

MR. WALTERS' previous chief contribution to æsthetics was a night club on Broadway called "The Latin Quarter." With Mr. Walters' new contribution, it still remains his chief one, even though I have never been in it and can only guess. His first effort in the theatre may be sufficiently described as an elaborate 225,000 dollar version of all the stale chorus numbers, cheap tunes, bad skits and old jokes that the worst of Earl Carroll's *Vanities,* along with *Viva O'Brien* and *Hairpin Harmony,* somehow overlooked.

The business begins with the "Parade of Models" in which a dozen lifted-nose zombies perfumedly named Velvet Night, Golden Day, My Sin, Midnight Madness, Bridal Blush, etc., walk elegantly down a flight of steps and stand at the footlights theoretically driving the customers crazy with their aloof beauty. A curtain comes down and out rush three supposed comedians with straw hats and canes who merchant a ditty informing the customers that, since the backers could not make up their minds (*laughter*) about what kind of show they wanted to produce they finally decided to throw everything into the pot and give the customers everything from vaudeville to burlesque and from ballet to the circus. Again the curtain, and now all the girls seated in minstrel show formation with the comics yodeling "Way Up North In Dixie Land." Then a female blues singer shouting "Swing Low" into a deafening amplifier.

This over with, one of the comics dressed as a candy
butcher appears in the aisles and goes through the business
of imitating a candy butcher in one of the old burlesque
houses. Follows on the stage a hard blonde in a short skirt
who with a fanatical coyness croaks a ditty called "How'ja
Like To Take Me Home?" And a number called "Strip-
Tease" in which a fully dressed sister act has various articles
of lingerie pinned on its backs and reaches around and
drops them successively onto the floor. Then out come
women billed wittily as Gypsy Rose Corio, Margie Smart,
Georgia Sudden, etc., who jiggle themselves, crack half a
dozen blue jokes, and eventually give way to a sketch
named "Hollywood, or The Road To Manasooris." It is
about a tropical island and its single repeated whimsicality, with winks, concerns the virginity of the island's Virgin
Princess. It also contains a song, "Sears-Roebuck," which
does not omit the venerable allusion to the use to which the
catalogue is put in the rural districts.

Three gentlemen who call themselves The Radio Aces
follow. Grouped around a microphone and intermittently
permitting themselves a pas seul, they howl a song called
"What Does The Public Want?", blandly unaware that the
subsequent lack of any applause indicates that The Radio
Aces are unmistakably not one of the things. Curtains again
and now another hard blonde who bangs swing out of a
piano accompanied by four female harpists, all of whom
apparently took xylophone lessons. More curtains and once
more the three comic gentlemen with straw hats and canes
in a facetious ton of lyrical coal called "North Dakota, South
Dakota Moon." Follows the female blues singer with a tear-
ful ditty, "My Heart Is On A Binge Again," and with the
amplifier shaking the customers out of their seats. First act
finale: a ballet, "New York Heartbeat," consisting of frantic dashes hither and thither and interrupted by pairs of
dancers squatting on the floor.

The second act opens with some acrobatic tumblers and
proceeds with the female blues singer giving out with "You
Are Romance," the amplifier now shattering what is left
of the audience's ear-drums; a sketch called "Submarine

U-Boat X37" in which the comedians bear the names Captain Anschluss and Lieutenant Eingemacht and which revolves about the discovery of the hard blonde as a stowaway; more songs by the female blues singer with the amplifier making with the boiler-works; a tap dancer with grin; some fifteen or twenty jokes that Joe Miller's grandfather heard from his uncle; and a finale in which the company gathers on the stage and doesn't look ashamed of itself.

The public, however, somehow didn't like it and it closed after 27 performances.

I'LL TAKE THE HIGH ROAD
NOVEMBER 9, 1943

A play by Lucille S. Prumbs. Produced as an erratum by Clifford Hayman and Milton Berle, the comedian, in the Ritz Theatre.

PROGRAM

MA BUDD	*Wanda Lyon*	MACNAUGHTON	*Betty Kelley*
SAM BUDD	*Len Doyle*	WESTERN UNION	*James Elliott*
PA BUDD	*John McGovern*	RAFFERTY	*Leslie MacLeod*
FLOYD BUDD	*Allan Rich*	KEENAN	*Ben Laughlin*
THERESA PACKETT	*Ethel Remey*	JOE KINDLE	*Larry Hugo*
JUDY BUDD	*Jeanne Cagney*	ED	*Gordon Hammill*
MRS. HALE	*Angela Willard*	CORP. STUART CHARTERS	
BEAVER	*John Bradley*		*Michael Strong*
CISSY	*Mona Graham*	V. PONIAKOFF	*Leo Chalzel*
KEWPIE	*Billy Sands*	MANAGER	*G. Swayne Gordon*
UNITED PARCEL	*Lester Lonergan*		

SYNOPSIS: Act I. *The Budd home, Masondale, Long Island. Time. The present — 7 a.m. Act II. Scene 1. Same as Act I — 8 p.m. Scene 2. Stage of the Masondale Theatre — 9 p.m. Act III. Same as Act I — Dawn.*

THE PROMISE which Miss Prumbs indicated in her first play, *Five Alarm Waltz,* produced in the 1940–1941 season, blew up with her second. Nowhere in it was there anything that glimmered even faintly. It took its place, in point of fact, with the season's worst. Intended at bottom as a comedy of the wacky *You Can't Take It With You* school, it again as in the case of various other such late imitations revealed itself critically as a spectacle minus the last two words.

Plot: Judy Budd, a young telephone operator in a Long Island aircraft plant and daughter of a family evidently descended from the original Cyrus J. Matteawan, suspects that the boss of the plant, ostensibly a patriotic American and public benefactor, is at heart a Fascist, Nazi, saboteur, and general secret enemy of the Republic. Aided by a movie actor who is to appear in a documentary film testimonial to him, she snoops around and finally not only gets the evidence against him but learns to boot that he has been harboring a dangerous Fascist sought by the FBI. The night the film is to be shown she jumps onto the stage and denounces the loafer. Her reward is the movie actor's hand in marriage.

Additional characters: the wisecracking kid brother, the mother and father who are always getting into each other's hair, the dialect movie producer, the acid spinster aunt, the uncle who exudes what is supposed to be droll philosophy, and the stencil like.

Acting: the kind in which the players invariably sit down with a plump and, when they get to their feet, make for conversation with the standing actors as if the latter were football goal-lines.

Incidental direction: the species that causes an actress not figuring in the immediate action to run to a sofa and begin frantically turning the pages of a magazine, that converts the ingénue into a bubble-bath with an unyielding darling smile, that presents the lovable old male folk in shirt sleeves and without neckties, and that, as a minor detail, doesn't see to it that the feminine love interest's stockings around the shoe tops do not resemble crow's feet.

Seven performances — and the storehouse.

WHAT'S UP. November 11, 1943

A musical show with book by Alan Jay Lerner and Arthur Pierson, lyrics by Mr. Lerner, and music by Frederick Loewe. Produced 63 times and at a considerable loss by Mark Warnow in the National Theatre.

Program

LOUISE	Sondra Barrett	SGT. HENRY WAGNER	Jack Baker
MARGARET	Lynn Gardner	1ST LT. ED ANDERSON	
MAY	Marjorie Beecher		Don Weissmuller
PAMELA	Honey Murray	2ND LT. MURRAY BACCHUS	
JENNIFER	Phyllis Hill		Robert Bay
SUSAN	Pat Marshall	SGT. MORONEY	Johnny Morgan
ELEANOR	Mitzi Perry	SGT. DICK BENHAM	
JAYNE	Mary Roche		William Tabbert
HARRIETT SPINNER	Claire Meade	VIRGINIA MILLER	Gloria Warren
DOCTOR	Frank Kreig	JUDY	Helen Wenzel
SGT. WILLIE KLINK	Larry Douglas	RAWA OF TANGLINIA	Jimmy Savo
CAPTAIN ROBERT LINDSAY		SGT. JIMMY STEVENSON	
	Rodney McLennan		Kenneth Buffett

SYNOPSIS: Act I. Scene 1. *The living-room. Afternoon.* Scene 2. *The men's bedroom. That night.* Scene 3. *The girls' bedroom.* Scene 4. *The Rawa's bedroom.* Scene 5. *The rumpus room. Following morning.* Act II. Scene 1. *The boys' and girls' rooms. Before the curtain, dance by Don Weissmuller.* Scene 2. *The living-room.* Scene 3. *The linen closet. In front of curtain, Jimmy Savo.* Scene 4. *The living-room.*

The entire action takes place in the Laurel House of Miss Langley's School for Girls, Crestville, Va. The time is the present.

ALTHOUGH THE BOOK was credited to the inspiration of the Messrs. Lerner and Pierson, it was probably first thought of by the Wright brothers on one of their off days, and quickly dismissed. It was the one about the boys, in this case aviators, who accidentally land in a girls' boarding school. As if that were not too superannuated, the Messrs. Lerner and Pierson added for bad measure the quarantine brought about by a case of measles, which was not altogether beardless when the Messrs. Hough and Adams borrowed it a quarter-century ago for their *The Time, The Place and The Girl.* Add further to this hardly springtime start the species of humor resident in such injunctions as "Chin up!" and a lady's rejoinder, "My, is it sagging already?"; lyrical wit implicit in such ditties as "How Fly Times," sung by the aviators; scenes in which the boys quartered in a spare room of the girls' dormitory become wildly delirious upon smelling the sachet in the pillows; and a dream ballet when the lights go down on a sentimental ballad; and the general nature of the evening may be suspected.

The theory advanced by the producer and press-agent that their show constituted in war-time a likely form of escapist entertainment eludes me, as it apparently also eluded the audiences that stayed away. Some such musical as *Rosalinda, The Merry Widow* or *Oklahoma!* may once in a while justify the theory, since Strauss and Lehar and even to some extent Rodgers are virtuosi of the necessary hypnosis, though the books may not be. But eight out of ten of such lesser shows as this not only do not provide any such mental and emotional jail-break; they rather operate the other way 'round.

It is occasionally possible that at a run-of-the-mill musical a competent clown, a gay tune, a nimble dance, or a lovely girl may momentarily divert the spectator from his deep and troubled concerns. But for the greater portion of the evening what goes on on the stage no more distracts him from such harassments than a bloody battle makes a distraught soldier think relievedly and happily of *Hairpin Harmony.*

The idea that when a man goes to a musical show he volitionally reduces himself to the status of a jolly ass, whereas at something like *The Two Mrs. Carrolls* he functions willy-nilly like a Hegel, survives only in the philosophy of the shows' producers. The truth, as any man of honor will tell you, is that he is actually much more critical of a musical show than of the average dramatic play he attends. If the girls aren't pretty enough, if the tunes don't make him hum, if the jokes don't make him laugh, if the book is a bit on the flat side, if the sets and costumes aren't sufficiently beautiful — if even so much as one of these items is glum, he will give issue to a pungent ouch. But let him go to a play that is as deficient on as many counts as, say, *Harriet, Janie, Lovers and Friends,* or anything else of the kind and you will not hear a complaining peep out of him.

So paradoxically exacting and challenging is the customer of a musical exhibit that, save it be more than usually good, he becomes in turn more than usually independently conscious of himself. He is thus jolted back to reality by a single dismal wheeze, by a single tune too obviously cabbaged from his favorite juke-box genius, by a chorus girl with a vaccination mark on her thigh, by any one of two dozen such things. And it is thus further that, when it comes to escape, he can achieve it more satisfactorily at some profound dramatic tragedy, or even by staring fixedly for half an hour at an electric fan, than at musical shows like this *What's Up.*

There is much fallacy in the theory of theatrical escape. In drama, escape does not lie in the mere themes, as so many producers imagine, but in the beauty with which, whatever they may be, they are handled. Nor can I believe that laughter provides the chief and most gratifying alley of escape; the escape is but momentary. Perhaps, as before observed, the only real escape is great and overpowering tragedy, since it to some degree minimizes the tragic circumstances of the immediate life and world in which we have our existence. The man who can forget his son's death on the battlefield, his house mortgaged because of burdensome taxes, and his ulcers in tapping his foot to some song like "You Wash And I'll Dry" in this show or in laughing at some such gag in another as "You get married at your age! Why, you're not heir-conditioned!" — the man who can vamoose from his cares and anxieties under such circumstances is either a congenital idiot or already drunk when he buys his ticket.

The only moments in *What's Up* that vouchsafed me any escape whatsoever — particularly escape from the conviction that I was wasting my time in not going home and reading the worst of the war news — were those in which a pair of attractive girls named Mary Roche and Pat Marshall just stood around looking attractive. As for the numerous tap dancers, I'd rather even have read the atrocity reports.

THE INNOCENT VOYAGE. November 15, 1943

*A play by Paul Osborn, derived from Richard Hughes'
novel,* A High Wind In Jamaica. *Produced by the Theatre
Guild in the Belasco Theatre, and a 40-performance box-
office failure.*

PROGRAM

CAPTAIN MARLPOLE	LAURA THORNTON
Ralph Cullinan	Mary Ellen Glass
MATE OF THE CLORINDA	MARGARET Lois Wheeler
Edgar Kent	CAPTAIN JONSEN Oscar Homolka
MRS. THORNTON Norah Howard	OTTO Herbert Berghof
MR. THORNTON Guy Spaull	MAGISTRATE OF SANTA LUCIA
RACHEL THORNTON	Boris Marshalov
Carolyn Hummel	SWEDISH CAPTAIN Arvid Paulson
JOHN THORNTON Dean Stockwell	MR. MATHIAS Clarence Derwent
EMILY THORNTON Abby Bonime	
EDWARD THORNTON	
Guy Stockwell	

SYNOPSIS: Prologue. *Aboard H.M.S. Royal William, a side-
wheeler, en route to England, 1860. Act I. Scene 1. Deck of the Clorinda.
Three months earlier. Scene 2. The same. Two days later. Scene 3. Deck
of the John Dodson. Partially simultaneous with Scene 2. Act II. Scene 1.
Deck of the John Dodson. Three weeks later. Scene 2. The same. Several
weeks later. Scene 3. The same. Some hours later. Scene 4. The same.
Later. Act III. Deck of H.M.S. Royal William, en route to England. Continuous with prologue.*

CLARE BOOTHE LUCE acquired the dramatic rights to the
Hughes novel several years ago but found after several attempts to make a play out of it that the job was baffling and
gave it up. Osborn subsequently undertook the task and,
though he fails to capture the impressive essence of the
novel, regrettably departs from the canny, cool and uncompromising analysis of the children's psyches and rather pret-
ties up the whole, his play yet manages to project what he
has selected from the tale with considerable charm, tender-
ness and humor. If, in point of fact, one puts the novel out

of mind and takes the play on its own, the evening amounts
to very acceptable pastime. And this, too, despite a group
of Fauntleroy stage youngsters in the present production
who suggested that they had been brought up on a home
diet of greasepaint and hand-mirrors, stage direction that
occasionally vacillated between comic opera and shriek melodrama, and the playwright's inclusion of a dully superfluous prologue that might readily, so far as its content goes,
either have been incorporated into the subsequent dialogue
or omitted altogether.

The fable you doubtless recall. A pirate ship of the last
century, after looting a clipper bound for England, finds
that it has taken aboard an unwelcome group of children.
It isn't long before the brats, theoretically innocent but actually a pack of he- and she-devils, begin to make life miserable for the buccaneers who, scratch their heads as they
will, can not figure out any way to relieve themselves of
the youthful burden. In the end and after the youngsters
have committed everything from simple mental torture to
actual murder, a British gunboat captures the ship, releases
the little fiends and takes the pirates prisoner, with hanging
in prospect for the leaders accused of the murder to which
one of the kids, at whom the authorities smile themselves
into disbelief, confesses.

The dramatic treatment here and there suffers from too
great a literality; the kind of treatment Barrie employed
upon his tale of Peter Pan would unquestionably have been
much better, had Osborn, who has written deftly and with
a nice touch of fantasy in the past, as in his dramatization
of *On Borrowed Time,* adopted it. That he might have
achieved something of the desired flavor is to be appreciated in his handling of his adult, if not always his children,
characters. The pirate skipper who wanted to be a preacher
but who, when his pirate father died, felt that he ought to
take over the family profession, and the first mate whose
awful job it is to wash the children, mend their sole wearing apparel, and keep an eye on them so they will not hurt
themselves — for, despite the agony they cause, the pirates
somehow can't help liking them — are in the exactly right

key and tone. (The roles, incidentally, were beautifully
acted by Oscar Homolka and Herbert Berghof respectively.)

In short, a play that misses the full approval of devotees
of the superior novel but one that nonetheless, even in its
paraphrastic form, contains the stuff of gentle, ironic, fresh
entertainment.

LADY, BEHAVE! November 16, 1943

A comedy by Alfred L. Golden. Produced for disaster by
High Bennett in the Cort Theatre.

PROGRAM .

GEORGE MORTON	*Jack Sheehan*	MRS. LANSING	*Madge Skelly*
ROLAND TALBERT	*Karl Weber*	MISS JONES	*Norma Winters*
LOUISE MORTON	*Pert Kelton*	MISS SHAW	*Carol Stone*
MARGARET BANNINGTON	*Lois Dow*	DR. BAKER	*J. Warren Lyons*
MIKE ROGERS	*Thomas Hume*	INSPECTOR WEISKOPF	*Dan Niels*

SYNOPSIS: Act I. *George Morton's apartment, New York City.*
Act II. *An afternoon, two months later.* Act III. *That night.*

SUCH PERSONS as went to this one deceived by its title
into imagining that it was a musical show like *Lady, Be*
Good! were doubly disappointed and triply grieved. Not
only wasn't it a musical show; it wasn't even a play. What
it was was an amateurish succession of dialogues involving a
spurious psychoanalyst and, in sum, another turkey that
vied with *Victory Belles* for garbage-can honors.

Characters: an oversexed, giggling female who ran hyena-
like around the stage snipping at men's clothing with a pair
of scissors; an iceman who teetered around ditto with a
shoe box containing a bomb which he every other minute
mournfully repeated he didn't have the courage to throw;
another sex-mad female who archly ogled everything in
pants; a balmy actress who talked drama but longed to take
her clothes off and be a strip-teaser; a tall, dark, greasy-
haired Don Juan who intermittently stole admiring glances
at himself in the mirror, none of them in the script; a mild
little husband who, prevailed upon to pose as a psychiatrist,
had all the women go through amatory posturings and
wrigglings by way of freeing their libidos; and the love interest, in the person of a wife about to divorce the husband,
who projected her great personal charm by maneuvering a
position close to the footlights, glueing herself to it in pro-

file, and purveying a fixed grin and pale stockings with seams as big and black as the Harlem river.

Humor:

> "Where in Heaven have I seen you before?"
> — "I don't know; what part of Heaven do you come from?"

> "Well, I must be off." — "You sure must be!"

> "Will the doctor relieve me?" — "Yes (indicating purse), of everything you've got."

> "She's got in the neighborhood of a million bucks." — "That's sure a nice neighborhood."

It closed, by popular acclaim, after a 23 trot.

A CONNECTICUT YANKEE. November 17, 1943

A "new" musical adaptation of Mark Twain's tale, book by Herbert Fields, music by Richard Rodgers, and lyrics by Lorenz Hart. Produced by Richard Rodgers for 133 performances and to minor returns in the Martin Beck Theatre.

PROGRAM

IN HARTFORD	IN CAMELOT
Lt. (j.g.) Kenneth Kay, U.S.N. *Robert Byrn*	Sir Kay, The Seneschal *Robert Byrn*
Judge Thurston Merrill *John Cherry*	Martin *Dick Foran*
Admiral Arthur K. Arthur, U.S.N. *Robert Chisholm*	The Demoiselle Alisande La Courtelloise (Sandy) *Julie Warren*
Ensign Gerald Lake, U.S.N. *Chester Stratton*	Arthur, King of Britain *Robert Chisholm*
Ensign Allan Gwynn, U.S.N. *Jere McMahon*	Merlin *John Cherry*
Lt. Martin Barrett, U.S.N. *Dick Foran*	Queen Guinevere *Katherine Anderson*
Capt. Lawrence Lake, U.S.N. *Stuart Casey*	Sir Launcelot of the Lake *Stuart Casey*
Lt. Fay Merrill, W.A.V.E. *Vivienne Segal*	Sir Galahad *Chester Stratton*
Corp. Alice Courtleigh, W.A.C. *June Warren*	Angela *Mimi Berry*
	Queen Morgan La Fay *Vivienne Segal*
	Sir Gawain *Jere McMahon*
	Mistress Evelyn La Rondelle *Vera-Ellen*

SYNOPSIS: Prologue. *A banquet hall of a hotel in Hartford, 1943.* Act I. Scene 1. *On the road to Camelot, 543 A.D.* Scene 2. *Courtyard of King Arthur's Castle.* Act II. Scene 1. *Corridor of the royal factory. Three months later.* Scene 2. *On the road from Camelot.* Scene 3. *The palace of Queen Morgan La Fay.* Epilogue. *Same as Prologue, 1943.*

FIRST SHOWN sixteen years ago and achieving a run of more than 400 performances, the exhibit was revised for the 1943 trade after a fashion one did not experience undue pains in anticipating. The characters in the prologue were dressed in military uniforms.

Otherwise, save for the incorporation of a few new tunes and lyrics, three or four procumbent topical gags, and one scene laid in a munitions factory with an incidental dance number called "Ye Lunchtime Follies," the show was just about what it was in its original incarnation. Which is to say that some of Rodgers' old tunes, notably "My Heart Stood Still," again fell agreeably upon the ear, that some of Hart's lyrics again merchanted a nice wit, and that the book was still about as sterile a contraption as one could imagine. To compare it with the book of a college show, as some of the reviewers very tartly did, was unseemly. Any number of the books for college shows have been genuinely amusing and infinitely superior. For example, some of the Harvard Hasty Pudding shows, the Pennsylvania Mask and Wig shows, the old Princeton Triangle shows, and the old Cornell Savage Club shows. The conceit that all such college shows rest for their humor on boys dressed as girls and on allusions to the football team and the more crotchety professors is ill-founded. There is frequently more invention and more honest fun in them than one will encounter in a round of at least half the Broadway shows.

Although once upon a time theatrically diverting enough — back in the remoter period of *The Road To Yesterday*, *When Knights Were Bold*, et al. — the Twain idea of placing a man of the present in a long past era and extracting humor, or in some instances drama, from the situation has long since lost its sauce. And when, as in the show under discussion, a single note is hit throughout the evening, as it was similarly hit in Rodgers' and Hart's previous season's *By Jupiter*, things are likely to become depressing. For such persons as find a copious jocosity in two hours of hybrid locutions like "thou louse!", "thou has put me on the beam," and "thee and thy nerve!" the occasion, however, was apparently rich in satisfaction. As for myself, what distraction I derived from the show was induced solely by one or two of Rodgers' old songs, Hart's comically macabre lyrics for a new one called "To Keep My Love Alive," his further lyrics for a ditty called "You Always Love The Same Girl," although the witty French revue writer, Rip, anticipated them some twenty-eight years ago, Vivienne Segal's sardonic vocal delivery, and — above all and like almost everyone else — the dancing girl who elects to go by the name Vera-Ellen (she might at least add You-All to it) , who was and is otherwise as beguiling a package of beguilement as has beguiled the beguileable in what the poets describe as many moons.

Footnote. The leading man, one Dick Foran, an erstwhile singing cowboy on the movie screen and here playing a U. S. Navy lieutenant, appeared with his lips made up with a beautiful pink rouge.

CAREER ANGEL. November 18, 1943

A play by Gerard M. Murray. Produced by the Blackfriars'
Guild for a brief run in the Blackfriars' Guild Theatre.

Program

Brother Gregory	Liam Dunn	Brother Ubaldus	John Young
Donnie McAdams	John Hickton	Joe Hurdles	Jack O'Neil
Willie Garvey	David Kelly	Walter Glinsky	Howard Berland
Brother Fidelis	Joseph Boley	Frank Thompson	Eddie Ross
Kurt Rheinhold	Eric Ladd	Johnnie Rinn	Gerard McLaughlin
Brother Seraphim		Bruno Chevoski	William Russell
	Angelo Benedetto	Dr. Volatov	William J. Connor
Angel Guardian		Heinrich Von Taushauer	
	David Carman Jones		C. Fabian Thomas
J. Mosely Barr	Paul Pettit		

The Blackfriars' Guild is a semi-amateur — more often amateur — Catholic theatrical organization that functions in a little playhouse two flights up at 320 West 57th
Street in Manhattan. The author of its first seasonal production is a young priest of the Church of Our Lady of
Mercy in Forest Hills, Long Island. Its scene laid in a boys'
orphanage in Georgia, the three acts detail the manner in
which a guardian angel given to the modern lingo descends
from above to assist the Brother in charge in putting the
shelter back on its financial feet. This is accomplished by
the angel's discovery and his bringing into the news of the
fact that the house is the long-lost one that General Sherman omitted to raze on his march to the sea. Forthwith,
contributions pour in and there is no further need to bring
on any dramaturgical Marines to save the day. Father Murray, however, overlooks this lack of need, at least figuratively, and tacks on for what he evidently persuades himself
is popular necessity a lot of extrinsic business involving
Nazi spies and saboteurs and the FBI, which, while it seemingly doesn't hurt the orphanage, wrecks his play.

Earlier portions of the play are fair enough, although it

is clear that the novice playwright is not averse to borrowing ideas freely from G. K. Chesterton (*Magic*), Anatole France (*The Revolt Of The Angels*), H. G. Wells (*A Wonderful Visit,* dramatized by St. John Ervine), Charles Rann Kennedy (*The Servant In The House*), Brian Doherty and Bruce Marshall (*Father Malachy's Miracle*) and Noel Coward (*Blithe Spirit*). The evening, indeed, frequently takes on the complexion of a dramatic revue of these authors' works. Father Murray here and there adds some observation and humor of his own geniture which is not without merit and now and again even contrives to make what is familiar seem a little fresh. His idea, for example, of making his Brother Seraphim a former Broadway ham actor and his Brother Gregory a retired dramatic critic is good waggery. And some of his guardian angel low-comedy has its points. When, in short, his play is bad it is very bad, but when it perks up a bit it amounts to a comparatively creditable first effort.

WINGED VICTORY. November 20, 1943

A show contrived by Moss Hart for the United States Army Air Forces. Produced under the latter's auspices for 212 performances for the benefit of the Army Emergency Relief Fund in the 44th Street Theatre.

Principals

Corp. Mark Daniels, Pvt. Richard Hogan, Pfc. Edmond O'Brien, Pvt. Don Taylor, Pvt. Barry Nelson, Sgt. Rune Hultman, Pvt. Lee J. Cobb, Pvt. Philip Bourneuf and Pvt. George Reeves. Also Phyllis Avery, Elisabeth Fraser, Olive Deering, Kathryn Eames, Genevieve Frizzell and Virginia Hammond.

MAKING USE OF 228 members of the Air Forces personnel, a number of them with previous stage experience, thirty civilian actresses, five big revolving stages, settings by the Army's theatre-wise Harry Horner, lighting by the ditto A. H. Feder, costumes by the ditto Howard Shoup, incidental music by the Army's Hollywood composer, David Rose, and playwright Moss Hart, author in part or solo of various such Broadway successes as *The Man Who Came To Dinner, Lady In The Dark, You Can't Take It With You, Once In A Lifetime,* etc., the exhibit was received by the press and public with the wildly enthusiastic acclaim that was to be expected. As a single but typical example, I quote my colleague of the *Sun*. Proclaimed he: "Here is a thrilling show that dwarfs all else of the current season and beside which the majority of productions of the present decade and century shrink to mediocrity. It is exalted stuff. It is truly magnificent. It is a memorable event. It is, I repeat, magnificent!"

What it was on the whole was a poor show.

The fundamental patriotic impulse which dictated the rapt reaction to the occasion was an estimable one, and not to be depreciated. But it seems to me that a patriotism which is worth its dignified salt should include a love and respect for things other than the obvious ones, and that among these is one's country's efforts in those departments that may go to make its arts finer, and fuller, and more soundly beautiful. The theatre and its drama are potentially one of these. And so when I write as critically as I do about this particular contribution, I write out of that feeling and surely with no slightest reflection on the admirable military body involved. After all, it is not the United States Army Air Forces I am talking about but a show about the United States Army Air Forces.

That show or play was, to tell the simple truth, an often tepid and even more often maizey business. What it in sum amounted to was a minor paraphrase of Maxwell Anderson's *The Eve of St. Mark* with unmistakable overtones of Rida Johnson Young's old college-boy handshaker and backslapper, *Brown of Harvard*. Worse, it was Grade-B movie stuff. In it there was none of the unstrained simplicity and high skill that made Irving Berlin's *This Is The Army* the memorable show it was. Nor was there in it the quality of at least two of the plays that served to make *The Army Play-By-Play* the relatively pungent and acceptable presentation it in turn was. Where Berlin's show smiled a profound pride of country into its audiences and where *The Army Play-By-Play* here and there took things almost as gracefully and easily in its stride, the Hart exhibit not only muscled its purpose down one's throat but shed so many noble and self-affecting tears in the process that it purged one of any but jingo response. Writing of the Berlin spectacle, I said that there were two points of view from which to report on it. One was the patriotic, which would warmly assert that it was grand stuff. The other was the critical, which would coolly assert that it certainly was. Writing now of the Hart spectacle, I repeat that there were two points of view from which to report on it. One was the patriotic, which would warmly assert that it was grand stuff. The other was the critical, which would coolly assert that it certainly wasn't.

The Berlin show, for all its soldiers dressed as girls and other such elements, projected a sense of size and gave the

Army an aura of powerful importance. The Hart show turned the Air Force into a troupe of actors mouthing sentimental and humorous hokum. To say that the boys in that Force may occasionally do that very thing is to beg the question. The boys in the Royal Air Force may equally on occasion comport themselves as do their stage types in such English plays as *Golden Wings* and *Flare Path* but that doesn't absolve those plays from being not only very bad plays but small honor to the body that inspired them.

There were some effective moments in *Winged Victory,* yet they were swallowed up in what went before and came after. The scene wherein the boys take their examinations was vigorous literal theatre. The graduation scene in which they get their wings was good spectacle. And the Christmas show they put on in the South Pacific was amusing. But the play in the aggregate simply was not up to its subject matter. Working with much the same basic materials, Maxwell Anderson's play about a Middle Western youth's career from the moment he plans to enter the armed services to his end in the South Pacific concealed the obvious to a degree in deft writing. Hart's play about several such youths' careers ditto was on the contrary composed almost entirely of the obvious unrelieved by any such deft writing. The aim was simplicity; what emerged was triteness. Its motives were lofty and absolutely honest; its purpose was high-minded and to be respected; its reception by the public was a sincere and thoroughly intelligible reception. But it remained an unimaginative, a juvenile, and an oversentimentalized job.

I illustrate this estimate's justice with a few typical examples of the play's rubber-stamp construction and content, culled both from the acted play and the published version sent to the critics.

1. Business of getting characters off the stage: " 'Scuse me — I've got a cake in the oven."

2. Wit: "I come from Oregon." "That's a nice place to come from — a long way from!"

3. Sentiment: "You know, I feel like I'm the first guy that ever got married in the world. Is it always like that?"

"Always, buddy. Wait till you become a papa like me. *That's* a feeling!"

4. Tragedy: "Oh, God — if they don't come back — if they don't come back . . ." "Perhaps God will be good to us, Helen." "I like to think He knows how little we've had — how we've only begun to live, and how much we love them."

5. Comedy: "For God's sake — my mother sends me a sweater! If we were in the Aleutians I bet I'd get a straw hat!"

6. Tears: "It just hit me, Irv, I'm afraid! I was never afraid before, but now I'm scared. I don't want to die, Irv; I want to see my kid."

7. Solicitude: "They're such kids, Mom — such babies! Even Allan!"

8. Jovial spirits: "Pick out some good bunks for us!" "Don't grab off all the women!" "Did you kiss the Sarge goodbye?" "Keep those latrines nice and clean!"

9. Nobility: Private: "Could I just get my coat, sir? I'm cold." Colonel: "Better take mine." Private: "You're very kind, sir." Colonel: "Kind? You boys do the dying! The word 'kind' sounds a little foolish. Sure you're all right?"

10. Heartbreak: Mrs. Ross (quietly) : "I want to freshen up a bit before supper." *(With an elaborate show of looking at her hands she starts quickly for the house.)*

11. Incidental humorous embroidery: 1. "What will you be having for dinner — purple hearts or oak leaves?" "Just the oak leaves — with parsley." 2. "Look, he comes from Brooklyn!" 3. "Hey, fellas, Betty Grable — with the legs!" 4. Helen: "Only the best man and his best friends haven't even tried to kiss the bride, and I want to know why." "We didn't want to be killed in the crush." 5. "Is leave taking one or two words?" "You mean going away?" "Well, I don't mean stealing leaves from trees."

I further illustrate the reaction of isolated intelligences in the audience through this communication from one Donald Maggini, a publisher: "Not since *The Great Waltz* have I been exposed to so tedious an evening in the theatre. The catalogue of clichés and obvious situations is as long as the play, which seemed endless. At each rise of the curtain it was possible not only to anticipate the argument but the phrasing of the lines. Probably the only thing that kept the audience from chanting the speeches with the actors was the incurable optimism implicit in theatregoing which engenders the hope that the author just could not dare to use such familiar stuff: 'Doctor, he's just got to get well!' — 'Go ahead, son, every man has to cry sometime,' etc. And that Moss directorial touch: the affectionate glancing blow on the shoulder delivered in every scene by some inarticulate soldier to an anguished buddy. Thespis should have stood in the foyer and done the same to the agonized theatregoers as they departed."

I illustrate still further the reaction of even infinitely more isolated intelligent professional criticism with this pointed reflection by Wolcott Gibbs: "As an attempt to report the emotions and behavior of young men at war, I'm afraid it has something of the high-minded but vacant quality of a moving picture . . . The adolescent effect of the play might have been avoided to some extent if Mr. Hart had chosen to include at least one character of a skeptical or even faintly disreputable nature, but he hasn't. There are 228 people in the cast, and there isn't an ignoble thought in the lot of them . . . Mr. Hart's plotting often seems to have come directly out of a Hollywood story conference . . . It occurred to me, in reading the reviews, that some of my colleagues might perhaps have been overpowered and slightly deafened by the scenery. Certainly they overlooked what seems to me one of the most peculiar lines I can remember. One of the cadets has just come back from his first night flight. 'Well, goddamit,' he says in response to some heckling, 'it *is* romantic! And you don't hate yourself in the morning, either!' The idea of sex as inseparable from disgust, especially in a healthy young man who happens to be married, made me wonder just a little about the nature of Mr. Hart's researches into Army life."

The great United States Army Air Forces, I think, deserve something better than that.

GET AWAY, OLD MAN. November 24, 1943

A comedy by William Saroyan. Produced and quickly unproduced by George Abbott in the Cort Theatre.

Program

Patrick Hammer	Edward Begley	Martha Harper	
Ben Manheim	Richard Adams		Beatrice Pearson
Harry Bird	Richard Widmark	Pianist	Sula Levitch
Rose Schornbloom		Bernice Fitch	Joyce Mathews
	Hilda Vaughn	Messenger	Mason Adams
Sam	Glenn Anders	Doctor	Jerome Thor
Correspondent of the			
N. Y. Times	Edwin Hodge		

SYNOPSIS: Act I. *Office of Patrick Hammer.* Act II. *Harry Bird's office overlooking a company street.* Act III. *Harry Bird's office. Three hours later.*
The Place. *California.*
The Time. *A day of the week.*

THE OCCASION PROVIDED an instructive example of what can happen to a play from the time it is written to the time it sees production. As first negotiated by the author, the comedy was at once an hilarious and touching appraisal of decency, artistic and otherwise, in conflict with the debased standards of Hollywood. Its basic fabric was simple: a movie executive, charlatan to the core, on the one hand and a young writer with ideals on the other — not too original but given renewed spirit by the author's observant treatment. It was the details that counted. They embroidered the theme with many illuminating critical threads, and the script as a whole left one with a mood half smiling, half a little sad, as happens with most of Saroyan's plays. It was by no means so good a play as *My Heart's In The Highlands* or *The Time Of Your Life* or even *The Beautiful People.* But it was Saroyan for those who like the way he approaches the theatre and often so freshly and imaginatively serves it. The script called for a few minor, obvious changes, such, for example, as eliminating the nonsensical series of quickly dropped curtains in the second act to indicate brief lapses of time, and also, certainly, the excessive and gratuitous use of profanity. But it was otherwise pretty sound as it stood.

The first producer who read the script was Eddie Dowling. Mr. Dowling wished the author among other things to elaborate the elliptical love story of the young writer and the movie extra into the conventionally romantic business and to constitute it the most important element in the play. He also urged that the "Ave Maria" story which the executive wanted the young man to write for the screen be altered to something that would not offend the hypothetical sensibilities of some elements in the audience. And he wanted several other such changes, all of which would have damaged the play. Saroyan, lending remote ear, declined to comply, and the script went to Billy Rose who allowed that he liked it as it was but let things go at that and did nothing more about it. So, too, with Michael Myerberg.

Michael Todd was the next recipient. Mr. Todd, who has infinite ideas for rewriting plays, however already all right they may be, had all kinds of notions, to which Saroyan, probably weakened by the powerful aroma of Mr. Todd's huge, black, two-dollar cigars, listened attentively. And it was not long before the play's eloquently long speeches were chopped up into so many strips of theatrical ham that the script began to take on the flavor of having been written on a telegraph instrument. Into the strips, incidentally, several more "son-of-a-bitches" and "God damns" were incorporated, the two dozen or so already there evidently not being deemed sufficient. All this duly done, Mr. Todd thereupon abandoned the script and devoted himself instead to that dramatic masterpiece, *The Naked Genius*.

Then came George Abbott. The first thing Mr. Abbott demanded — and, although he does not smoke huge, black, two-dollar cigars and no poison gas overpowered Saroyan, the latter peculiarly agreed — was the elimination of the nun's costume in which the little extra girl makes her first appearance and the substitution for it of a star-spangled classical robe like that worn by Shakespeare's Juliet. The nun's costume was a vital touch in Saroyan's scheme; without it, the whole first scene which the girl plays goes for little. By way of injecting more comedy into another act, an episode was ordered in which the movie executive instructs an employe to jump on the train, follow the young writer and get the better of him, which not only flattened the action but amounted to little more than a cheap paraphrase of a similar and capital episode in the Hecht-MacArthur play of some years ago, *The Front Page.* Worse, the original ending of the play which showed the defeated and broken executive going back for consolation to the faded old movie actress who had long been his mistress and of whom he was sick to death but who was the only living creature left to him was cast aside, and the play with it. Substituted was the venerable Broadway curtain gag situation in which the man, getting on his feet again, calls up another girl. And topping this was a tacked-on scene (double happy-ending hokum) wherein the rejected, faded old actress (cast with a beautiful young blonde show-girl from the Broadway musical comedies) danced gayly around the stage with the boozy friend of the young writer. There were a number of other such "improvements," not the least being the inclusion of a ten-minute-long spoofing of the Dr. Kildare films.

Combine with all this the casting of a radio soap-opera actor in the role of the movie executive and another radio soap-opera actor as the idealistic young writer, and the picture begins to take on the necessary blur. And if anything else were needed to reduce the script to approximate zero, add stage direction that, strangely enough for the customarily ebullient Mr. Abbott, paced the comedy in terms of Gorki, lost sight entirely of the delicately vagrant mood in which Saroyan writes, caused the movie executive to alternate the acting technique of Edward G. Robinson with that of Jimmy Durante, allowed the young writer to indicate his aloof and contemptuous genius by walking forevermore back and forth across the stage with eyes meditatively on the floor, shoulders geniusly huddled and hands in pockets, and gave to the young extra girl so coquettish and superficial a quality that any sincerity the love motif might have had went flying.

Result: thirteen performances — and the storehouse.

LOVERS AND FRIENDS. November 29, 1943

*A tot by Dodie Smith. Produced for a run of 168 perform-
ances by Katharine Cornell and John C. Wilson in the
Plymouth Theatre.*

Program

Rodney Boswell		Lennie Lorrimer	Carol Goodner
	Raymond Massey	Martha Jones	Anne Burr
Stella	Katharine Cornell	Edmund Alexander	
Agnes	Katherine Hynes		Henry Daniell

SYNOPSIS: The scene is London. Prologue. *In Regent's Park.
Spring evening, 1918.* Act I. *The Boswells' drawing room. Early evening,
May, 1930.* Act II. *The same on a day in mid-July, 1930. Scene 1. Early
afternoon. Scene 2. Late afternoon. Scene 3. Very late evening.* Act III.
The same. Late on an autumn afternoon, 1930. Epilogue. *In Regent's
Park. Spring evening, 1942.*

THE ENGLISH Miss Smith, author of such paper-napkin
tea-room comedies as *Autumn Crocus, Call It A Day, Touch
Wood, Bonnet Over The Windmill,* and *Dear Octopus,* has
here fashioned another of equal substantiality. It is of the
species that was wont to show up on the local stage years ago
after Charles Frohman had rejected it and some lesser producer had laid hold of it as something either for his actress
wife, who was getting unruly around the house because of
a long lay-off, or for his turtle-dove, who was beginning to
look at other men. Miss Smith, whose antecedent plays of
similar quality succeeded in building her up to the lofty
estate of a Hollywood movie scenario writer, has now again
offered a smear of childish, sentimental greasepaint which
is less a play than a vehicle, like a baby carriage. And when
it comes to baby carriages on the stage, I prefer Ray Dooley
in them. To discover on the other hand a dramatic actress
of Miss Cornell's status smiling and sobbing, albeit effectively, in such an artless conveyance is hardly gratifying to
those with whom she has found fond favor in drama worth
its and her salt. She is, in addition to and quite apart from

her acting ability, very popular with that liberal portion
of the box-office which doesn't recognize such ability when
it sees it and lays out its money primarily for favorite stage
personalities. She has, therefore, no slightest need for recourse to this kind of spun candy to be a success in that
quarter. She can make as much money from reputable plays
like *The Three Sisters, Candida,* and *The Doctor's Dilemma.*

I mention this because I am not one of those reviewers
who consider it the God-given duty of an actress to go bank-
rupt in catering to their dramatic prejudices. As I see it, an
actress has just as much right to make money out of a bad
play, if she sorely needs it, as a reviewer has to make it out
of writing about the bad play, when he doesn't need it.
What is more, the bad play doesn't always get such bad notices, which gives the actress an ethical advantage of sorts.

The theme of Miss Smith's perambulator has been familiar to theatregoers since the days of programs printed in
Old English, to wit, the threat to a happy marriage offered
by an attractive intruder, male or female, and — after the
usual alarms — the triumph of the old and tested love. Since
these alarms on the stage are necessarily for the most part
conversational — in life, after the first explosion, I am informed by reliable sources that they take the form of grim
and painful silences — any play espousing the venerable
theme calls for either very deft dramaturgy or witty writing
if it is to pass critical muster. Otherwise its old bones are
likely to give off a considerable rattle. Miss Smith is neither
deft nor witty, and the result is such a bone rattling as needs
only a couple of end-men with tambourines to constitute it
a first-rate Piccadilly minstrel show.

Miss Smith's dramaturgy, furthermore, closely follows
the old Al G. Fields minstrel show pattern in its inclusion
of what used to be called a fore-part and an after-part or,
dramatically, a prologue and an epilogue. As in the shows
noted, the former, here exhibiting the first meeting of the
lovers, is in the tender ballad mood of "Swanee River" and
the latter, exhibiting their reunion after the troubled years,
in the bring-down-the-curtain allegro mood of "My Gal's
A Highborn Lady."

Miss Smith, further still, is the kind of playwright who is enraptured by the idea of lovers being brought together in the first place by a mutual appreciation of music. Her husband character accompanies a strange young woman to a harpsichord recital and they are in each other's arms (platonically, for Miss S. never forgets that she is an English lady) before you can say Mozart. Her wife character listens to a phonograph record of Bach in the company of another man and they in turn are in each other's arms (ditto) before you can say Bologny.

Miss Smith, yet still further, like the English lady she is, views intercourse chiefly as of the verbal variety. Her male and female lovers are consequently and merely so many conversational orgasms.

Miss Smith, in short, writes mush.

I observed in a review after the opening night that to praise Miss Cornell and her company for their performances in a play to which they were so embarrassingly superior would be to praise the Notre Dame backfield for a performance against Miss Spence's school. Miss Cornell, usually magnetic in anything she does, although the suggestion of a single approach to whatever role she may be appearing in becomes increasingly manifest, here again pitted her soft and melodious voice against the strident amateurishness of the lines the playwright had provided her and even contrived to make some of them slip from the auditor's ear with not too much discomfort. But I might have been a little more receptive to her performance as a whole had Guthrie McClintic, whose direction was otherwise nutritious, eliminated her business of lighting a cigarette at what seemed five minute intervals by way of indicating that she was collecting her thoughts or bridging a mood of uncertainty and hesitation. I might also have reacted a bit more fully to her personal attraction if he had cautioned her not to slap her thigh loudly whenever she wished to indicate sudden resolution. The sound of a loudly whacked thigh somehow doesn't seem to be associated in my fancy with delicate and desirable femininity.

CARMEN JONES. DECEMBER 2, 1943

A modern paraphrase of the Georges Bizet opera (libretto by Meilhac and Halévy after Prosper Mérimée's romance) by Oscar Hammerstein 2nd in the way of the libretto and lyrics and by Robert Russell Bennett in the orchestral arrangements. Produced with great success by Billy Rose in the Broadway Theatre.

PROGRAM

CORPORAL MORRELL		FRANKIE	*June Hawkins*
	Napoleon Reed	MYRT	*Jessica Russell*
FOREMAN	*Robert Clarke*	RUM	*Edward Lee Tyler*
CINDY LOU	*Carlotta Franzell or*	DINK	*Dick Montgomery*
	Elton J. Warren	HUSKY MILLER	*Glenn Bryant*
SERGEANT BROWN	*Jack Carr*	MR. HIGGINS	*P. Jay Sidney*
JOE	*Luther Saxon or*	MISS HIGGINS	*Fredye Marshall*
	Napoleon Reed	PHOTOGRAPHER	*Alford Pierre*
CARMEN	*Muriel Smith or*	GIRL FROM CUBA LIBRA CLUB	
	Muriel Rahn		*Ruth Crumpton*
SALLY	*Sibol Cain*	PONCHO	*William Dillard*
T-BONE	*Edward Roche*	DANCING	*Sheldon B. Hoskins*
TOUGH KID	*William Jones*	BOXERS	*Randolph Sawyer*
DRUMMER	*Cosy Cole*	BULLET HEAD	*Melvin Howard*
BARTENDER	*Melvin Howard*	REFEREE	*Tony Fleming, Jr.*
WAITER	*Edward Christopher*		

SYNOPSIS: Time. *The present.* Act I. Scene 1. *Outside a parachute factory near a Southern town.* Scene 2. *A near-by roadside, immediately after.* Scene 3. *Billy Pastor's cafe, three weeks later.* Act II. Scene 1. *Terrace of the Meadowlawn Country Club, south side of Chicago, two weeks later.* Scene 2. *Outside a sport stadium, one week later.*

BILLY ROSE, hitherto known chiefly as a purveyor of swimming girls and night club entertainment, typified respectively by his Aquacades and Diamond Horseshoe cabarets, is responsible for this quite extraordinary theatrical achievement. It is very far from being merely the clever stunt one might think in connection with a paraphrase. To fashion a sound and intelligent paraphrase of a classical work is a much more difficult task than criticism usually gives it credit for being. I plainly do not mean to elevate Mr. Hammerstein (and Mr. Bennett) into the company of the great, but it may be permissible to note casually in passing that such greats as Racine were not particularly successful in achieving paraphrases of the Greek drama, nor such as Gerhart Hauptmann in their attempts to paraphrase the Elizabethan. Nevertheless, on their own level the two boys have come off with considerable honor. Hammerstein's contemporary version of the Meilhac-Halévy libretto after Mérimée's romance, though some of its observation of the Negro is on the routine theatrical side, is a handsomely maneuvered affair. And Bennett's adaptation to that libretto of the Bizet score, with no interpolations in the original composer's work, is an equally skillful one.

The libretto, laid in the American South and in Chicago and dealing with Negroes, parallels the original as to the basic story. Carmen becomes a worker in a parachute factory; Don José a soldier named Joe; Michaela Cindy Lou, a girl from his home town; and Escamillo Husky Miller, a champion prize-fighter. The cigarette factory becomes the parachute factory, the inn a night club, the smugglers' den a Negro country club, and instead of the bull-ring there is the prize-ring. There is no travesty; the fable of passion and the tragedy it leads to is allowed to retain its elementary complexion. If a leaven of humor lightens the whole, it is a fully relevant humor, and never gratuitous. And the net effect is in this day and time a factually more impressive libretto than the original, which, though opera house classicists may deride the idea, here and there takes on, by virtue of its very intensity, a recalcitrant and misfitting air of whimsicality.

Bennett's rescoring is extremely ingenious and rich in subtlety. Obedient to Bizet, he intrudes solely in the matter of arrangements and artfully maneuvered rhythms which do no slightest violence to the originals yet which at the same time are so perfectly suited to the new libretto that they seem to have been born simultaneously with it. Even

the pastiche for the burlesque ballet number in the paraphrase of the smugglers' scene — the single small departure from the serious handling of the original score —
amounts to an honorable arrangement. The elimination of
the recitatif passages in favor of spoken dialogue is also entirely within the exhibit's rights since, as Mr. Hammerstein
points out, Bizet and his collaborators originally wrote *Carmen* with spoken dialogue scenes between the airs that
were sung and since *Carmen,* the opera comique, did not
become so-called grand opera until after the composer's
death. The music set to the dialogue was not Bizet's but
Ernest Guiraud's.

Hammerstein's lyrics are, furthermore, a delight. The
Negro idiom which they employ is fantastically faithful to
the spirit of the originals; their wording is wonderfully
adroit; and whether they sing of passion or of frivolity they
ring true to the immediate setting.

There have been, of course, the anticipated protests, most
of them from old stand-patters, and most of them, it seems
to me, a little ridiculous. The very idea of paraphrasing the
libretto has aroused some indignation. Why not stick to the
original, which is satisfactory enough as it is? goes the argument. Why not, we might reply, stick to Schiller when it
comes to Joan of Arc and put Bernard Shaw in his place?
Why not still Augustin Daly's version of *The Taming of
the Shrew* instead of the Lunts'? Why not condemn Basil
Sydney's modern dress *Hamlet* and hail Leslie Howard's
conventionally costumed *Hamlet*? Why not, finally, when
it comes to Negroes, go back to the old ways and arbitrarily
insist upon some Robert Downing or Walter Hampden as
Othello instead of a Paul Robeson?

Carmen, in short, has had many things done to it in the
past, and without undue complaint. The things done have
ranged all the way from the Moscow Art Theatre Studio's
engaging *Carmencita and The Soldier* to the scoreless *The
Pretty Sister of José,* which offered in its stellar role that
hardly Spanish actress, Miss Maude Adams.

The alteration of scene has promoted further qualms.
Yet such qualms have not been articulated when a similar

alteration has several times been made in the scene of Verdi's *Un Ballo in Maschera,* among others.

Adaptations of librettos, further still, have long been a commonplace and highly welcome, on the Russian and other stages, as, for example, Mihail Galperin's new libretto for Lecocq's *The Daughter of Madame Angot* and for Offenbach's *La Périchole.*

The idea of Negroes singing French music, with its flavor of Spanish, has yet further grossly offended the sensibilities of one or two of the music critics. But they do not seem to be in the least offended when, at the Metropolitan, German music is sung by Italians and Americans, Italian by French and Germans, French by Italians, Americans and Swedes, and Russian by Italians.

"What would the art world say," shouts Mr. Oscar Thompson, of the *Sun,* "if some one were to overpaint a black man's face on a portrait by Rembrandt?" What does the critical world say when a music critic overpaints any such Coney Island comparison on this paraphrase by Hammerstein and Bennett?

It is true that some of the voices in *Carmen Jones* are hardly the equal of some of those that have sung *Carmen* at the Metropolitan. But it is equally true that some of the acting in the opera house's presentations of *Carmen* has been hardly the equal of some of that in *Carmen Jones.* And certainly the Metropolitan can not hold a candle to the latter's pictorial staging and lighting. All in all, and in short, a real gift to the theatre. Everyone connected with it deserves an unusual amount of credit: Hammerstein for his book, Bennett for his orchestral arrangements, the Messrs. Bay and du Bois for their settings and costumes, Eugene Loring for his choreography, Hassard Short for his admirable staging, and — last but far from least — Billy Rose himself for being the general behind this unaccustomed non-amphibious operation.

Do I forget another? I do not. That other is John Henry Hammond, Jr., whose job it was to scout the country from coast to coast and dig up the Negro singing and dancing talent for it. Using trains, airplanes, buses, bobsleds, bicycles, street-cars, taxis and in some desperate instances roller-skates and coaster wagons to get places, he penetrated into the lairs of bellhops, chauffeurs, chicken-kitchen cooks, policemen, photograph developers, crap game professors, stevedores, steer-busters, and countless other such bizarre haunts to find what he and Impresario Rose wanted. And he came away with such a new, fresh and exciting lot of musical play competences as has not been seen on a single stage in years.

That is one of the most applaudable elements of the show. It isn't good manners, and certainly it is worse criticism, to say so, but just the same one does in time get a little tired of seeing the same old established and talented players proving again and again that they are everything we long have known them to be. It is a relief to look at something newfledged and vernal for a change and to give ear to newfledged and vernal talent, for that way lies the hope, and life, and happy future of the theatre.

THE WORLD'S FULL OF GIRLS
December 6, 1943

A play by Nunnally Johnson, based on a novel by Thomas Bell titled Til I Come Back To You. *Produced by Jed Harris, with the financial backing of the Twentieth Century-Fox movie company, in the Royale Theatre, it lasted for but 9 performancs.*

Program

Mr. Bridges	*Thomas W. Ross*	Edward	*Charles Lang*
Mrs. Bridges	*Eva Condon*	Miley	*Berry Kroeger*
Dave	*Thomas Hume*	Sally	*Virginia Gilmore*
Hannah	*Julie Stevens*	Sergeant Snyder	*Harry Bellaver*
Florie	*Gloria Hallward*	Mel Fletcher	*John Conway*
Adele	*Frances Heflin*	Mrs. Fletcher	*Cora Smith*
Nick	*Walter Burke*		

SYNOPSIS: Act I. *The living-room of the Bridges family in Brooklyn. Sunday morning.* Act II. *The same. Sunday afternoon.* Act III. *Miley's room in Greenwich Village. Sunday night.*
The time of the play is the autumn of 1942.

J OHNSON'S PLAY is a compound of the stencils of its familiar later day species. There is the feeble distillation of the Sycamore family out of *You Can't Take It With You*, with the scene laid in Brooklyn by way of affording an opportunity for the customary jocosities about Brooklyn. There are the old paterfamilias (in shirtsleeves and galluses) and the plump old materfamilias who long for the money wherewith to buy a small farm and get away from it all. There is the married daughter with a baby whose husband has lost his job and who is bitter over the future — "I haven't even seen a movie in months!" she moans. There is the flighty younger daughter who cajoles her boy-friend lover into matrimony with the news that she is pregnant. There is the injured soldier returned from Guadalcanal and given to modest, halting monosyllables by way of guaranteeing his audience acceptance as a hero. There is the young fascist given an elaborate build-up as an odious character in order to draw the audience's applause when the time comes for him to be punched on the jaw. There is the wheeze, when several characters disturb the lovers by coming into the room for a book or magazine, that it's just like Womrath's. There is the other one about the baby wetting itself. There is the girl alarmed because her soldier beau must be off to the front the next morning and, as in *Those Endearing Young Charms,* etc., giving herself to him without benefit of wedlock. There is the loving young married couple whose fond expectancy of a baby induces in a young wife who hasn't one the overpowering desire for one even if she has to adopt it. There is the bewildered old mother of the family who simply can't make out all that is going on around her. There is the hair-pulling act on the part of two irate females. There is the gag about the draft boards taking men even if they are paralyzed. There is the other gag about the near-sighted man who says if they take him he may very probably shoot General Eisenhower. And there are two or three dozen other such ingredients.

Mr. Johnson, the author, is a well-known Hollywood movie scenario writer who some months earlier performed an interview for a New York newspaper in which he declaimed that he was sick and tired of the theatre's condescension to the films, that writing for the latter was an even more difficult craft than writing for the former, and that the plays on the Broadway stage were on the average considerably worse than the things shown on the screen. Mr. Johnson has now written a play for the Broadway stage. It proves conclusively that he knew what he was talking about, at least as regards one of the plays on the Broadway stage.

The Hollywood champion has proved otherwise, however, that it still seems to be a somewhat more complex business to satisfy the theatre than to gain celebrity in the celluloid arts. He has also proved, to the unanimous conviction of his reviewers, that the theatre's condescension to the films will not be materially lessened by the epiphany of such plays as his.

Augmenting the occasion's strain was some very poor stage direction by Jed Harris and some poorer acting, only two or three of the players avoiding the impression that they had overnight been hurried into the cast from *Lady, Behave!*

THE VOICE OF THE TURTLE. December 8, 1943

A comedy by John van Druten. Produced for a long and prosperous run by Alfred De Liagre, Jr., in the Morosco Theatre.

Program

Sally Middleton	Olive Lashbrooke
Margaret Sullavan	Audrey Christie
	Bill Page
	Elliott Nugent

SYNOPSIS: Act I. Scene 1. *Friday afternoon.* Scene 2. *Friday evening.* Act II. Scene 1. *Saturday morning.* Scene 2. *Late Saturday night.* Act III. Scene 1. *Sunday morning.* Scene 2. *Late Sunday afternoon.*

The action, throughout, takes place over a weekend in early April in an apartment in the East Sixties, near Third Avenue, New York City.

Like Johnson's play, this also deals with a soldier bound shortly for the fighting front and his amorous adventure with a girl, but the difference is the vast difference between an expert dramatist on the one hand and an expert movie writer on the other. Utilizing only three characters to tell his story, van Druten has achieved a comedy that for smoothness, wit, humorous understanding and all-around satisfaction has not been surpassed on the local stage in several seasons. What is more, it is the most engaging of all the miniature-cast plays, including its author's own meritorious four-character comedy, *There's Always Juliet,* that have been written and displayed hereabouts in the later years.

Such plays are often less plays, strictly speaking, than clever tricks, and frequently not even that. They range from one-character exhibits like August Stramm's *Power,* which goes to the absurd length of reducing its dialogue to one-syllable words, and Irving Kaye Davis' *Courtesan,* whose telephone bill is at least 5,000 dollars, to two-character dodges like Cosmo Lennox's German-derived *Close Quarters,* whose drama occurs largely off-stage, and various three-character and four-character affairs which would be much better were the characters arbitrarily kept off the stage brought on. I speak, of course, of plays of the full-length species which have been confected by present-day writers, since a number of shorter ones that belong to the past — Strindberg's *Countess Julie,* for example, and, in the even shorter form, his *The Stronger* — are in a critical category apart. Incidentally, however, when it comes to modern playwrights, Eugene O'Neill will reveal himself an exception when his *By Way Of Obit* is produced; it is a remarkable achievement.

Van Druten's comedy succeeds in every department where the great majority of other such recent attempts have failed. It avoids any suspicion of tricky approach and, to boot, has been directed by the author himself with high dexterity. So wily is that direction, in point of fact, that one never becomes conscious that he is dealing with merely a trio of actors. With similar small-cast plays in the past, that consciousness has generally provided a considerable measure of discomfort, what with the endless transparent chicanery to deceive one into imagining that there are enough actors somewhere around the premises to serve a couple of *Winged Victory* companies. Van Druten's devices are absolutely plausible throughout. He pays the telephone only the Equity minimum; he doesn't have milkmen, icemen, letter carriers, messenger boys, and a mob who have mistaken the number of the house assail the doorbell or buzzer; newsboys don't yell out their extras in the street; telegrams are not slipped under the door every fifteen minutes by unseen hands; and maids, butlers and footmen aren't paid wages to entertain themselves by making peculiar noises in the wings. What one gets, rather, is a genuinely literate evening's entertainment and one devoid of any slightest trace of stunt.

Deriving its title from the Song of Solomon: "The flowers appear on the earth; the time of the singing of birds is come; and the voice of the turtle is heard in our land," the comedy's tale is the fundamentally conventional one of the young man who meets a young girl through the offices of

an older one with whom he has had a passing affair; their
mutual distrust, based upon their past experiences, of love
taken too seriously; their own affair in a spirit of careless
gaiety; the girl's desire to keep it in that spirit lest the unhappiness of the past repeat itself; and the young man's effort to win her over to a deeper love. In van Druten's hands,
however, the story takes on a simple impressiveness that is
rare in the theatre. He knows his characters to the last little
quirk; he knows deeply the emotions that they treat lightly;
and he writes with restraint and gentleness and humor.
Only a few times does he fail himself. One might wish, so
perfect is the rest, that he did not descend to such an outworn jocosity as observing of sex or something of the sort,
"So you have given it up for Lent!," to such another as
teases a laugh out of a reference to *Tobacco Road,* to such
coyness as "I haven't the faintest idea what goes on in that
funny little head of yours," and to a quotation on fidelity
from a Dorothy Parker verse whose amatory philosophy is
a bit on the débutante side. These, however, are readily
dismissible flaws in a fabric that is otherwise irreproachable.

The three members of the presenting company were excellent. Miss Sullavan caught her director's purpose exactly
and made the character of the young girl — not an easy one
to play — thoroughly believable. Miss Christie was made to
avoid any of the acting tricks generally associated with the
interpretation of the routine character of the sophisticated
actress-friend. And Nugent entered into none of the histrionic details customarily negotiated by actors in similar
roles. One other item in the adroit direction. Among the
more foolish conventions of the stage is that which arbitrarily imposes upon actors the necessity for making gestures. Believing that such gesticulations, whether they correctly suit the occasion or not, assist in giving a sense of life
and movement to the scene, directors become white in the
face if an actor, even in the role of a paralytic, keeps his
hands in his pockets or at his side for so long as one or two
minutes. The result is a stage which, even when it purveys
the politest and most socially punctilious of comedies, frequently suggests that it has been directed by Potash and

Perlmutter. Van Druten's actors conducted themselves like normal human beings, not like windmills.

A bloom in conclusion for Stewart Chaney's stage setting showing a cross-section of living-room, bedroom and kitchenette. Such settings in the past have seemed no more liveable than Ludwig Baumann's shop windows. One might, however, well sit in Chaney's living-room without momentarily expecting Lee Shubert, Al Woods and Blanche Yurka to sweep into it, or scramble an egg in his kitchenette without smelling it up like Belasco, or sleep singly or otherwise in his bedroom without fearing the imminent intrusion of a couple of stagehands.

In the sense that the moralists use the word, let it be recorded that there has never been a more completely immoral play on the American stage. It isn't so much that it deals from beginning to end with illicit sex; many plays have done that. It is rather that from beginning to end it makes the miscellaneous relations of men and women charming, highly desirable and something happily and satisfactorily to be indulged in by all and sundry. If there has been any other play that so consistently has operated to the same end I have certainly neither seen it nor heard of it.

Consider.

Its three immediate characters are (*1*) a young girl who has had two easy affairs before the play begins, who has another during its course, and who is presented and accepted as a delightful heroine by virtue of them; (2) a slightly older woman who has had so many she can't count them and whom the audience is made to embrace as a thoroughly companionable creature; and (*3*) a young hero who has also taken things where he has found them and who persuades the audience that he is an enviable romantic fellow. The affair between this hero and the heroine is strictly casual; it is unadorned carnality; the girl forbids the young man to regard it as anything emotionally deeper with the demand that he not get in the least serious about it and that he "keep it gay"; the scene is her bedroom; and the audience is made to admire it and love it. And the young man has already had relations with the older girl, who tries to resume them in the lightest possible manner. So much for the principal characters.

The characters who have figured or who figure in the lives of these three are not seen on the stage but become alive to the audience nonetheless. They include a theatrical producer with a wife and two children who has been the pleasant lover of the heroine; a gallant in the form of a popular star actor who tries to seduce her as he has dozens of other young women; the man who has long been the lover of the older girl; a boy who has been the first sexual experience in the heroine's career; a girl in Paris with whom the hero has had an impressive go; and a comprehensive assortment of other such glandular instruments. All, save possibly alone the actor Lothario, are projected as very charming people and beyond moral criticism.

The play, in short, is an apotheosis of the sex life and irresistible in its implications. It exercises triple the persuasion in its particular field that any dozen *The Sign of the Crosses* and *The Stranger in the Houses* exercise in theirs. It is convincing, infinitely appealing, and beautifully indifferent to the morality held sacred by the bluenoses. Yet the latter seem to have not the slightest suspicion of the fact and, save for one negligible protest from a Brooklyn padre, no voice has been lifted against it. That is van Druten's triumph. For he has written it so very skilfully; he has, without the least chicanery or subterfuge, gone about his business with such deceptive immaculateness and simplicity; and he has so astutely avoided any slightest sense of smirk or vulgarity that he has managed to make the moralists themselves not only eat his play but digest it and like it. I know of no other play even remotely approaching the essence of this one that has succeeded to that extent.

In the history of the local sex drama, professional morality seems most often paradoxically to have been offended into action by plays that far from defending their so-called immorality have either debated it or condemned it. The only exception I can think of is Schnitzler's celebrated *Reigen,* a merry-go-round of sexual intercourse that in its circular movement brings its protagonist back to his anatomi-

cal starting point. Yet even *Reigen* is hardly an exception,
since there is the implication of moral retribution in terms
of physical disability inherent in it. Furthermore, *Reigen*
has been shown in the theatre of our time in its unexpur-
gated form for only a single, subscribed performance, and
that one was interrupted by the police.

What of the others? *The Captive,* which treated of Les-
bianism but which indicated its tragic consequences, was
pounced upon by the outraged authorities. *The God of
Vengeance,* one of the most moral tragedies ever displayed
on the American stage, suffered a like fate simply because
a house of ill-fame figured in it. Two trashy plays by the
ineffable Mae West drew the prurientsia down upon them
although one of them, *Sex,* wound up in a relatively ecclesi-
astical manner, and although the second, *Pleasure Man,*
(originally called *The Drag*) , which dealt with homosexuality, threw Sunday school confetti at its theme before the
last curtain. The same with George Scarborough's trashy
The Lure, one of its scenes having to do with a sporting-
house, but morally circumspect withal. *The Girl With the
Whooping Cough,* an adaptation from the French, got under the skins of the official muckmoochers for no other reason than that it had been whispered about that the whooping cough of the title was originally a sly synonym for a
social disease, although you couldn't tell it from anything
spoken on the local stage. *The Rubicon,* a light French comedy beside which the sex of *The Voice of the Turtle* is stuff
for Cinderella audiences, was at one time also frowned upon
because it contained a scene in which a man has designs
upon a fair lady and notwithstanding the fact that, though
he accomplishes his purpose, matrimony is hanging around
the corner waiting to rear its head. And *The Demi-Virgin,*
a farce, though it ended on an immaculate enough note,
caused a moral rumpus because of a mild paraphrase of the
game called strip-poker.

Dismissing the police wrath over any such innocent and
profoundly moral play as Shaw's *Mrs. Warren's Profession,*
recollection of which today doubtless makes even the bluest
nose blanch with amused shame, we conjure up the picture

of moral indignation over such a farce-comedy of years ago as *Naughty Anthony*, which had the snoopers by the ears because, while the rest of the play had nothing in it to bring blushes to the cheeks of even a Postmaster General, one scene showed the heroine taking off her stockings in preparation for the night's slumber. *Sapho*, a vehicle concocted for Olga Nethersole, further and actually had the moralists of the period screaming because it contained a kiss that lasted for a full thirty seconds and because one scene showed the hero gathering the heroine into his arms and grunting his slow way up a winding staircase with his load. And a play called *The Turtle* in the years before and with Sadie Martinot in the leading role caused the professional pureboys to gasp because, while the rest of it didn't materially offend them, it contained an episode in which the heroine undressed behind a tall, broad and fully concealing screen.

There have more recently been similar examples of moral idiosyncrasy. Robert Sherwood's *Idiot's Delight*, whose theme is a denunciation of the imbecility of war, was suppressed in one American city because it offered a scene in which a man humorously allowed he had once spent the night in a hotel with the heroine. This, it was alleged, made the whole play immoral. And *Tobacco Road* was outlawed in a half dozen communities on the ground of an episode showing a Georgia cracker girl attempting to arouse the libido of a male cracker, although the play as a whole is a sociological study and tragic in its final impression.

Meanwhile, in whatever period of the theatre, the moralists have missed the train in their mad running after a stray little weed along the tracks. While they have been indignantly howling against plays that for the greater part have been basically clean and often even morally elevating, they have been inveigled into passing up plays that, were they shrewd critics of immorality, or what they are pleased to regard as immorality, have been considerably more censorable (according to their peculiar lights) than those against which they have pitched themselves. *The Voice of the Turtle* is only one such, and a dandy. Another beauty was *Women Go On Forever*, which had to do with the contentful rewards of female promiscuity, and still another, un-touched by a single bluebeak, was Thoma's famous *Moral*, along with such of its derivatives as Starling's *Weak Sisters*, all proving convincingly that the occupants of fancy houses are a far more decent lot than the moralists themselves.

Sacha Guitry's *Let's Dream*, done locally as *Sleeping Partners*, didn't get a peep out of the lewdheads, yet it was sexually magnetic with a vengeance. Giraudoux's *Amphitryon 38*, which was as naughty as they come, missed the attentions of the professional dirty boys entirely, probably because its leading rôles were occupied by the duly married and eminently respectable Lunts. *The Great Magoo*, a really foul play by the Messrs. Fowler and Hecht, didn't attract the notice of even the corner cop and was allowed peacefully to pursue its course until it expired from a natural death. The same with the Langners' *Susanna and the Elders*, which was constituted of smut from start to finish. The same with such earlier dirtbags as the Hattons' *Love, Honor and Betray* and *The Squab Farm*. And exactly the same with such smut as Kirkland's *Tell Me, Pretty Maiden*, Wilson Collison's canon, Paul Hervey Fox's *Foreign Affairs*, William Grew's *The Mating Season* (although his *My Girl Friday*, which was not any worse, drew the moralists' notice), Ernest Pascal's *The Marriage Bed*, Elmer Harris' *A Modern Virgin*, and Henry Rosendahl's *Strip Girl*.

The circumstance that the great majority of these plays were trash brings up a confounding point. It is frequently argued — in point of fact, I myself have so argued in connection with *The Voice of the Turtle* — that skilful writing can often get away with murder and that it is cheap writing that gets itself into trouble with the moralists. But in many cases, as the above catalogue in sufficient part proves, it doesn't seem always to be true. *The Captive* was not only skilfully but beautifully written, yet the puritanos descended upon it. What holds out of the theatre seemingly also at times holds in it. A *Jurgen* is suppressed and a *The Common Law* not; in the theatre a decent dramatization of Tolstoi's *Resurrection* gets into trouble and an indecent one of Steinbeck's *Tortilla Flat* goes scot free.

It thus in general becomes impossible to guess how the winds of official morality will blow. The idea that times and morals change and that the standards of the moralists change with them does not always hold water. If the moralists a full three decades ago frowned upon the scene in Wilde's *Salomé* wherein Salomé indulges in an anatomical cajolery of the prophet, they frown today upon the not essentially dissimilar so-called horsing scene in *Tobacco Road*. If, contrariwise, they shut their eyes for the antecedent half-century at the spectacle of homosexuals in the burlesque shows, they opened them wide and furiously when *Pleasure Man* eventually came along, albeit it handled the creatures equally in terms of comedy. If in the past they saw nothing objectionable in the strip-tease — it flourished for years with no interference — they see something objectionable in it in this later and supposedly much more sophisticated day. And if nowadays they become white in the face over the double entendre of a song called *My Bunny* in a *Star and Garter* and force its elimination, they failed to think one way or another about one equally fertile in innuendo called *I'm a Cooler For the Warmest Coon In Town* sung for years on end by the esteemed Messrs. Williams and Walker.

The whole business becomes confusion twice confused. From a strictly moral viewpoint, Lonsdale's recent *Another Love Story* was many times more immoral in both line and act than the musical show *Wine, Women and Song*, yet the moralists let it alone and raided the latter. There has never been a more forthright, dirty seduction scene on the American stage than that in *Brother Cain,* produced a few seasons back, yet the blueboys did nothing about it. Instead, they waited for a harmless forty-year-old burlesque skit in *Star and Garter* and demanded that it be bowdlerized. This season in *Try and Get It* we engaged a rubbishy farce that was of cheap smut all compact. It didn't get so much as a nervous twitch from the lascivii. But let someone add tunes and a line of chorus girls to it and I'll lay odds of five to one that License Commissioner Moss will, in Wilson Mizner's old phrase, begin foaming at the mouth like a cream-puff.

PILLAR TO POST. December 10, 1943

A comedy by Rose Simon Kohn. Produced as a mishap by Brock Pemberton in the Playhouse.

Program

Mrs. Bromley	Ruth Gates	Private Curley Hart	
Sgt. Jackson	Paul Kirk Giles		Guy Gillette
Private Corliss	Alfred Porter	Alabama	Hamtree Harrington
Miss Dawson	Jean Mann	Capt. Jack Ross	Richard Hart
Frances Bass	Elaine Perry	Col. Michael Otley	
Private Pearl Hart			Franklyn Fox
	Susana Garnett	Mrs. Kate Otley	
Jean Howard	Perry Wilson		Frances Woodbury
"Pudge" Corliss	Lorraine Pressler	Milly Ross	Elsie Hanover
Private Dixon	Bob King	Lt. Thompkins	Lee Parry
Vera Marsh	Judith Cargill	Dotty Thompkins	
Private Peters	Henry Michaels		Frances McCabe
Lt. Don Mallory	Carl Gose	Sgt. Tommy Withers	Kip Good
Mrs. Harley	Agnes Scott Yost	Mrs. Mallory	Suzanne Jackson
Hattie Beekman		Sgt. Jones	William Christal
	Margaret Power	Cab Driver	Robert Clark

SYNOPSIS: Act I. Scene 1. *USO Housing Bureau, early evening.* Scene 2. *Colonial Auto Court, half hour later.* Act II. *Colonial Auto Court.* Scene 1. *Jean's cabin, that evening.* Scene 2. *The Otleys' cabin, that evening.* Scene 3. *Jean's cabin, immediately afterward.* Act III. *Colonial Auto Court. Jean's cabin, next day, noon.*

Time. *Present.* Place. *Near a large army camp.*

THERE ARE SOME PLAYS that you can tell all about after a quick glance at the cast of characters and the list of scenes. Just as in the old melodrama days you knew pretty well what was in store when you saw in the program the names Harold Tremaine, Simon Black and Nellie and such scenes as *A Tenement Room, Marsh's Department Store,* and *A Mansion On Fifth Avenue,* so it is in these days of comedy when you detect a Lieutenant and a girl named Jean, along with *Jean's Cabin That Evening* and *Jean's Cabin Next Day.* If, in addition, you see *Place: Near A Large Army Camp,* you might just as well have stood in bed.

Before the curtain went up on this specimen you accordingly knew that the Lieutenant and Jean would find themselves under embarrassing circumstances sharing the bungalow or cabin or whatever it be called and that it would be necessary for them to pose as a married couple. You also knew that, such plays being backed by a movie company and such movie companies being regularly fetched by duplications of the film, *It Happened One Night,* the lieutenant would sleep on the floor that night so as not to disturb the Hays office. And you knew that, come the dawn, pure love would lift its ugly head and that holy matrimony would again be just around the corner. If Miss Kohn is not already a successful movie scenario writer, it will not be long before she is one. Her characters, her dialogue and everything else about her play stamp her as something of a Hollywood ace.

Footnote: When will the producers of these plays about the Lieutenant and Jean stop casting the Jeans therein with young actresses suffering from suppressed desires to be Billie Burke?

Appropriate statistic: The carbon-copy shut down after twenty-seven performances, twenty-six of them to seats but one-sixth occupied.

ARSENIC AND OLD LACE. DECEMBER 12, 1943

The travesty melodrama by Joseph Kesselring. Presented by the Professional Children's School in the Hudson Theatre for 2 performances.

PROGRAM

ABBY BREWSTER	*Patsy O'Shea*	MR. GIBBS	*Teddy Rose*
THE REV. DR. HARPER		JONATHAN BREWSTER	
	Mack Twamley		*Paul Porter, Jr.*
TEDDY BREWSTER	*Roy Robson*	DR. EINSTEIN	*Johnnie Ven*
OFFICER BROPHY	*Edwin Bruce*	OFFICER O'HARA	*Jackie Ayers*
OFFICER KLEIN	*Richard Dalton*	LIEUTENANT ROONEY	*Jack Irwin*
MARTHA BREWSTER	*Lorna Lynn*	MR. WITHERSPOON	
ELAINE HARPER	*Mary Ellen Terry*		*Edwin Zimmerman*
MORTIMER BREWSTER			
	Charles Howard		

THE BEST PERFORMANCE by children in my local experience was that in the melodrama, *Alias Jimmy Valentine,* at Wallack's Theatre some thirty years ago and if anyone arises to proclaim the old rebuke that memory has a way of cheating I denounce him out of hand. I have seen many performances of plays by youngsters since then and none has equalled it. The presently considered exhibit was drolly acted by the little boys and girls bent on future histrionic careers in some of its roles but travesty melodrama nevertheless offers difficulties that straight melodrama does not, and some of the children found it beyond their resources.

There is, of course, something about these performances that is irresistible to the more sentimental of adults, and the exhibition was duly greeted by such with the customary raptures. I like children myself; I think that some of them are cute; I even think that some of them are peculiarly very good in the acting craft; but I could not find it in my critical psyche, as most of my colleagues did, to be overawed by competences that seemed to me to be here and there hardly significant. My sentimental gifts, like my patriotic in the instance of *Winged Victory,* are apparently not sufficiently developed to discern genius in even the sweetest kids when it is not in evidence.

SUSAN AND GOD. DECEMBER 13, 1943

A week's revival of the comedy by Rachel Crothers. Produced by John Golden on behalf of the New York City Center of Music and Drama in the City Centre Theatre.

PROGRAM

IRENE BURROUGHS		LEONORA STUBBS	Doris Day
	Jeannette C. Chinley	CLYDE ROCHESTER	
MICHAEL O'HARA			William Weber
	Douglas Gilmore	SUSAN TREXEL	
LEEDS	Earl McDonald		Gertrude Lawrence
CHARLOTTE MARLEY		BARRIE TREXEL	Conrad Nagel
	Eleanor Audley	BLOSSOM TREXEL	Jean Sampson
HUTCHINS STUBBS			
	Francis Compton		

SYNOPSIS: Act I. Scene 1. *The terrace room in Irene Burroughs' house in the country — a Saturday afternoon in June. Scene 2. The same room — four hours later. Act II. Scene 1. A guest room in the same house. Seven o'clock the following morning — Sunday. Scene 2. The terrace room. Eleven o'clock the same morning. Act III. Scene 1. Susan's sitting room in her house in the country. Three months later — late afternoon. Scene 2. Two days later — about nine o'clock in the evening.*

THE CITY CENTER of Music and Drama, founded in the old Mecca Temple by a group of artistically minded citizens, is New York's gesture toward a municipal theatre. Its soberly announced aim is to present the very best in drama and music at prices within the reach of the masses. One might have wished that it had inaugurated its policy with something a little more important than this six-year-old Broadway box-office knickknack. It seemed rather difficult to get excited over a venture of the sort that began business with any such thing as *Susan and God*. It may be all very well to open a Broadway commercial playhouse with *Susan and God* but, when it comes to something proudly designed as a City Center of Music and Drama and heralded as an institutional contribution to the metropolis' culture, *Susan*

and God doesn't seem to have been exactly an inspiration.
Dedicating a municipal theatre with *Susan and God* is
much like having launched one of the famous European
municipal theatres not with Goethe's *Faust* or Molière's
Tartuffe or Chekhov's *The Cherry Orchard* but with *Whose
Wife Is Emily?*

Another thing. The advance advertisements grandly
promulgated the fact that the guest of honor at the opening
would be Mr. Noel Coward. Mr. Noel Coward was accordingly and duly signalized by Mayor La Guardia, who acted
as the master of ceremonies, as the guest of honor, though
haplessly detained by the flu. There is no doubt that Mr.
Coward is perfectly all right in his way, but the idea of
Mr. Coward as the star guest at the dedication of a municipality's theatrical and dramatic dream strikes me as like
having had Sam Bernard as the guest of honor at the opening of the Dresden Municipal Theatre or Theodore of the
Ritz as the big event at the opening of the Odéon. My notion of the launching of a civic temple of dramatic art ded-
icated to "educational and cultural purposes" somehow
does not include as the outstanding guest of honor a con-
cocter of trivial Piccadilly and Broadway sex comedies.

There were further misfortunes. *Susan and God,* the
Latter knows, is a poor enough specimen of dramatic writing as it is but, when the sound system went askew and filled
the auditorium with echoes, having to listen to it twice was
asking a bit too much. The acting company, in addition,
apparently thought it necessary, in view of the theatre's size,
to overshout and overplay to such a degree that the stage
took on the aspect of an amateur hockey game. Gertrude
Lawrence, the star of the occasion, treated the play, moreover, as if it were an airplane on which she had booked
passage, which had inconsiderately taken off just as she was
about to get aboard, and which she thereupon frantically
dashed after all the way from 8:45 to 11 o'clock. Excellent
comédienne that she otherwise is, Miss Lawrence here once
again as in *Skylark* elected to regard every line of dialogue
as a Benzedrine tablet and the moment it got into her
mouth to enter upon such a demonstration of animal vital-

ity and so much hopping, gliding and jumping about that the impression was of a ballet directed by Frank Buck. It was certain when the evening was over that her industrious sweeping up and down and around the stage obviated the necessity of the theatre's employment of any scrubwomen and cleaners.

If you do not happen to be familiar with the play which served the gala occasion, I may sufficiently picture it to you as the kind in which, just after the first curtain has risen, what the author describes as "a healthy, out-doorsie woman" comes on and is informed by another woman, "You look like a lobster!", to which she wittily retorts, "I feel like a crab!"

THE PATRIOTS. December 20, 1943

Sidney Kingsley's Critics' Circle 1943 prize play. Presented by the Playwrights' Company in association with Rowland Stebbins for a one week holiday engagement in the City Center Theatre.

Program

Captain	Matthew Ayres	Ned	Paul Ransom
Thomas Jefferson		Mat	Philip White
	Walter Hampden	James Monroe	John P. Boyd
Patsy	Julie Haydon	Mrs. Hamilton	Sonya Stokowski
Martha	Marie Dow	Henry Knox	Joe Byron Totten
Jupiter	Ken Renard	Butler	Paul Mosnar
James Madison	Ross Matthew	Mr. Fenno	Freeman Hammond
Alexander Hamilton	Guy Sorel	Mrs. Conrad	Leslie Bingham
George Washington		Frontiersman	John Stephen
	Cecil Humphreys	Thomas Jefferson Randolph	
Sergeant	Peter Emery		Allan Martin, Jr.
Colonel Humphreys		George Washington Lafayette	
	John Stephen		Theodore Leavitt
Jacob	William C. Tubbs		

SYNOPSIS: Prologue. *The deck of a schooner, 1790.* Act I. *New York, 1790.* Scene 1. *The presidential mansion.* Scene 2. *The smithy of an inn on the outskirts of New York.* Act II. *Philadelphia, 1791–93.* Scene 1. *Hamilton's home.* Scene 2. *Jefferson's rooms.* Scene 3. *The same. A few days later.* Act III. *Washington, 1801.* Scene 1. *Jefferson's rooms at Conrad's boarding house.* Scene 2. *The interior of the Capitol.*

R ECORDED IN DETAIL in *The Theatre Book of the Year, 1942–1943,* this meritorious play would better have served the opening of the City Center than the puny Rachel Crothers comedy. A drama dealing with the birth struggles of the American Democracy seems after all to be slightly more suitable to the dedication of a municipal theatre than a Broadway concoction about a female nitwit who spouts Buchmanism and is finally and somewhat gratuitously reunited with her dipsomaniac husband through the agency of their small child. The presenting company, moreover, was on the whole superior to that which performed the play last year, as was the simplified scenic production. Walter Hampden, less rhetorical than is his wont, was rather too old for the role of the younger Jefferson, which now and again gave the stage the effect of having two Washingtons on it; but even so it was agreeable to have a professional actor in the role in place of last year's radio actor, although the latter was paradoxically not unimpressive, doubtless because of the generic force of the role itself. It was similarly satisfactory to engage a professional, albeit one far from immaculate, in the Hamilton part, since the radio actor who filled it last season seemed to regard it primarily as a microphone and Hamilton as Boake Carter broadcasting the Kingsley script. As Jefferson's daughter, Miss Haydon — the part was originally occupied by the felicitous Madge Evans, Mr. Kingsley's wife, for whom he had written it — brought once again to the role that half soft-cloud, half distant-sunshine quality which is so gratifying to a stage too often in my prejudice ridden by a semimasculine harshness and which is shared on the British stage by the lovely Celia Johnson. Cecil Humphreys, of the original cast, was again the Washington in a performance nominated as last season's best. Patsy Jefferson's little boy on this occasion was Allan Martin, Jr., who will go down into the record as the only stage child in the history of the American theatre who has looked like H. L. Mencken.

FEATHERS IN A GALE. December 21, 1943

A comedy by Pauline Jamerson and Reginald Lawrence. Produced for prompt failure by Arthur Hopkins and Martin Burton in the Music Box.

Program

Matilda Phinney	*Louise Lorimer*	Felipe	*Stuart Brody*
Phoebe Fuller	*Paula Trueman*	Josiah Abner	*Richard Garrick*
Zeb Hibbitt	*John Hamilton*	Town Clerk	*John Robb*
Lucy Abner	*Zamah Cunningham*	Captain Ebenezer	
Annabelle Hallock			*Alexander Campbell*
	Peggy Conklin	Abigail	*Aileen Poe*
Reverend David Thatcher		Mr. Otis	*Cyrus H. Staehle*
	Harry Ellerbe	Mr. Carey	*Edwin Cushman*
Captain Seth Barnabas			
	Norman MacKay		

SYNOPSIS: Act I. Scene 1. *Afternoon.* Scene 2. *Evening.* Act II. Scene 1. *Two weeks later, afternoon.* Scene 2. *Late that night.* Act III. Scene 1. *The following morning.* Scene 2. *An hour later.*

Scene. *The Great Room of Annabelle Hallock's house in Sesuit, Cape Cod, June, 1804.*

Every so often in glancing through an encyclopædia someone runs across an item describing some quaint, little known, old American custom and promptly concludes that in it cries out the germ of a likely comedy. It is thus that every so often we are visited by a play dealing, as in *The Pursuit of Happiness,* with bundling, or one, as in *Susanna and the Elders,* dealing with sex as practised in the Oneida community, or one, as in *Feathers In a Gale,* having to do with the old New England custom of the widow's vendue. It is most frequently the misfortune of the hopeful playwrights, however, that their acquaintance with dramaturgy is based upon a mere flirtation, and the misfortune of their audiences that their plays accordingly amount to little more than the drama's more aged platitudes with the customs in point wound 'round their middles like a gingham sash.

This is again true of the play in question. The basic story is the routine one of the widow trying to snare a husband and exercising all her routine wiles to that end, the story here being laid in the New England of 1804 and multiplied, in the case of the widow, by three. The business of the vendue, that is, the selling of indigent widows to the highest bidder for service as housekeepers or worse than death, has little to do with the play save as a stimulus to the women to get themselves married as quickly as possible. The dramaturgy, further, is even less expert than is commonly the case. It consists almost wholly in actionless dialogues; the phraseology takes such standard old Cape Cod stage forms as "glory be!", "tarnation!", "he's a fine, upstanding young man," and "I swan!"; the humor has to do with drinking out of a saucer and in leering at any reference to upstairs; the characters are introduced by periodic looks out of the window on the part of someone on the stage and such exclamations as "Why, it's the Reverend Thatcher! Hurry and open the door for him"; and the audience is provided with further identification by having everyone on the stage regularly to refer to one another by their full names, as, "Why Matilda Fuller, how can you?", "Now, then, Annabelle Hallock!", or "Captain Seth Barnabas, you have certainly traveled a lot!"

Nor have the authors overlooked the device of causing a sailor to mistake the house wherein the widows live for a brothel. Nor again, the establishment of atmosphere by additional looks out of the window accompanied by remarks on the aspect of the sea, the aforesaid remarks being further accompanied by the noise of a wind-machine.

Mr. Hopkins' staging and direction did not help matters. The coquettish widow was permitted the familiar pit-a-pat geisha gait; the shy widow was made shrinkingly to put her hands over her face when the occasion called for her to be embarrassed; and the practical, hard-headed widow duly and defiantly rolled up her sleeves and stalked intermittently into the kitchen. The hired hand was directed to comport himself like Hi Holler out of *Way Down East;* the indignant clergyman upon each of his appearances was

stood near the door from which he had entered and made
to read his lines without penetrating into the intimacy of
the room; the sea captain was vouchsafed the old bellowing vocal delivery; and the town's selectman was instructed
per formula to look like, speak like, and comport himself
like the late Cal Coolidge.

Box-office statistics: seven performances.

LISTEN, PROFESSOR! December 22, 1943

A play by Alexander Afinogenov, adapted by Peggy Phillips. Produced for 29 performances by Milton Baron in association with Jean Muir and Toni Ward in the Forrest Theatre.

Program

Anya	*Virginia Farmer*	Dr. Pavel Tumansky	
Professor Vassily Okayemov			*Alexander Clark*
	Dudley Digges	Senya Marshak	
Masha	*Susan Robinson*		*Michael Dreyfuss*
Leonid Karayev	*Martin Blaine*	Lyolya Spirina	*Peggy Allardice*
Nina Alexandrovna		Galya Chikova	
	Frances Reid		*Anne Marie Macauley*
Victor Tumansky		Vera	*Viola Frayne*
	Peter Fernandez		

SYNOPSIS: Act I. Scene 1. *Early evening, October.* Scene 2. *Late afternoon, six weeks later.* Act II. Scene 1. *Evening, several days later.* Scene 2. *Early afternoon, two weeks later.* Act III. Scene 1. *New Year's Eve.* Scene 2. *The next day.*

The action takes place in 1936, in the home of Prof. Okayemov in Moscow.

It entertained the late venerated Prof. Hugo Münsterberg to project various words at the students in his psychology clinic and to bid them forthwith respond with their personal connotations. Thus, "top" would seem almost invariably to have suggested "hat"; "whiskey" to have suggested "soda"; "blue," "Danube"; and so on. It entertains the present somewhat less venerated Prof. Nathan at this juncture to project various modern national drama at his readers and to bid them do likewise. He need not, however, as in Münsterberg's case, wait even momentarily for the connotations, since they will in all probability be even more routine than the Harvard boys' replies. Thus, French drama will in nine instances out of ten undoubtedly suggest "infidelity" and in the tenth maybe "bedroom"; English will connote "drawing-room" and in the tenth perhaps "butler"; German will betoken "stodgy" and from the facetious back row in the tenth either "beer" or "fat actresses"; and the Russian, in all ten cases, surely and following tradition "gloomy."

That there is a measure of accuracy in all these is plain. But the measure is materially smaller than is generally thought. For one modern French play treating of infidelity there are at least three that do not. For one English play set in a drawing-room there are at least four or five otherwise set. For one stodgy German play there are at least five far from stodgy. And though the modern Russian drama often leans to the gloomy there is plenty of evidence that the Russians can chuckle with the best of them.

The popular fundamental picture of Russian drama, fairly justified by the examples of it usually shown on the stages of the western world, remains still that which I impressionized all of twenty-nine years ago in *Another Book On The Theatre:*

Cast

Miska Vasalenavitch Klooglosevtloff (a retired professor)

Anna Vladimirovna Klooglosevtloff (his ailing wife)

Andrievna, Elizavetna, Marina, Marfa, Varvana, Binga, Maska, Ginka, Paulina (his daughters)

Volgutz, Savel, Kuligin, Boris, Constantin, Alexis, Ivan (his sons)

Michailovsky Alexandrovitch Distcheff (his wife's brother, a failure)

Astroff Leonidivitch Zowski (his first cousin, a failure)

Marina Konstantinova Petrishtsheff (his second cousin, a failure)

Bimboff (his third cousin, a neurotic)

Butkevitch Spiffvitch Kokoklinghin (his wife's step-uncle, a paralytic)

Kudrash Ilia Psychovitch (his grandfather)

Dmitri Binghoff Korotskoff (his half-brother, a half-wit)

Natasya Paulovitchna Vitch (his imbecile great-aunt)

Leonidas Dostevski Klishavitch (his uncle's brother-in-law, a dipsomaniac)
Pavel Paulovitch Sonoff (his doctor)
Klinghoff Abrezkovitch Statchoff (his wife's doctor, a paranoiac)
Pishkin, Dlthidor, Borapatikin (other doctors)
Gamboff, Pisk, Kudrash, Gregorovitch (epileptics)
Sergius Vodkaroff (chief of police)
Diapera (an old nurse)

The entire action is laid in the country home of the Klooglosevtloffs, near Moscow, during a thunderstorm.

In the popular imagination the plot of the Russian drama follows, with minor variation, one of three courses. In the first, all the characters are filled with a deep longing for something they haven't got, and never get it. In the second, someone murders someone else for a Principle and, apprehended by the police after an hour and twenty-five minutes' colloquy with his conscience, escapes the law by suicide. In the third, everybody except an old man with white whiskers goes crazy from drink, dissipation, and philosophy.

That the Russian drama — the recent war plays, as in the case of those of other nations, eccentrically and naturally aside — is frequently far from the accepted tombstone pattern and of some considerable humor is customarily overlooked. Katayev's farce-comedy, *Squaring The Circle*, hasn't a paralytic in it from beginning to end and is approximately as pessimistic as Sacha Guitry. The same with Peter Ustinov's *Blow Your Own Trumpet*. Evreinoff's *The Chief Thing* is, thematically, Pirandello dancing with the Irish Lennox Robinson. His *The Theatre Of The Soul* is satirical humor all compact. And his *The Merry Death* is as entertaining a harlequinade as his *The Beautiful Despot* is droll irony. Ostrovsky's *The Forest* and *Little Snowdrop* glint with pleasant humors. Nemirovitch-Dantchenko's prize-winning *The Value of Life* is frisky comedy; gay farces like *Strange Child* popularized Moscow's Satire Theatre; and Saltuikoff-Shchedrin's *The Death of Pazuhin* added to Moskvin's high standing as a comedian.

If you think all Russian plays contain speeches like "Yes,
I am well. It would be better if I were ill — but something
is wrong. Such a fancy keeps flitting through my head and I
cannot escape from it. I begin to think and I cannot collect
my thoughts; I try to pray and I cannot. I murmur words
with my lips but my mind is on something else. What is the
matter with me? Some misfortune is going to happen! At
night, I cannot sleep; I no longer dream those old dreams
about the trees of paradise and the mountains," etc., — if
you think that, disabuse yourself of the notion by taking a
look at Zamiatin's *The Flea* or Faiko's *Teacher Bubus*. If it
is loud sex farce you seek, you won't find a louder one than
Shkvarkin's *Another Man's Child,* which was so great a success in Soviet Russia that it brought its author more than a
million roubles in royalties in its first year. Pushkin's *The
Stone Guest* is given to smooth Don Juan humors; and
Turgenieff's *A Month In The Country* is certainly far from
being the grim business the Theatre Guild made it out to
be by casting the tragic Nazimova in the leading woman's
role but rather a high comedy, as the Moscow Art Theatre
properly realized (Moskvin scored one of his biggest comedy successes in it) and as the local Gilbert Miller, taking a
hint from the St. James's Theatre in London, appreciates
in his hope to revive it with the comédienne Ina Claire.

The delusion of the insistent gloom of the Slav drama in
toto, spreading to the majority of our local producers, ambitious stock company actresses and one-tongued translators
and adaptors, has helped further to mislead audiences. It is
such as these who, unlike Guthrie McClintic, have banished
the periodic comedy from Chekhov's *The Three Sisters,*
unlike the Lunts from his *The Sea Gull,* and unlike Jed
Harris from his *Uncle Vanya.* It is such as these who have
ignorantly tricked audiences into imagining that a people
who could give birth to world-famous witty ballets, Balieff
vaudeville, operas like Rimsky-Korsakov's *The Girl from
Pskov* and Prokofieff's *The Love For Three Oranges,* orchestral scherzos like Borodin's, and jolly belles lettres like
Andreyev's *Satan's Diary,* Dostoievski's *Another Man's
Wife* and Gogol's *How The Two Ivans Quarreled* — that

such a people could produce only dramatists who invariably have seen their world as an admixture of desolation,
despair, and lingering death.

What is further generally overlooked is the two-sidedness
of many Russian playwrights. Thus, if one of the leading
dramatists of the past like Tolstoy wrote in terms of tragedy
he wrote also in allegro terms, as *The Fruits of Enlighten-
ment* guarantees. Thus, in the past, if one like the celebrated Griboyedov wrote in the vein of tragedy, he also
wrote in *Gore ot Uma* what is generally considered to be
one of the great classic Russian comedies. And probably
even the Quiz Kids can tell you that the Chekhov whom
their elders somehow view as an apostle of gloom was a
pretty hand at lively farce and satire, as *A Marriage Proposal, On The Harm Of Tobacco* and *The Entr'-acte Under The Divan* attest, and as his delightful tale of a lovesick
carp fully attests in another quarter.

For every deep-dyed woe-is-me playwright, the Russian
theatre in point of fact has offered one who has often approached the world with a genial smile: the witty Ostrovsky before mentioned, Alexander Ivanovitch, Sologub (his
Vanka the Butler is a comedy lark) , Luiboff Stolitsa (*The
Mirror Of The Virgin* will give you some sardonic grins) ,
Evreinoff (*The Foundation of Happiness* is a three-act
spoof of gravediggers) , Kuzmin, Merezhkovsky and, surely,
Griboyedov with his *The Misfortune of Being Clever*. And,
doubly surely, if there remain any slightest doubt in the
matter, Gogol with his grand satirical comedy, *The In-
spector-General*.

The occasion under immediate scrutiny contributed, at
least in a measure, to the evidence. Afinogenov, haplessly
killed in an air raid on Moscow three years ago, was one of
the leading younger writers for the Russian stage. If with
one hand he wrote serious plays like *Distant Point, Second
Roads* and *Salute To Spain,* with the other he wrote a number of comedies like this *Listen, Professor!* (Its original title was *Mashenka.*) The story is hardly a novel one: the
introduction into the household of a set, old man of a representative of the younger generation and the change the

latter effects in the life of the ancient. It has served scores
of plays, from the tragic *The Master Builder* to all kinds of
popular comedies like *The Rainbow, Peg o' My Heart,* et
al. But Afinogenov has avoided most of the later-day clichés
and has wrought a simple and generally pleasing little play
with an agreeable warmth to the whole of it. It is a distinctly
minor effort and far too tranquil for an American stage
that usually venerates hustle and bustle above everything
else; it belongs to the past of *The Professor's Love Story*
and gentle comedies of the species; but, though in the lesser
critical groove, it has its lief and homely points.

The adaptor, working from a literal translation by J. J.
Robbins, has not been particularly successful in her under-
taking. Her phraseology takes such close to travesty turns
as "You have no right to stand in the way of that child's
welfare!"; "Love? You don't know the meaning of the
word!"; and "You came here to tell me all this?" And the
very title she has given to her adaptation, *Listen, Professor!*,
in its suggestion of such musical shows as *Oh, Boy!, Oh,
Kay!, No, No, Nanette!,* and *La, La, Lucille!* hardly indicates the proper mental approach to the job she took in
hand.

DOCTORS DISAGREE. December 28, 1943

A play by Rose Franken. Produced as a misstep by William Brown Meloney in the Bijou Theatre.

Program

Celia	Eda Heinemann	Laura	Ethel Intropidi
Dr. Margaret Ferris		Dr. Stanley Bates	Judson Laire
	Barbara O'Neil	Miss Kelly	Ann Thomas
Mrs. Deane	Dolly Haas	Mr. Deane	John Ireland
Pete	Jack Willett		
Dr. William Lathrop			
	Philip Ober		

SYNOPSIS: Act I. *Apartment and office of Dr. Margaret Ferris. Seven o'clock in the evening.* Act II. Scene 1. *The Deane nursery. A few minutes later.* Scene 2. *Same as Act I. Shortly afterwards.* Act III. *Same as Act I. Early the next morning.*

It is a far cry from the author's *Outrageous Fortune* to this play. Written originally as a serial for a popular women's magazine, it betrays its geniture, with but slight interruption, from first to last curtain. Also, since the serials in the women's magazines most often seem to hark back for their themes to the matinée favorites of the theatre of more than a quarter-century ago, it betrays an old-auntie attitude toward the contemporary stage surprising in a playwright whose previous work has in considerable part assumed a quite different stance.

For her thesis Miss Franken has had recourse to one already stage-rusty when Rachel Crothers some three decades ago dispensed it in *A Man's World,* to wit, women's struggle (which in these days is necessarily about as bloody as a pillow fight) to gain recognition and equality with the male sex in the sphere of the professions. Aside from making her heroine for a change a surgeon, Miss Franken not only contributes nothing new to the general treatment of the subject but contributes so much that is theatrically and otherwise ham that her play takes on in sum the dramatur-

gical architecture of Cain's storehouse. She has overlooked
nothing that bad playwrights have incorporated into similar plays for the last fifty years, and while her talent for
character appraisal and pointed dialogue fitfully comes to
her rescue, the exhibit in its entirety seems like the kind
of thing that back in the brainless theatrical era used to be
put on once in a while in one of the smaller off-Broadway
houses and was regarded by Broadway, if by no one who
had got beyond the first year in a high-school, as "a play of
ideas."

The climax of Miss Franken's drama is, as may be suspected, the scene wherein the female surgeon tells off a
male colleague who hesitates in performing an emergency
operation on an apparently dying child and herself peremptorily performs it with such jiffy success as hasn't been witnessed on a stage since Will Rogers first jumped through a
lariat. If only the chairs in which the several movie directors present on the opening night had had their names
painted in large letters on the backs, one would have been
convinced that one was not in a 1943 theatre but on a Hollywood movie lot, except possibly for the circumstance that
the scene in a film would be laid on board a ship and that
the emergency operation would be performed either by a
heroine whose previous experience in surgery had been confined to plucking her eyebrows or, if the actress had had an
argument over raising her salary from $20,000 a week to
$30,000 and had been temporarily suspended by the studio,
by the actor playing the first mate who had apparently
gained his knowledge of surgery in turn from operating on
Dave Chasen's porterhouse steaks.

Among the other items in Miss Franken's hokum slaw
are the separated husband and wife who are reunited by
their child's mortal illness, the wisecracking old-maid house-
keeper, the wisecracking, brash young nurse, the joke about
sweetbreads, the business with the cigarette lighter that
doesn't work, the dog that is brought on with a broken leg
and the proof that the seemingly hard-boiled female surgeon is a sweet human being after all through her solicitude
for the animal, and the woolly toy dog the recuperating

child prizes above all else and beamingly clasps to his cute
bosom. Among the scenes is the one in which the heroine
bent on a career declines an offer of marriage from her neurologist admirer — "there are more important things we
two have to do; we can not allow domesticity to interfere
with them" — and offers instead to be his mistress, which
offer he morally spurns with the words, "I love you too
much to love you." Also the inevitable one in the concluding act wherein the heroine observes, "I thought to be a
surgeon was all I wanted — I thought it was enough to
want," and decides upon marriage after all. "If you have
only one person who loves you, you're rich," she whispers,
adorably crawling up on a couch with her 150 pounds and
pulling down the neurologist's head to kiss him. Previous
to all this, her neurologist beau has given vent to such titbits as "You're too young to understand" and "You have
the art of making men comfortable." The earlier sentimental conversations of the delightful couple at the dinner table have an obbligato of clinical remarks on cancers and
gall bladders, the parties being reminded about the former
by the calves' brains they are eating, which may be allowed
hardly to induce the desired Alt Wien mood in an audience.
Nor were matters greatly mellowed by the actress cast as
the heroine, who throughout the evening indicated puzzled meditation by sucking violently at a back tooth.

Let there also be report of the scene in which the female
surgeon, desirous of recalling his duty to the famous neurologist, enters upon a long harangue in which, employing the
third person, she tells him the story of a determined young
doctor — "I remember a wonderful young man years ago,
etc." — and finishes at length with a gentle pat on his shoulder, whereupon he gets up with the old resolute look in his
eyes and decides to do her bidding.

The stage direction by the hitherto highly proficient
Miss Franken was almost as reprehensible as her play. The
heroine, for example, was made to conduct herself after the
ritualistic, outdated stage formula in the case of characters
representing business or professional women, resulting in
such a masculine striding back and forth, so much firm

mouth-setting and such abrupt speech (indicating sharp mentality) that the picture was less that of a competent professional woman than of a bad actress auditioning for the leading role in *The Captive*. The neurologist hero was permitted to model a dinner suit, evidently dreamed up in some Broadway smart shoppe, with such a plethora of trouser pleats that every time he put his hands into the pockets the pantaloons bloomed expansively forth like bagpipes and, when he negotiated the doggy business, made his profound utterances on materia medica ridiculously alien to the scenic display. Nor was it easy to believe that the same director who had done so handsomely by her directly antecedent play could be responsible for having the dying child's governess stand tearfully beside his empty bed and deliver a long monologue attesting to her deathless affection for him, or for having the wisecracking young nurse periodically nibble at whatever edible was in sight, or for causing the fashionable Park Avenue doctor to suggest his superior social status by having him stand to one side like an expressionless statue of Albert Jay Nock, or for making the father of the dying child stand head bowed with his back to all the other characters to indicate his overpowering grief, or for having the child's mother indicate hers in turn by resorting to the acting devices of Creston Clarke's old-time road tragédiennes.

Twenty-three performances — and finis.

SOUTH PACIFIC. December 29, 1943

A melodrama by Howard Rigsby and Dorothy Heyward.
Produced for quick failure by David Lowe in the Cort
Theatre.

Program

Sam Johnson	*Canada Lee*			*Gordon Heath*
Captain Dunlap		Natives		*Kaie Deei*
	Wendell K. Phillips			*George Fisher*
Ruth	*Wini Johnson*			*Ruby Dee*
Daniel	*Rudolph Whitaker*			*Ledia Rosa*
Liliboi	*Dan Johnson*	Native		*Gloria Robinson*
Dr. John	*Louis Sharp*	Children		*Emanuel Gillard*
The Luluai	*Frank Wilson*			*James Reason*
				Clyde Goines

SYNOPSIS: *The entire action of the play takes place in the present on a small island in the South Pacific. The scene is the Government Community House.* Act I. *The Government Community House. Late afternoon.* Act II. *Scene 1. The same. A month later, in the evening. Scene 2. Later that night.* Act III. *Scene 1. The same. A few days later. Scene 2. Later that night, just before dawn.*

HERE A CAPITAL IDEA for an intelligent melodrama was undone by the deficient dramatic imagination and impatience of the authors. The idea in brief: A Negro out of Georgia and the New York streets is landed through the agency of a Japanese torpedo on a Japanese-held island in the South Pacific. With him, off the raft, is a white American captain. Once on the island, the Negro finds that for the first time in his life his color does not count against him, that it is in point of fact in his favor not only among the dusky natives but even among the Japanese, and that it is the white captain who is out of place and out of key. In America the Negro has since childhood been kicked around and condescended to; here he is not only an equal but superior to many. He finds friendship, admiration (for he has been, among other things, a prize-fighter of sorts), and the love of the prettiest native girl.

Suddenly, in these comfortable surroundings, the war means nothing to him. The whites have done little for him; why should he do anything for them? "Ain't there just one place in the whole world they'll let alone?," he demands. But presently the Japs kill not only a little native boy of whom he has become fond but also a native doctor who has been kind to him. And, also, the white captain who has gone out with a borrowed rifle to snipe the enemy. Gradually there dawns on the Negro that no man, whatever or whoever he may be, can stand alone in this world, that there are things he must do in spite of himself and, as the boom of guns from an American invading fleet is heard off-shore, he too grabs up a gun and makes through the jungle.

For most of the first act and part of the second the authors have not done badly by the idea, but thereafter force and invention fail them and action stops in favor of rhetoric. They thenceforth talk their play out of movement. The result, after a sufficiently lively beginning and a middle section that up to at least the half-distance mark is holding enough, is one of those plays whose failure to satisfy always leads an audience to remark, "Well, anyway, it would make a good movie," which is pretty much the most pointed criticism of the movies anyone can think of.

The stage direction, while apt to a degree, further invalidated much of the melodrama by allowing the actors to pick up their cues too deliberately. Since melodrama calls for sharp and vibrant delivery, any such slowing down of dialogue inevitably goes a long way toward debilitating it. The sound effects of rain, native drums, gunfire, stealthy tread of enemy feet, etc., were nicely handled, but the cannonading of the fleet at the final curtain — an effect that should in a booming crescendo have lifted an audience's excitement — sounded like nothing more than the popping of a lot of flat champagne bottles.

Canada Lee's performance in the main role missed much of the power of his performance in *Native Son;* it had an air of the self-consciousness of a star actor which took it out of its frame. Wini Johnson, who seven years ago was just about the most ornamental young colored dancing girl on the local theatrical premises, in her first dramatic role disclosed herself to be not only the most ornamental colored actress on those same premises (and with not too much competition in the white department), but also a curiously convincing one, and this despite the fact, or maybe because of the fact, that her speaking voice would in no wise be deemed strong enough by nine producers or actors out of every ten.

It is a matter for regret, when playwrights hit upon material for a play as fresh and valid as did these in question and succeed in doing the job thus half well, that they do not refrain from such quick productions and experiment further until their play is properly whipped into shape. With a few weeks' more attention and some luck they might have converted *South Pacific* into an all-around prosperous exhibit. The delay would have been worth the gamble, whatever the tryout expense. There are all kinds of plays seemingly doomed to failure which by chance or pure accident have been turned into great successes. I content myself with a pair of historic examples. The celebrated French play, *Riche d'Amour,* known in English as *Lend Me Five Shillings,* found itself by sheer accident. The plot you know. A young man becomes deeply infatuated with a fashionable woman at a subscription ball. She bids him see her home. Not having the five francs for the hiring of a cab, he is frantic. The action consists in his mad efforts to obtain them and in their slipping from his grasp each and every time he thinks he is about to lay hands on them. As the play was originally written, he fails to get them and the lady of his heart is gone.

Since repetition was necessarily involved in the young man's attempts to get the money, the play became monotonous. And since he didn't get the money and lost the lady, the final effect of the comedy was unsatisfactory. The authors were at a loss what to do, when one day at a desperate rehearsal luck came to their rescue. At the end of their play as written, the young man bade an attendant fetch his overcoat which he had left in the cloak-room. The attendant duly fetched the coat and, following the prescribed business, the young man fumbled in its pockets and turned them inside out, only to find not only not five francs but nothing else in them. On this occasion, however, he fumbled in them and to his dismay found a fat purse. It appeared that the attendant had brought onto the stage the overcoat of the stage manager which the latter had unintentionally thrown on the off-stage table over the property overcoat.

The play was saved. By inserting the line, "Who put a purse into my overcoat? Why, it *isn't* my overcoat!," discovering to the audience the mixup in the cloak-room because of the crowd at the ball, and thus leaving their hero free to take his lady love home, the authors eventually shared in a box-office fortune. (The device has since been often imitated.)

Labiche's *The Two Timid Men* was saved by a similar trick of chance, and after its author had despaired of it. The plot hinges on two bashful men, one of whom wishes to ask the other for his daughter's hand but is too blushfully hesitant to do so, and the other of whom is too shy to allow that he would be delighted to have him as a son-in-law. The prolonged situation proved killingly monotonous and got nowhere, and the little play expired of its own inanition. One day, during the endless rehearsals, one of the actors in the two main roles found himself exhausted, lost his patience, and interrupted his soft speeches to bellow forth his decision to give up his part. Labiche let out a yell of joy. He rushed to a desk and in short order caused the young heroine to take first her father and then her swain aside and confide to each in turn that the other was the more timid and that all either had to do to gain his point was to lift his voice and swagger the other out of countenance. The scene went in; the two men bawled at each other; the monotony went flying; and the play went over with a bang.

South Pacific, if the authors had had just a little patience with it and had bought a rabbit's-foot, might similarly have found some way to kick up its monotonous last act and might have become a tip-top melodrama. As it was, it expired after five performances.

OVER TWENTY–ONE. January 3, 1944

A comedy by Ruth Gordon for Ruth Gordon. Produced to big box-office returns by Max Gordon in the Music Box.

Program

Jan Lupton	Beatrice Pearson	Mrs. Armina Gates	Jessie Busley
Roy Lupton	Tom Seidel	Col. H. C. Foley	
Paula Wharton	Ruth Gordon		Carroll Ashburn
Max Wharton	Harvey Stephens	Mrs. Foley	Dennie Moore
Robert Drexel Gow		Joel I. Nixon	Philip Loeb
	Loring Smith	Miss Manley	Kay Aldridge
An Elderly Gent	Eddie Hodge		

SYNOPSIS: Act I. *June.* Act II. *July.* Act III. *August.*
The scene is the living-room of 26D, Palmetto Court, Miami, Florida, summer, 1943.

Miss Ruth Gordon is celebrated as the actress who invariably speaks some such simple line as "Will you please hand me a glass of water" with more tonal variety than Richard Strauss put into the whole of *Also Sprach Zarathustra.* The "will" will have the sound of a violin; the "you" that of a clarinet; the "please" will take on the color of a 'cello; the "hand" suddenly that of a zooming Stuka; the "me" will bring out all the percussion instruments; the "a glass of" will be sounded on trombones, with an obbligato of automobile sirens; and the "water" will flow from her throat like a cymbalon. Miss Gordon's play, which she has manufactured as a vehicle for herself, provides her with every opportunity to make Paul Whiteman seem in comparison a mere paper-comb virtuoso. It also provides her with other opportunities, of most of which she takes equal advantage.

When an actress writes a play for herself, a number of things are, of course, duly to be expected. It is to Miss Gordon's credit that she has avoided at least a few of them. She has not incorporated the business of exhibiting herself via a reincarnation or dream sequence as her own sixteen-year-old daughter looking too theoretically ravishing for words. She has not presented herself as being so excruciatingly attractive to men that the whole cast, including even the neighbor's boy, have a tragic time controlling their libidos. Nor has she done what actress playwrights in the late forties or early fifties often do in the way of triumphing in the affections of a lover or husband over half a dozen young girls who look like Wini Johnson. But she has nevertheless hardly failed herself. She presents herself suitably embellished by a bewildering succession of recherché dressmaker's creations, although the scene of her play is a cheap tourist bungalow. The character she has confected for herself is a Bar Harbor-Paris Ritz elegantess who is also a famous author and, at least in intention, a brilliant wit who is pursued by a swooning populace. She has seen to it that if any other character is vouchsafed a choice bit of repartee she will be right back with a mot to top it. She has further not neglected to give herself the scene beloved of actress playwrights wherein she disrobes for the night and reveals herself adorable in adorable lingerie. Nor the scene in which, by way of displaying her gifts of pantomimic expression, she engages in a lengthy droll telephone conversation. Nor yet the business of being the wise little woman who maneuvers her husband's career for him, with the latter hardly aware that she is really the brains of the two. Nor even yet the scenes wherein she lovingly instils confidence in her mate when he is dejected and about to give up. Nor still even yet the scene in which she charms her husband's boss, a gruff old curmudgeon, into doing her will.

She has, in a word, as a playwright done pretty well by herself as an actress, though as an actress she might have done better by criticism in supplying herself with a playwright somewhat less personally prejudiced in her favor. Any such playwright might have stopped to think twice before causing another character, upon Miss Gordon's delivery of a decidedly feeble wisecrack, to gaze upon her in awe and inquire, "When you say such beautifully witty things, do you know you are going to say them or do they just come out?" Any such playwright, further, might have doubted if a character offered as a trenchantly witty woman would be deeply impressed upon an audience as being one through replying to another character who ecstatically observes that she feels like pinching herself, "Well, go right ahead!" Or, when her husband gloomily remarks that he is nearly forty, through observing to another character, "We've been everywhere about it but it seems nobody can do anything about it." And any such playwright might have hesitated to resort to the old device of trying to make a more or less familiar jocosity seem relatively fresh by identifying it with some real person like, in Miss Gordon's case, Felix Frankfurter, Orson Welles, or Spencer Tracy.

In her treatment of character, Miss Gordon, in addition, here and there tries to emulate the bitter irony of her fellow-playwright, Miss Clare Boothe. But instead of bitter irony she achieves only a shallow meanness, it being apparent that her observation, unlike Miss Boothe's, is grounded less on human experience than on theatrical.

George Kaufman, who is an expert in the technique of filling in the holes in Swiss cheeses and who undertook the direction of the play, did much to cover up its lapses, rushing to its rescue every few minutes with so many property gags and extrinsic monkeyshines that one imminently expected either Ward and Vokes or W. C. Fields to come on. By playing it so fast that one wasn't sure of what was going on, he further managed to make the audience accept even the play's nonsensical conclusion in which Miss Gordon's self-created heroine who also writes movie scenarios and who during the whole play has not uttered a single thought unworthy of a movie scenario writer is suddenly made the editor-in-chief of an important liberal newspaper. It was that way throughout. If the script bogged down at one point, he was on the spot with a vaudeville act in which the characters, given nothing else to do to keep things moving, comically assault a refractory icebox and make a wreck of it. If the script tottered at another point, he was there with leaking drinking cups or something of the laugh-cadging sort. It was thus largely due to his legerdemain that the audience was persuaded to take as a play what was and is essentially only Joe Cook on the loose in a series of Mainbocher frocks.

RAMSHACKLE INN. January 5, 1944

A melodramatic comedy by George Batson. Produced with good box-office results by Robert Reud in the Royale Theatre.

PROGRAM

ARBOTHNOT	*Mason Curry*	GAIL RUSSELL	*Helen Heigh*
JOYCE ROGERS	*Ruth Holden*	ALICE FISHER	*Maurine Alexander*
PATTON	*Joe Downing*	DR. RUSSELL	*Richard Rober*
MAME PHILLIPS	*Ruth Gates*	BILL PHILLIPS	*William Blees*
CONSTABLE SMALL	*Harlan Briggs*	MR. TEMPLE	*Royal Dana Tracy*
BELINDA PRYDE	*ZaSu Pitts*	MARY TEMPLE	*Mary Barthelmess*
COMMODORE LUCIUS TOWSER		GILHOOLEY	*Robert Toms*
	Ralph Theadore	FRED PORTER	*John Lorenz*

SYNOPSIS: Act I. *Seven o'clock in the evening.* Act II. *One hour later.* Act III. *A few minutes later.*

The interior of Ye Olde Colonial Inn, not far from Gloucester.

IF MISS GORDON is celebrated as the stage actress with the Cab Calloway directed Philharmonic-Symphony larynx, Miss ZaSu Pitts is equally celebrated as the motion picture actress with the unceasingly fluttering hands. Had Miss Pitts' hands been tied behind her at the beginning of her career there probably would have been no career. Her histrionism, aside from funny hats, is entirely manual. If she is called upon to address another character, she prefaces her speech with a finger pantomime of two sizeable butterflies dancing a minuet. If it is trepidation she must indicate, her hands enter into a weaving movement of such proportions that one is disappointed not to see a parlor rug emerge. If it be demanded of her that she register archness, she executes in the surrounding ether a digital *Merry Widow* waltz. And if the moment calls for nervous doubt and hesitation, her hands massage the air like a couple of frightened osteopaths. Meanwhile, in each case, she pops out her eyes and jolts her funny hat askew.

The lady and her hands selected Mr. Batson's little number for their introduction to the dramatic stage. The little number may be roughly described as what *Seven Keys To Baldpate* might have been had George M. Cohan not written it, only worse. Trying his luck at a similar comedy mystery melodrama, the author's comedy relies almost wholly upon such lines as a fat man's remark that he is an outdoorsman and the retort, "You surely need more space," to say nothing of a spinster's reply to why she is single, "Well, I was born that way." His mystery in turn relies largely upon the identity of the leader of a bootlegging gang and at the last moment is explained by the introduction of a character whom the audience has not seen before and with whom it hasn't the slightest acquaintance. And his melodrama is a compound of all the prescriptive corpses in trunks and closets, loud screams, eavesdroppings, suddenly extinguished lights, disappearing bodies, and doors occultly opened and closed. Even the comic village constable is again in evidence.

The exhibit, in short, is a reunion of the class of 1900 mystery melodrama alumni. Present is the veteran about the corpse removed from the room and the allegation that the woman who swears she saw it must be crazy. Also the dodo, borrowed from the well-known French story, about the girl who registers at a hotel, who disappears as if the earth had swallowed her, and whose name they can't even find on the register. Also the ding-dong one about the bizarre doings down in the cellar, and the one about the terrible thunderstorm going on outside, and the other one about the concealed identity of the FBI investigator, and the line what-was-that-scream?-that-was-only-the-wind, and the scene wherein the heroine who has been tied into a chair by the villain manages to extricate herself when he isn't looking but continues to pretend that she can't move until the moment arrives for her to slip out and assist in cornering the scoundrel.

Although it has advanced in many other directions, the popular stage seems very definitely to have retrogressed in the matter of these mystery and detective divertissements.

There hasn't, in point of fact, been a really appetizing one in some years now. I am not speaking of the later order of so-called psychological thrillers, of which two specimens in the last dozen years — *Rope's End* and *Angel Street,* both, incidentally, by the same Patrick Hamilton — have been lively enough. What I am speaking of is the plain, out-and-out mystery or detective play without any fancy assistance from Freud, Jung, Stekel and Co.

There have been several of this latter species that have had pretty good basic ideas, but that was about all. The notion in *Trick For Trick* of pitching the skill of one prestidigitor against another in ravelling and unravelling the plot mystery was a savoury device. And the scene in which one of them conjured the corpse of the murdered woman in another room to float out upon the stage and thus confound the other, who was the culprit, handily caught the breath. Yet the general writing was too shabby to make the whole acceptable. The same with *Subway Express,* the entire action of which was laid on a moving subway train and which involved the spectacle of the murdered man, supposedly still alive, seated throughout the evening in one of the cars with wide-open eyes staring at the audience. (To achieve the effect, the eyes were painted on the outside of the actor's eyelids.) And the same to a degree with *Margin For Error,* the theme of which was the possibility that three different persons had committed the murder simultaneously but which finally went to pieces on the uninventive notion of the old switched poisoned drinking glass.

All the other exhibits in the same long span have suffered not only from poor writing and generally poor craftsmanship but from lack of ingenuity and a reliance for the most part on the familiar stencils. Of them all, only *The Fatal Alibi,* derived from one of the Poirot detective novels, offered the faintest novelty in its story of the murderer being the detective himself. But even it could embroider the fancy with nothing more original than the overworked tell-tale phonograph record and, to boot, with dramaturgy so shaky that interest faded long before the climax.

The bulk of the plays have been mere carbon-copies and

paraphrases of earlier and better cockrobins. The venerable locked room device has been one favorite and, except for a slight variation in *Whispering Wires* wherein the murder was accomplished by a revolver secreted in a telephone and discharged by the electrical connection, has followed the old tracks of chandeliers rigged to drop on the victim's head, revolving bookcases concealing the killer, and the like. The business of the fixed clock (*Ten Minute Alibi*), the escaped lunatic (*Goodbye In The Night*), and the hooded malefactor (*The Cat Screams*) has been vainly merchanted in the guise of novelty. And thunderstorms, shrieks, clutching hands, doors opening and closing of their own accord, and all the other stale appurtenances have been fallen back upon in lieu of fresh imagination. Or, worse, there have been so-called comedy mysteries like this *Ramshackle Inn*, patterned after the George M. Cohan early, excellent *Seven Keys To Baldpate* noted, which, failing Cohan's dexterity, have had recourse to all the chestnuts and have accordingly succeeded in being neither particularly mysterious nor comical.

The wits-addlers of an earlier period were certainly superior. *The Unknown Purple,* one of the best of the lot, was a highly original affair in which the protagonist, a scientist, invented a ray to make himself invisible and via the ray sought out and wrought his revenge on the evil-doer. The moving of objects on the stage by the unseen hand, the sound of the man's voice coming seemingly from nowhere, and the purple light recurring threateningly during the action constituted the stuff of exciting theatre. (The movies have appropriated the idea many times since and, I am told, with much the same impression upon their audiences.) The locked room device in *Arséne Lupin,* the first time it was employed effectively on the local stage, was built up to a genuinely thrilling climax through the presence in the room, apart from Ars, of another character masquerading as a totally different person and hence free from suspicion. And the missing murder weapon has never since been treated with the cunning that Bayard Veiller employed in *The Thirteenth Chair,* wherein throughout two acts and

undetected by the audience the fatal knife remained stuck
in full view into the ceiling.

Gillette's dramatization of Sherlock Holmes was, of
course, a masterpiece and is well recalled, even by persons
who never saw it. For the lighted cigar butt that helped
Sherlock escape from Moriarty's gas-chamber has become
one of the theatre's legends. But there were other artifices
that were just as fetching: the picture on the wall that when
slightly moved provided Sherlock with a view of anyone
entering the house; the mirror that in turn provided him,
when his back was turned, with a view of Moriarty's machinations; his rapid, nervous dash toward the front door upon
the sound of the ringing bell and his slow, measured steps
when within a few feet of it; his knocking at the stage's non-
existent fourth wall with his cane by way of emphasizing
its solid presence; etc. And surely not less skilful was the
Hopwood-Rinehart *The Bat,* with its tale of the murderer
waylaying the Hawkshaw in a garage at the play's beginning and thereafter passing himself off as the masternose
who was in quest of him. Here, too, were various original
dodges to heighten suspense: the shadow of a bat appearing mysteriously on the walls of the house (it had been covertly painted on an automobile headlight) ; the swathing of
the murderer's person in black until the ultimate surprising revelation of his true identity; and, meanwhile, all the
dirty work inexplicably negotiated right under the characters' eyes by the very man, posing as the detective, whom
they were looking for.

Another toothful specimen was *The Dummy,* with its
sleuth in the person of a deaf-mute boy; and still others, of
a somewhat later period, were *The Spider,* with its mur-
derous shot supposedly coming from the theatre's auditorium, and *The Trial of Mary Dugan,* with the lifelike
effigy of the murdered man brought shockingly into the
court-room and with the sudden tossing of the murder
weapon at a suspect on the stand and his self-betrayal in
catching it with his left hand. And still another worthy pair,
shown in the seasons before, were A. A. Milne's *The Perfect
Crime,* though not nearly so expert as the story of the same

name, never dramatized, by Austin Freeman, and Mrs. Belloc-Lowndes' Jack-the-Ripper spasm, *The Lodger.*

In subsequent years, though a falling off was perceptible, an occasional exhibit nevertheless hinted that the old art was not entirely dead. *Kind Lady,* dramatized from a Hugh Walpole story, succeeded in creating an atmosphere of evil and mystery that nicely worked its spell. The slow driving insane of the woman held prisoner by the gang of scalawags and her last-minute turning of the tables exercised much of the power of the Grand Guignol at its most devilish. And *Payment Deferred* similarly hypnotized an audience with the spectacle of its murderer's gradual self-betrayal. But for the greater part the other plays began clearly to indicate the decline that lately has hit the low-water mark.

What this later period has brought has been mainly either the British species of murder play involving perversion and degeneracy or the American involving an altogether too obvious and unsuccessful strain for freakish novelty. The British plays, things like *Love From A Stranger* and *Night Must Fall,* have inclined more and more toward the horror angle and have seemed little more than unduly expanded one-act Guignol shockers. In addition, they have, as noted, offered central characters so remote from normality that they have stacked the cards against themselves from the outset. Some of them have been fairly well written but the thick murk of degeneracy that has hovered over them has made them seem less mystery plays in the locally accepted sense than studies in abnormality. And their reliance for shudders on such devices as the murdered woman's head in a hat-box resting on the mantelpiece have frequently operated less toward the hoped-for shudders than unwelcome snickers. Of them all, *Ladies In Retirement* was perhaps the best, since it concerned itself not with clinical perversion but with the simple, suspensive story of a woman desirous of getting two burdensome relatives out of the way and with her eventual exposure by a suspicious nephew who happens unexpectedly into the house.

The American specimens, on the other hand, have relied so greatly upon a veneer of novelty, and with nothing underneath, that the great majority have made snoozers of even the staunchest addicts to such pastimes. An exhibit like *Mr. Big,* unable to think up anything better than the poisoned dart projected by striking a certain chord on the piano (shade of the old *Strand* magazine!), has vainly tried to sell itself by spilling part of the action into the auditorium (shades of *The Spider, The Gorilla,* et al., to say nothing of such non-mystery plays of forty-odd years ago as *Pretty Peggy!*). Another like *The Night of January 16,* essentially little more than a pulp magazine version of *The Trial of Mary Dugan,* has similarly sought to win trade by culling the members of the jury from the audience and having them nightly pass the verdict upon the heroine accused of the murder. Still another like *Seen But Not Heard* has endeavored to put over an intrinsically outworn murder plot through bringing about its solution by three children of the household. And something like *Dark Tower* has feebly battled the box-office by making the disguised character of the plays of four and five decades ago an actor who makes himself up as another man, commits the murder, and by then removing the makeup escapes detection.

The flashback technique, originally popularized back in 1914 by Elmer Rice in his expert crime play, *On Trial,* has been retrieved from oblivion and the moving pictures and made to pose as something novel in a dozen such failures as *Eight O'Clock Tuesday.* By confining the cast to women, it has been hoped to sell the customers on something like *Nine Girls,* which was otherwise approximately as suspensive in mystery as Louisa M. Alcott. By laying one scene in the Braille room of the Public Library, the author of *Escape This Night* imagined that he might hoodwink an audience with an otherwise wholly commonplace mystery plot. And the producer of such a turkey as *Cuckoos On The Hearth* has vainly looked for audiences who would accept as something wonderful a silly mystery story acted out twice in order to show the two different points of view of those involved in it.

Just why there should be so little invention and ingenuity in this form of drama is hard to make out, especially since one frequently encounters both in the current mystery and detective novels. Yet for one play like *Uncle Harry*, with its relatively fresh story of a murderer who freely confesses his crime but can find no one to believe him, you will find any number like *I Killed The Count, Angel Island* and *The Cat Screams* that are nothing more than rehashes of similar exhibits of twenty and thirty years ago and that hope to be accepted as something vernal by making laboriously and foolishly complex mysteries that are generically simple of solution. The height of the ridiculous in this regard was the last named play, which introduced a supposedly ferocious mechanical cat that had absolutely nothing to do with the plot by way of augmenting its hypothetically terrifying puzzle.

The most effective mysteries seem paradoxically to have figured not in the mystery plays of the later-day stage but in the non-mystery plays. The air of mystery which permeates *Outward Bound,* for example, and which involves characters who are not aware that they are dead, surpasses that in any ten recent straight mystery plays that one can name. And the mystery of spiral time in Priestley's *I Have Been Here Before,* for another, is infinitely more provocative than that in any two dozen murder jigsaws like *Timber House, Cue For Passion,* or *They Walk Alone.*

OUR TOWN. January 10, 1944

A three weeks' revival of the Thornton Wilder play. Produced by Jed Harris in the City Center Theatre.

Program

Stage Manager	Marc Connelly	Woman in the Balcony	
Dr. Gibbs	Curtis Cooksey		Alice Hill
Joe Crowell	Richard Dalton	Man in the Auditorium	
Howie Newsome	Donald Keyes		John Paul
Mrs. Gibbs	Evelyn Varden	Lady in the Box	Frederica Going
Mrs. Webb	Ethel Remey	Simon Stimson	Walter Swetland
George Gibbs	Montgomery Clift	Mrs. Soames	Doro Merande
Rebecca Gibbs	Carolyn Hummel	Constable Warren	Owen Coll
Wally Webb	Teddy Rose	Si Crowell	Roy Robson
Emily Webb	Martha Scott	Sam Craig	Jay Velie
Professor Willard	Arthur Allen	Joe Stoddard	John Ravold
Mr. Webb	Parker Fennelly	Mr. Carter	Walter O. Hill

SYNOPSIS: *The entire play takes place in Grover Corners, N. H.*

A second view of the play is reassuring to one's first critical estimate of it, to wit, that not only is its widely admired "winning simplicity" much that of a shrewd theatrical confidence man ingratiating himself with his prospective victims by giving their children some penny candy but, further, that its excursion into metaphysics is of a weight with that of the aforesaid children's after they have eaten too much of it. Under the circumstances, the award of a Pulitzer prize to the play was therefore not too surprising.

As has been pointed out before, Mr. Wilder's play is essentially an amateur paraphrase of Andreyev's *Life of Man* placed in a New England small town setting and produced with an economy in stage scenery and properties which cleverly imposes upon the actors the business of entering hypothetical houses and drinking non-existent ice-cream sodas. It also cleverly imposes upon an audience the business of imagining that it is seeing what is actually an equally hypothetical and non-existent play. Its success is a tribute both to the imagination of an audience and to the author's faith in its virtuosity.

Succeeding Frank Craven in the role of the narrator was Marc Connelly, who was making his first official professional stage appearance. Mr. Connelly is an able and amusing fellow, but a natural big-town sophistication ill-suited him to the down-East Yankee role and suggested that he would constitute a far likelier compère for something like the Chauve-Souris or a lively Broadway revue. Sinclair Lewis would have been a better choice, if the city fathers who are in charge of the theatre had been theatre-wise. Unless, indeed, they achieve such wisdom in a more general way and see to it that their municipal stage offers plays of rather more distinction it is to be feared that the City Center will eventually end up as merely another side-street, cut-rate revival showhouse, like one of the Leventhal subway circuit theatres.

STORM OPERATION. January 11, 1944

A war play by Maxwell Anderson. Produced for failure by the Playwrights' Company in the Belasco Theatre.

Program

1st Sgt. Peter Moldau		Lt. Dammartin	*Walter Kohler*
	Myron McCormick	Corp. Ticker	*Bertram Tanswell*
Abe	*Joseph Dorn*	Capt. Sutton	*Bramwell Fletcher*
Winkle	*Alan Schneider*	Mabroukha	*Sara Anderson*
Simeon, a Technical Sgt.		Arab Guide	*Maurice Doner*
	Cy Howard	Chuck, a Technical Sgt.	
Mart, a Technical Sgt.			*Charles Ellis*
	Millard Mitchell	Corp. Hermann Geist	
Dougie	*Michael Ames*		*Louis Fabien*
Bread Seller	*Maurice Doner*	Squillini	*Nick Dennis*
The Muezzin	*Mehem Simone*		*Marianne Bier*
Stefano	*Carlo Respighi*	Arab	*Julie O'Brien*
Lt. Thomasina Grey		Women	*Elizabeth Inglise*
	Gertrude Musgrove		*Lela Vanti*
Lt. Kathryn Bryne		Arab Boy	*Neil Towner*
	Dorothea Freed		

SYNOPSIS: Prologue. *An invasion barge. Somewhere on the Mediterranean.* Act I. *In front of an officer's tent near Maknassy. Several months later.* Act II. Scene 1. *The tent. Now pitched on a rocky desert hill. A week later.* Scene 2. *The dry bed of a stream in the mountains above Mazzouna. Late afternoon.* Scene 3. *Same as Scene 1. Evening of the same day.* Epilogue. *The invasion barge.*

THERE IS SOMETHING in common between certain of Mr. Anderson's plays and those religious cults which believe that great exaltation of the spirit is a direct consequence of lying on sharp nails, walking over hot embers, and not having anything to eat for a couple of weeks. It seems to be the conviction of both that considerable suffering has to be negotiated by the client before he assimilates the ultimate invigorating manna. This play is an illustration in point. It calls upon one to endure any number of theatrical pains, including nothing in the way of dramatic food for a couple of hours, and then bids one to accept as an intoxicating compensation for faithfulness and patience the spoonful of greasepaint uplift implicit in a hitherto reluctant female's surrender to love and the collateral philosophy that the soldier protagonist now at last has something to fight for. Before, presumably, he had nothing but the honor and safety of his native land and home, fairness, decency, the splendor of thrilling adventure, and his own hide.

For two solid hours Mr. Anderson's play assiduously concerns itself with a multiplicity of such depressing attributes of war as death, disaster, despair and a diet of foul camel meat and then his cute little blonde Army nurse tells his sergeant hero that she will be his, thus theoretically recompensing both the bedevilled sergeant and the audience with the necessary holy faith in the future and the resolve at all costs to do battle for it. It is rather like being rewarded with a five-cent cream-puff after a protracted and agonizing siege of the mumps. Save for the inclusion of an amusing double-talking comic relief character, the play plods its way through a succession of afflictively moist episodes involving everything from a soldier physically paralyzed from grieving fright to the extensive reading of letters from home until it reaches this super-maudlin climax of the wedding of the little nurse and sergeant under a hail of bullets from the Stukas. Rarely has Mr. Anderson committed himself to such an excess of sentimentality. His view of war, in point of fact, frequently takes on the aspect of a pillow fight between Peg o' My Heart and Channing Pollock.

This sentimentality reaches its flower not only in the wedding which, incidentally, is nobly performed by the English officer from whom the American sergeant has stolen the little nurse, but in Mr. Anderson's key philosophy which precedes and follows it. That philosophy is expressed by the author in the line, "The best soldier is the one with a picture of a girl in his pocket." Aside from being news to the greatest fighting men that the world past and present has known, the idea provides a sufficient clue to the general tenor of Mr. Anderson's writing. For empty theatricality, his play would be hard to match.

Literally to set down all the ingredients and their dramatic treatment would be to make accuracy seem unnecessarily cruel. The derision of the British officer for the American way of things is laboriously built up to the old brother Elk business in which he warmly takes the American sergeant by the hand, slaps him on the back, and genially and expansively calls him by the when-you-say-it-smile bit of profanity. The death of the Arab girl beloved of an American soldier is accompanied by the gentle removal of her veil by the nurse, with the awed and tremulous remark, "Why, she is beautiful!," and with the soldier standing pokerlike behind her bier, gazing lugubriously into space and swallowing a silent tear. At the height of danger, the sergeant proceeds to make love to the little nurse and is brushed aside by her with the observation, "Not now! There are other more important things to do." In the way of humor there is the letter to a sex-starved soldier enclosing a photograph of his wife in a bathing suit and his remark, "I haven't seen her for nine months and she sends me a picture of herself looking like that!" And in the way of original fancy there is such bonbon stuff as, "All right, I'll go ahead and learn to be ruthless and learn to be hard and learn to be a better soldier, but I can't do it unless there is something beyond, unless there is something to come back to — a hope of somebody that loves you and doesn't let go." These are only a few samples.

No man writing for our theatre has greater sincerity than Anderson, and no man a higher goal. But none, also, has a mind more critically incapable of meeting the demands it imposes upon itself and none presents himself so in the light of a stuffy college professor trying to mix with the boys and have himself accepted as a good fellow. His excursions into worldly philosophy have a classroom ring, and his efforts at daring humor — such, for example, as a soldier's remark that "you can't use words ending in *it, itch, uck* and *astard* over the 'phone" — give the impression of a schoolmaster on the loose after one beer.

That Anderson is a dramatist by rote, he himself some time ago gave self-incriminating evidence in an address to the students at Rutgers. "I did discover that there were rules of playwriting which could not be broken," he stated emphatically. And then went on:

1. "The story of a play must be the story of what happens within the mind or heart of a man or woman. It cannot deal primarily with external events."

   Required playgoing for Mr. Anderson: *Plague,* by Walter Hasenclever; . . . *one-third of a nation,* by Arthur Arent; etc.

2. "The story of a play must be a conflict — and specifically a conflict between the forces of good and evil within a single person."

   Required playgoing for Mr. Anderson: *The Time of Your Life,* by William Saroyan; etc.

3. "The protagonist of a play must represent the forces of good and must win, or, if he has been evil, must yield to the forces of the good and know himself defeated."

   Required playgoing for Mr. Anderson: the famous *Earth Spirit* of Frank Wedekind; etc.

4. "It might be possible to write a play in which the hero was evil and thought himself victorious — but the playwright would have to indicate that he did not agree."

   Required playgoing for Mr. Anderson: The illustrious *Countess Julie* of Strindberg; etc.

5. "The protagonist of a play cannot be a perfect person. If he were he could not improve, *and he must come out at the end of the play a more admirable human being than he went in.*"

   Required playgoing for Mr. Anderson: *The Man Who Came To Dinner,* by Kaufman and Hart, to say nothing of Mr. Anderson's and Laurence Stallings' *What Price Glory?*

6. "The protagonist of a play must be an exceptional person. . . . The man in the street simply will not do as the hero of a play. If a man be picked from the street . . . he must be so presented as to epitomize qualities which the

audience can admire. Or he must indicate how admirable human qualities can be wasted or perverted — must define an ideal by falling short of it, or become symbolic of a whole class of men who are blocked by circumstances from achieving excellence in their lives."

Required playgoing for Mr. Anderson: Rutherford Mayne's *Red Turf;* Lady Gregory's *The Bogie Men;* etc.

7. "Excellence on stage is always moral excellence. A struggle on the part of a hero to better his material circumstances is of no interest in a play unless his character is somehow tried in the fire, and unless he comes out of his trial a better man."

    Required playgoing for Mr. Anderson: The celebrated *Business Is Business* of Octave Mirbeau; etc.

8. "The moral atmosphere of a play must be healthy. An audience will not endure the triumph of evil on the stage."

    Required playgoing for Mr. Anderson: the memorable *The Father* of Strindberg; etc.

9. "The plays that please most and run longest . . . are representative of human loyalty, courage, love that purges the soul, grief that ennobles."

    Required statistical study for Mr. Anderson: *Tobacco Road, Craig's Wife, The Bat, The Women, Ladies In Retirement, The Front Page,* etc., etc.

10. "Put on a play which sets out to prove that dishonesty is the best policy and vice is triumphant in human affairs, and the audience will refuse it coldly."

    Required playgoing for Mr. Anderson: The distinguished *Les Corbeaux* (*The Vultures*) of Henri Becque; etc.

11. "There is a place in the dramatic scheme for *The Beggar's Opera,* in which the hero is a footpad, and for *Pal Joey,* in which the hero is a rat. But . . . the audience must know that he (the author) is fooling. . . . If he tries to be serious in such matters, no audience will follow him."

    Required instruction for Mr. Anderson: 1. *Robin Hood;* 2. The author of *Pal Joey,* he assures me, wasn't fooling.

In *Storm Operation,* Mr. Anderson has accordingly and inevitably contrived simply another routine war play. Not only doesn't it measure up even to his antecedent *The Eve of St. Mark;* it doesn't improve noticeably upon various earlier commonplace war plays from other hands. One can say all the kind and gentle things one can usually say about his plays — that it is honest, sincere, dignified, lofty in purpose, etc. — but there critical grace ends.

It isn't that the play treats of materials altogether too familiar. So, for that matter, in another direction does *The Voice of the Turtle,* but observe what van Druten has done with them. It is that Mr. Anderson views them in altogether too familiar a fashion. He brings nothing new to them in the way of sharp observation, philosophy, or dramatic life and they lie at the end where he first found them. What we get, in other words, is much the same old thing merchanted by much the same old characters: the inability to put one's heart into fighting unless one has something to fight for, be it a woman or what not, and all the rest of the often-mouthed sentiments. The invention to give renewed vitality to the materials is lacking, and what results is merely a high-minded depressant.

Statistics: Twenty-three performances — and amen.

SUDS IN YOUR EYE. January 12, 1944

A farce comedy by Jack Kirkland, based on the novel by Mary Lasswell. Produced without luck by Brown and Del Bondio in the Cort Theatre.

Program

Chinatown	Chueck Ming Chin,	Kate Logan	Janet Tyler
	Frederic Munn Szeto	Mrs. Ferguson	Lujah Fonnesbeck
1st Buyer	Russell Morrison	Mr. Wilson	Robert Rhodes
Mrs. Feeley	Jane Darwell	Mrs. Katz	Marie Kenney
Mr. Fitzgerald	John Adair	Mac	Kenneth Tobey
Miss Tinkham	Brenda Forbes	Mrs. Miller	Cynthia Latham
Shipyard Worker	Bruno Wick	Danny Feeley	Will Hare
Conchita	Ruth Gilbert	Policeman	Bert James
Mr. Reynolds	Tom Hoier	Armond Hansen	Frank Tweddell
Mrs. Rasmussen	Kasia Orzazewski	Pinky Kennedy	Tom McElhany
Mrs. Rasmussen's Daughter		Moe	Loy Nilson
	Wanda Sponder	June	Helene Young
Elmer	John Gerard		

SYNOPSIS: Act I. *A summer afternoon.* Act II. *That evening.* Act III. Scene 1. *Early evening, three days later.* Scene 2. *Several hours later.*

The action of the play takes place in Mrs. Feeley's junk yard, San Diego, California.

Time. *The present.*

In the Theatre Comique in New York back in the year 1881 Ned Harrigan of the famous team of Harrigan and Hart produced his comedy, *Squatter Sovereignty*. It dealt robustiously with the poor families who were living in squatters' shanties, without payment of rent, which cluttered the tin-can-strewn and goat-inhabited rocks on the upper West Side of the city, and it was sensationally successful. *Suds In Your Eye* deals robustiously with three impecunious old hussies who live in a junk yard in San Diego, California, without payment of rent if they can help it, and, while it does not otherwise bear a close resemblance to *Squatter Sovereignty*, frequently suggests it. It further sug-

gests a distaff version of other such Harrigan and Hart exhibits as *The Mulligan Guards' Ball*, *The Mulligan Guards'
Picnic*, *McSorley's Inflation*, and at least in part the equally
celebrated *Reilly and the 400*. There is also a lot of *McFad-
den's Flats* and *Krausmeyer's Alley* in it. It accordingly is
welcome to those of us oldsters who chortle reminiscently
over that grand old bygone era of slapstick.

Out of the story of the boozy harpies who swill enough
beer to flood Johnstown and who meanwhile swindle the
authorities who would dispossess them from their junk-pile,
Kirkland may not have contrived much of a play in the
strict critical sense. But he has managed for the most part
to contrive a pretty jolly roughhouse evening. What is more,
he has contrived it without any of his former insistence
upon gutturals, guts and guano, and the result, while far
from délicat, is infinitely more acceptable. The hilarity derived from the spectacle of the tosspot trio engaging officers of the law, cheating money out of a guest on the junk-
pile with marked cards, without a nickel to their names
extravagantly bidding in at auctions, bellowing over such
jokes as a policeman's assertion that his feet have got so
tough he wears out his shoes from the inside, and every
other minute howling loudly for more suds is large and
juicy. And in its forthright Gargantuan quality it is all the
more acceptable in a theatrical day given generally to the
humor either of feeble double entendre or cheap smut.
There is health and breadth and a wonderful good-nature
in most of the humor here; no mincing, no dirt for dirt's
sake, no pink.

As the lagerish Mrs. Feeley, Jane Darwell was right out
of all the old Irish corner saloons; as her alcoholic partner,
Mrs. Rasmussen, Kasia Orzazewski was to the life the old
Polish-Swede dame fed up with living with a daughter who
tolerated her only for the thirty dollars she got monthly
from the relief charities and devoting herself rebelliously
to a beery fling; and as the absurdly elegant Miss Tinkham
from Ohio who, with no place to live and without a sou,
accepted the invitation to live in the beery milieu, Brenda
Forbes contributed such a portrait to the gallery of bur-

lesque as has not been surpassed since Isaac Levy first changed his name to Billy Watson.

Low stuff? Crude stuff? Most assuredly. But mighty funny. Yet it lasted for only 37 performances.

JACKPOT. January 13, 1944

A musical comedy, book by Guy Bolton, Sidney Sheldon and Ben Roberts, music by Vernon Duke, and lyrics by Howard Dietz. Produced for 69 performances at a great financial loss by Vinton Freedley in the Alvin Theatre.

PROGRAM

BILLIE	*Billie Worth*	GIRL	*Flower Hujer*
MR. DILL	*Morton L. Stevens*	TOT PATTERSON	*Althea Elder*
BILL BENDER	*Ben Lackland*	SGT. NAYLOR	*Wendell Corey*
NANCY PARKER	*Mary Wickes*	SGT. MAGUIRE	*Betty Garrett*
SALLY MADISON	*Nanette Fabray*	HELEN WESTCOTT	
DEXTER DE WOLF			*Frances Robinson*
	Houston Richards	SNIPER	*Bob Beam*
EDNA	*Jacqueline Susann*	MONICA	*Drucilla Strain*
HEDY	*Helena Goudvis*	PAT	*Pat Ogden*
HAWLEY	*John Kearny*	BETTY	*Betty Stuart*
JERRY FINCH	*Jerry Lester*	SHERRY	*Sherry Shadburne*
WINKIE COTTER	*Benny Baker*	MARY LOU	*Marie Louise Meade*
HANK TRIMBLE	*Allan Jones*	CONNIE	*Connie Constant*

SYNOPSIS: Act I. Scene 1. *Assembly room of the Duff and Dill Engine Corporation.* Scene 2. *Hawley's bar.* Scene 3. *A broadcasting studio.* Scene 4. *Recreation room, Priscilla Manor, Turtle Beach, S. C.* Scene 5. *A cornfield.* Scene 6. *The recreation room.* Act II. Scene 1. *Garden of the Priscilla Manor.* Scene 2. *Bedroom of the bridal suite.* Scene 3. *The balcony.* Scene 4. *Garden of the Manor — the next day.*

Book: Three marines combine to buy a war bond in a lucky number contest, the prize being the leading lady. They win. After two hours, the baritone marine marries her and the other two, the comedians, reconcile themselves with, respectively, the saucy soubrette and the tall, angular comédienne.

Humor: Fat comic in a woods scene: "I'd like to look like a slender birch." Second comic: "You look like a big ash to me."

Business: The comics eat pills that are supposedly aphrodisiacal and thereupon instantaneously grab at the tall, angular, pieface comédienne.

Staging imagination: The leading lady disrobes in silhouette behind a window curtain, the while the leading man stands below the balcony and sings of his heart's pure desire.

Ballet wit: A travesty of the Agnes de Mille ballets in *Oklahoma!* and *One Touch of Venus,* called "Grist For de Mille," in which the men carry the women pig-a-back and trot back and forth, the while an unclad six-foot female "pagan" shakes her legs at the bass drummer.

Biggest comic invention: A soldier is camouflaged as a tree and a woman comes on with a dog.

Sample lyric delicacy: "I've Got a Piece of a Girl."

Music: Plugged song: "One-Track Mind." *Cf.* Lehar's "Vilia."

Finale: The leading lady kisses various men to determine by the taste the one who kissed her in the dark.

Unanimous critical report: Rubbish.

THE DUKE IN DARKNESS. January 24, 1944

A play by Patrick Hamilton. Produced for 24 performances by Alexander H. Cohen and Joseph Kipness in the Playhouse.

Program

Gribaud	*Edgar Stehli*	The Count D'Aublaye	*Albert Carroll*
The Duke of Laterraine			*Dorman Leonard*
	Philip Merivale	Guards	*Ralph Douglas*
Voulain	*Raymond Burr*		*Joseph Vernay*
Chauvet	*Horace Cooper*		
Marteau	*Wells Richardson*		
The Duke of Lamorre			
	Louis Hector		

SYNOPSIS: Act I. Early evening. Act II. Late that night. Act III. Late afternoon, two days later.

The action of the play takes place in a room high in the Chateau Lamorre, in France, at the time of the civil wars, about 1580.

If Mr. Hamilton were as artful in other directions of playwriting as he sometimes is in the matter of suspense he would be a dramatist of some position. Suspense, however, seems often to be the especial gift of minor playwrights who have little of consequence beyond it. Any number of fabricators of simple melodrama or detective and mystery plays have been pretty smart at the business of making audiences nervously anticipative. Mr. Hamilton is one of these, much better than the majority but otherwise still one whose genius inclines immeasurably more toward inducing in his clients a childish wonder as to what will happen next than toward evoking in them emotions somewhat less closely associated with the feverish tearing of eight or nine layers of gaudy paper off a ten-cent Christmas present.

In this critically negligible way Mr. Hamilton, as noted, has indicated himself a relatively superior fellow. The presents which he bestows upon the stage sometimes might cost as much as a quarter or even half dollar. Some persons, indeed, who view the theatre as being desirably of a piece with whiskey, cocaine, or the House of Frankenstein have esteemed his opera as being worth as much as $3.85. It is these who see in his *Rope's End* and *Angel Street* not simply much better than ordinary "psychological" thrillers but genuinely profound psychological dramas, damnigh worthy of Strindberg. To this way of looking at them, however, they remain simply the much better than ordinary thrillers. Which should be sufficient praise.

In *The Duke In Darkness*, Mr. Hamilton has attempted the relatively more costly dramatic form of historical romance wherein certain elements other than mere curiosity over what is coming next are necessarily called for and has discovered himself in such unaccustomed surroundings that even his former knack of suspense deserts him. What he has essayed to write is a "literary" melodrama laid in the sixteenth century and concerned with a ducal follower of Henry of Navarre whose faith is in the people, who has been imprisoned for fifteen years by a rival and dictatorially minded duke, and who by one stratagem and another succeeds eventually in managing his escape. Aside from a gratuitous identification of the subject matter with the current world situation the play is a slack throwback to the stage of a half century ago and to the exhibits of the period wherein Don César de Bazan with drawn sword held his captors at bay and effected his getaway by diving headlong through an open window or wherein the handsome Gil de Berault, to the delight of the peanut-gallery, told Richelieu in no pianissimo terms where to get off.

Mr. Hamilton's writing is of the "Very well, don't stand there gaping; go!" school. It also is the kind in which no character is permitted to say simply, for example, "It can not be," but must needs invariably say it twice over. The acting was in perfect key, and likewise the stage direction by Robert Henderson. Mr. Merivale, as the heroic duke, alternated between the chill reserve of a statue of William Faversham and the warm exuberance of a bust of Edmund Breese. As the villainous duke, Mr. Hector growled like an over-indulged stomach. As the heroic duke's faithful servant who goes insane, Mr. Stehli negotiated a histrionic repertoire which included everything that even the late Richard Mansfield forgot to incorporate into his Baron Chevrial in *A Parisian Romance.* And the other items in the company duly comported themselves like traveling salesmen for the Dazian, Eaves, and Brooks Costume Companies.

THE CHERRY ORCHARD. January 25, 1944

A revival of the play by Anton Chekhov. Produced for 96 performances by Margaret Webster and Carly Wharton in the National Theatre.

Program

Lopahin (Yermolay		Semyomov-Pistchik	
Alexeyevitch)	*Stefan Schnabel*		*Carl Benton Reid*
Dunyasha	*Elizabeth Eustis*	Yasha	*Stanley Phillips*
Epihodov	*Rex O'Malley*	Petya Trofimov	*Eduard Franz*
Firs	*A. G. Andrews*	A Tramp	*Bruce Adams*
Anya	*Lois Hall*	The Station Master	
Varya	*Katherine Emery*		*Michael Gray*
Lyubov Andreyevna		A Post-Office Clerk	*Jack Lynds*
	Eva Le Gallienne		*Lois Holmes*
Leonid Andreyevitch		Servants	*Beatrice Manley*
	Joseph Schildkraut	and Guests	*Annette Sorell*
Charlotta Ivanovna			*H. Etienne*
	Leona Roberts		

SYNOPSIS: *Act I. A room in the house. The old nursery. Spring. Early morning. Act II. The open country. Sunset. Summer. Act III. Living-room. Evening. August 22nd. Act IV. The same as Act I. Fall. The action takes place on the estate of Lyubov Andreyevna.*

MISS WEBSTER, who was mainly responsible for the staging, apparently confused *The Cherry Orchard* with The Cherry Sisters. The result was something to behold.

It seems to be the dour resolve of some of our producers and directors, Miss Webster notably among them, to lighten the dramatic classics, whether the latter intrinsically bear lightening or not. This famous work of Chekhov's was the latest victim. It is quite true that it is not the grim and glum thing that certain stage stewards have made of it in the past. But it is, or should be, equally manifest that neither is it quite the jolly parlor comedy that the lady in question, in collaboration with Miss Le Gallienne, constituted it. I am always suspicious of producers and directors who exploit this kind of interpretation. I fear that, whatever their august pretensions, they are thinking a deal more about the box-office than about a sound and honest internal job. They seem to say to themselves, sotto voce: "After all, what the public wants these days is not tragedy but entertainment and the way to win it is by hook or crook to work out a fairly plausible light treatment of the play which if played otherwise might depress the customers and keep too many of them away from the ticket-window.

Operating on this cagey principle, the director proceeds forthwith to the Public Library and buries his (or her) nose deep in the dramatist's diaries, letters to tailors, grocers and old servant girls, and other such esoterica in the obdurate hope that he (or she) may dredge up something that will provide a faint justification for making the suicide of one of the characters, say, the result not of unbearable misery but of an unconstrained psychological jocularity and maybe the bankruptcy of the family, with starvation staring it in the face, something not more serious than just another of life's little contretemps.

Coming upon the scantiest clue and stretching it to the limit, the overjoyed director thereupon rushes home and composes a treatise for the papers arguing his (or her) box-office dodge in terms of a superficial scholarship. Impressive names, only remotely connected with the issue in hand, are dragged into the argument by further means of convincing the susceptibles that they never before had the correct idea of the play and of its author's real intention. And additional wile is exercised in such artifices as contending that when, in the script of a Russian dramatist, the stage direction as in the present case is something like *Through tears,* what the dramatist, being a Russian who had once written several one-act comedies, really meant was that the tears were not those of grief but of uncontrollable happiness. (In this connection, it will be casually pointed out that the dramatist, though he never in relation to the play in hand realized it himself, was a sly satirist.)

This frequent diminution of the serious elements in a playwright's work and the insistence upon lightening them as a gesture toward popular favor will, if it keeps up at the later-day pace, probably culminate in a day when insane Lear will be indistinguishable from the crackpot in *Arsenic and Old Lace* who imagines he is Teddy Roosevelt and when Banquo's ghost will be played by Leonora Corbett.

The Cherry Orchard in Miss Webster's hands thus came figuratively to be to Chekhov what *The Great Divide* in the hands of the Messrs. Weber and Fields came to be to Moody, maybe unintentionally but certainly ridiculously. The tenderly affecting drama was sacrificed to the groundlings' passion for humor at any cost, and the fine and moving play was brought down by the slapstick long before its axes brought down the treasured orchard trees. Almost every old vaudeville device save alone the idea of having Andreyevitch fall over the footlights and land on the bass drummer was introduced: the slap on the maid Dunyasha's backside, the stumbling over the furniture, the slapping of the forehead too forcibly and the resultant comical staggers, the bumping into the door on an exit, etc. And the acting for the most part belonged similarly on the old Palace stage, with Sam Mann and the trained seals.

On this occasion Miss Webster once again spread herself antecedently in the Sunday journals informing me and my colleagues that our previous views of *The Cherry Orchard* and other of its author's plays had been all wrong, that being in the cozy confidence of their author she alone was privy to his secret intentions, and that it would accordingly be well for us, save we were willing to be considered prime numskulls, to subscribe to her present interpretation. All this would have been meet had the lady's pronunciamentos been slightly more convincing than they were. At least to us older hands in the theatre. Thus, when in relation to this revival of *The Cherry Orchard* she sternly argued that all of Chekhov's plays call for a pervasive light treatment and supported her contention by stating that "in our country every one of the revivals on record has been greeted with cries of astonishment because it has emerged so clearly that the plays are not gray and gloomy but volatile, gay and even farcical, etc." — when she argued so, she proved rather handsomely that she did not entirely know what she was talking about. She did, true, convince some of the juniors whose acquaintance with the theatre dates from the Vera-Ellen period but hardly those of us war-horses who have been in harness a little longer.

The aforesaid cries of astonishment which Miss Webster must have dreamed in her sleep were assuredly not audible to these elder ears at Bulgakov's production of *The Sea Gull,* the Washington Square Players' production of the same play, the Co-operative Company's ditto some fifteen years ago, the Surry Players' more recent production of *The Three Sisters,* the Moscow Art Theatre company's local productions of either *The Cherry Orchard* or *The Three Sisters,* or for that matter even the Eva Le Gallienne production of this same *Cherry Orchard* at the Civic Repertory Theatre, to name only a few.

Again, when Miss Webster charitably essayed to compose our criticisms for us by informing us that when Chekhov indicated such directions as *yawns* and the like he unquestionably meant quite the opposite, we suspected that her astral body must have made the mistake of contacting not Chekhov but Gogol or Griboyedoff. And still again when she hoped to seduce us to her general coggery with the argument that "there has not since been any play in which man's faith in man was so clearly, so ringingly, proclaimed," we feared that we must unchivalrously grin not only at her very evident lack of knowledge of the modern drama but, considerably broader, at her peculiar appraisal of the drama under direct consideration.

As I have hinted, it is barely possible that Miss Webster is just a foxy advance press-agent intent upon bamboozling the more youthful reviewers and thus guaranteeing something of a sale at the ticket-window. It may well be. When she originally produced the Robeson *Othello* at Princeton, the experienced John Mason Brown went down to see it and subsequently reported that, among other things, Robeson was not ready for New York and that the costumes and settings were woeful makeshifts and hand-me-downs. Miss Webster telephoned him, he apprises me, in high indignation. "Why did you print such things?" she exploded.

"I knew it!" To which Brown gently replied, "Well, I just wanted you to know that *I* knew it too."

There is assuredly ample justification, as I have pointed out in an earlier section, for treating certain passages of *The Cherry Orchard* and of the other of Chekhov's three major plays with a relatively light touch. But to view any of them as being in substantial part not the fundamentally serious and even grave plays they are is, I think, to misunderstand them even more seriously and gravely. Too often, furthermore, they are cagily tricked to the limitations of their players. It is thus that we get a *The Sea Gull* intermittently directed to conceal the tragic delinquencies of a Lunt and Fontanne and to give play to their lighter talents. It is thus that we get a *The Three Sisters* here and there staged prettily to balance the lighter resources of a Katharine Cornell against the profounder ones of a Judith Anderson. And it is thus that now we get a *The Cherry Orchard* jockeyed into a box-offce vaudeville for the actress who once memorably played Hedda Gabler in a short sports skirt and insouciantly smoked Lucky Strikes during the play's most solemn scenes.

The younger reviewers duly and blissfully swallowed it whole. The older ones, however, mumbled something that sounded like *Carmen Chekhov* and thought of a certain other person who once similarly with a child's little ax chopped down a very beautiful and very precious cherry tree.

WALLFLOWER. JANUARY 26, 1944

A farce-comedy by Mary Orr and Reginald Denham. Produced with success by Meyer Davis in the Cort Theatre.

PROGRAM

JESSAMINE LINNET	Kathryn Givney	CHET	Michael King
BRIGITTE	Vilma Kurer	WARDWELL JAMES	Fred I. Lewis
WARREN JAMES	Joel Marston	DIXIE JAMES	Leona Powers
MRS. HENNICUT	Ann Dere	JASPER	Kurt Richards
ANDREW LINNET	Walter N. Greaza	BOBBIE	Charles Laffin
JOY LINNET	Sunnie O'Dea	RUTH HENNICUTT	Mary Orr
JACKIE LINNET	Mary Rolfe	LARRY OAKLEAF	Frank McNellis
BRUCE	James McMahon		

SYNOPSIS: *The rumpus room in the Linnet home, Ironville, Ohio.* Act I. Scene 1. *A Saturday morning in early June.* Scene 2. *Saturday evening, about three weeks later.* Act II. Scene 1. *Later the same evening.* Scene 2. *Wednesday evening, four days later. (During Scene 2, the curtain is lowered to denote the passing of a few hours.)* Act III. *The following morning.*

HERE IS A GOOD, saucy French farce-comedy idea executed more or less in the George Abbott manner. The two central characters are young stepsisters, one pretty and with a way with the boys, the other less blessed by nature and shunned by them. Upon this latter it slowly dawns that the reward of virtue is social neglect and boredom and she takes steps to rectify matters. Having duly appeared to have compromised herself with a young man, she finds that, once the news gets around that she is not too biologically pure, the boys who hitherto had avoided her forthwith take a rapt interest in her. And all thereafter is roses.

In the hands of some Frenchman like Guitry or Hennequin or Coolus the notion might have been developed with an amusing subtlety. In the hands of the present authors it is developed with an amusing vulgarity. There is a ribald drollery implicit in the theme that even their occasional deficiencies, both in writing and dramaturgy, can not quash.

That writing discloses itself every once in a while to be of the kind that, for example, stiffly substitutes the word "presume" for "suppose," and the dramaturgy here and there permits a situation to extend itself beyond its meat. In addition and as is to be expected, there is moral recourse to the stereotyped apology for the wallflower's sexual delinquency in the revelation that she was secretly married all the time. A Frenchman would shoot himself before compromising the theme in any such Abbott manner. (The Abbott impression was furthered by co-author Denham's stage direction, which, at least in the earlier part of the evening, had the actors rattle off their lines so quickly by way of imparting movement to the proceedings that it was sometimes difficult to distinguish whether one was attending a play or a radio news broadcast.) On the whole, however, the exhibit conceals its critical shortcomings in the veils of palliative laughter. The Viennese servant girl who learns English from the sporty daughter of the household and instructs guests, "Park your fannys," bids them on their departure, "So long, you bums," and the like is a comical creation. And not less so are the small-town lawyer who embarrassingly sends the chief of police to jail, the bespectacled small-town idiot youth who fancies himself a Casanova, the Princeton boy in his cups who undertakes to forget his jilting by the pretty sister in having an affair with the homely one and then for the life of him can't recall that he has been in bed with her, and the fat, middle-aged, gurgling wife of the small-town banker who rejoices in the name of Dixie.

It was difficult under the generally diverting circumstances to understand the moral indignation of those reviewers who heatedly denounced the occasion as "thoroughly offensive" and as using "sex only for the snickers and guffaws in it" when these reviewers happened to be largely the same who had joyfully swallowed the pregnancy snickers of *Kiss And Tell*, the obstetrical guffaws of *Three Is A Family*, and the offensive smut of *Strip For Action*.

MEXICAN HAYRIDE. January 28, 1944

A musical comedy by Herbert and Dorothy Fields, with tunes and lyrics by Cole Porter. Produced to standing room only by Michael Todd in the Winter Garden.

Program

Lombo Campos	*George Givot*	Henry A. Wallace	
Mrs. Augustus Adamson			*Byron Halstead*
	Jean Cleveland	Lolita Cantine	*Corinna Mura*
Eadie Johnson	*Edith Meiser*	Dagmar Marshak	*Luba Malina*
Augustus, Jr.	*Eric Roberts*	Bolero	*Alfonso Pedroza*
Mr. Augustus Adamson		Chief of Police	*Richard Bengali*
	William A. Lee	Lottery Boy	*Hank Wolff*
Joe Bascom (*alias* Humphrey		Mrs. Molly Wincor	
Fish	*Bobby Clark*		*Jeanne Shelby*
Montana	*June Havoc*	Lottery Girl	*Eva Reyes*
Billy	*Bill Callahan*	Paul	*Paul Haakon*
Senor Martinez	*David Leonard*	Eleanor	*Eleanor Tennis*
Miguel Correres	*Sergio De Karlo*	Lillian	*Marjory Leach*
David Winthrop	*Wilbur Evans*		

SYNOPSIS: Act I. Scene 1. *The Plaza de Toros, Mexico D. F.* Scene 2. *The bedroom at the Reforma Hotel.* Scene 3. *The bar at Ciro's.* Scene 4. *A street in the Merced Market.* Scene 5. *An outdoor corridor of the National Palace.* Scene 6. *Terrace of the palace at Chapultepec.* Act II. Scene 1. *Xochimilco.* Scene 2. *A gas station (on the Paseo de la Reforma).* Scene 3. *Taxco.* Scene 4. *Terrace of the palace at Chapultepec.*

Take a show in the best pictorial Ziegfeld tradition; have the great Bobby Clark blow his inimitable stogie smoke at it and razzle it with his inimitable cane; sprinkle it with such facetiæ as a woman's derisive remark, upon observing a dozen Mexicans sprawled on the ground in a siesta, that she wouldn't want a Mexican as a lover, with the retort, "How do you think they got that way?"; add some ingenious dancing and some pretty girls like Eva Reyes — and you have a bird's-eye view of *Mexican Hayride*.

Getting a little closer to the ground you may possibly detect certain other less whetting elements in the form of the

omnipresent corps of female Alps who intermittently come
on with the mien of show-girls' ideas of elegant ladies, posture themselves frigidly at stage right and left, and with
bland unawareness that anything is happening about them
serenely scan the audience; a butterball of a ballet dancer
whose art seems to consist solely in tossing herself into the
right arm of her male partner, bending in her stomach, and
curling her left leg in the air; the baritone lover resplen-
dent in the latest Broadway sartorial cri with its three-feet-
wide shoulders; a song number called "The Good-Will
Movement" with an anatomical dance accompaniment apparently based upon the theory that the good neighbor
policy consists in a denial of the policy of the Tenth Com-
mandment; several tunes that are familiar to the point of
garter-snatching; etc.

It is, however, a rare show that hasn't flaws of one kind or
another and this one, despite its share, comes off rather salubriously. Clark, playing a numbers racket impresario from
the States, finds himself the recipient of a slain bull's ear in
a Mexican arena and accordingly by local tradition something of an all-around lion. At the height of his glory the
FBI appears on the premises in search of him, and the rest
of the evening is devoted to his attempts to escape detection. The boy has never been more hilarious.

Hassard Short and his terpsichorean aides deserve especial credit for at least one item in the general staging, and
that is the suppression, or at any rate relative suppression,
of the customary bogus bonhomie of the ladies of the ensemble. The present lot have been made in some part to
comport themselves with a fairly reasonable approximation
to natural human beings. I am not speaking of the show-
girl dummies who always, as in this show, are enough to
freeze one's ears off, but of the dancing girls. Invariably
these are directed to whirl around so quickly that they
haven't time fully to resolve their grim frowns when their
backs are turned into the genial smiles which they subsequently beam at the audience. We see a line of darlings
prance on exuding enough sunshine to melt the Arctic re-
gions. Then, no sooner have they executed the second twirl

than we catch them on the three-quarters turn with a chill
grouch on their faces which the speed of the number hasn't
given them space enough to wipe off and to go back into the
exuberant grins. Since maybe it is too much to ask of the
girls that, when they aren't facing the audience, they smile
at the backdrop in happy recollection of the dog-meat frankfurters they had for dinner, probably the best thing would
be also to cut out the smiles when they turn around. There
is altogether too big a dose of synthetic good-nature in the
shows as it is. The average one, in the case of the boys as
well as the girls, may be summed up as a hundred rows
of teeth bared to the spectators in a pertinacious jollity. A
little lockjaw here and there would help.

There is generally no end to the facial and molar buoy-
ancy. Only once in the whole two and one-half hours are
we spared it and that is only for a few moments at the climax of the first act when the leading lady tells the leading
man that he is a loafer and that she no longer loves him.
Otherwise the evening from first to last is just one firm, big,
set, terribly gay and happy smile, if you can believe it.
There's no let-up even when the soprano finds the tenor
making up to her French maid or when the comedian
cracks a joke that everybody in the company heard when
they were playing in half a dozen previous shows.

In *Jackpot,* which was pretty dreadful all around anyway,
the misery was doubly accentuated by such a comprehensive
display of ferocious conviviality as couldn't be matched by
a mass convention of highly inebriated brother Moose.
While *Mexican Hayride,* true enough, is not without a
measure of the artificial animal spirits, again interpreted
mainly by baring the teeth in a simulation of irrepressible
glee, it has its nicely spaced periods of surcease which come
as a novel relief. But the only show of the season whose
cast's features comport themselves naturally throughout its
course remains *Carmen Jones,* and the cast of *Carmen Jones*
happens to be made up of darkeys who in popular legend
wear broad grins twenty-four hours of the day.

Most of Cole Porter's songs, especially the lyrics, are below his mark. Which brings one to reflect that the death

during the year of Lorenz Hart removed from our theatre one of the only two American lyric writers (the other is Hammerstein) gifted with any real penetration into the human emotions. In any number of his songs Hart disclosed a sly sagacity in the matter of the peculiar quirks of people's minds and feelings. They betrayed a sharp, if wistful, knowledge of men and women in various departments. Love to him was not simply the business of hearts and flowers that it is to most of the other lyric fashioners; it was something slightly more hintful than that, and he seemed to appreciate its odd tremors just a little more delicately than these others. He was far from being like many of his colleagues in their juvenile cardiac reactions to or juvenile cynical spoofing of the sentimental facets of human existence. There was an amiable critical tone to his lyrics, even when they touched the E-string of the imagination, which combined intelligence and undoubtedly experience with the gentility of their verbal melody.

DECISION. FEBRUARY 2, 1944

*A play by Edward Chodorov. Produced for 159 perform-
ances by Edward Choate in the Belasco Theatre and subsequently in the Ambassador.*

PROGRAM

MISS BAINES	Jean Casto	FITZGERALD	Paul Huber
FELIX	Dickie Van Patten	TOMMY RIGGS	Larry Hugo
HARRIET HOWARD	Gwen Anderson	VIRGIE	Georgia Burke
RIGGS	Raymond Greenleaf	MRS. MAY HOWARD	
ANDERSON	Len D. Hollister		Merle Maddern
BROWN	Homer Miles	MASTERS	Matt Crowley
MRS. BOWEN	Grace Mills	ALLEN	Howard Smith
JIM MORGAN	Herbert Junior	PETERS	Lee Sanford
BENNETT	Rusty Lane	SERGEANT CAREY	Paul Ford

SYNOPSIS: *An American city, in the present.* Act I. Scene 1. *Riggs'
office at the high school.* Scene 2. *The Riggs home, later that night.* Act II.
Scene 1. *The high school, several days later.* Scene 2. *The Riggs home,
that evening.* Act III. *The Riggs home, early the following morning.*

THERE IS NO SMALLEST DOUBT that in this case Mr. Chodorov is a passionately sincere man. Passionate sincerity, however, often unfortunately seems to be an attribute of inferior playwrights and here again he discloses himself to
be of that class. His indignation over the latent forces of
Fascism in the nation is tall, dark and handsome, and his
motives are unimpeachable. But he simply has not the
dramaturgical gift to make them seem otherwise than
cheaply melodramatic. The delicate tone of his cast of mind,
taste, and writing is, furthermore, readily to be anticipated two minutes after his first curtain rises. The conversation of a pair of his women characters in that short space
of time consists primarily of an allusion to the unpleasant
condition of the stomach of one of them, the necessity on
the part of the other of a trip to the John (his term), and a
reference to vomit.

What the play fundamentally amounts to is merely another paraphrase of the *It Can't Happen Here* business, of

which there has been an increasing surfeit. The thesis, as intimated, is still a perfectly valid one. But Mr. Chodorov brings nothing new to it and further corrupts what is old in it with character drawing negotiated with penny crayons, soap-box speeches of the standard cut, and such obdurate hokum as the fat, jolly, old female Negro servant, the young heroine who injects stamina into the vacillating young hero, the brash, slangy, but gold-hearted female friend of the heroine, the photograph of the deceased mother which the characters periodically take down from the mantel and gaze at wistfully, etc. His young soldier hero in whom he reposes his final trust for the defeat of the fascist higher-ups is, in addition, presented as such a consummate moron — his vocabulary consists chiefly in the expression "O.K." — that the play's optimistic conclusion impresses any analytical member of the audience as being just a little on the travesty side.

The genealogy of the exhibit may be traced back thirty-five years or more. In that period the present young soldier on sick leave who pitches himself against the corrupt fascist element was a young district attorney who pitched himself against a corrupt political machine. In the period following, the young soldier was a scion of a family of wealth and position who, disgusted with the family's way of life, set himself to teach it a different and more wholesome viewpoint. In the next period, the young soldier was a young journalist or an officer of the law who made it his mission to corner the gangsters who at the time were a menace to society. And in the period following that, the young soldier was a young radical who swept into the rich upper classes and brought at least the daughter of one of the families to a realization of the plight of the poor and to a sympathy with the Communist philosophy.

Whatever the specific nature of the plays, their courses have been and are for the most part uniform: Act I, indifference followed by doubt; Act II, doubt followed by alarm and challenge; Act III, alarm and challenge followed by battle and victory, either factual or potential. *Decision* does not materially depart from the formula.

PEEPSHOW. February 3, 1944

A comedy by Ernest Pascal. Produced by the author in association with Samuel Bronston to 28 scant audiences in the Fulton Theatre.

Program

Jonathan Mallet	John Emery	Jessica Broome	Joan Tetzel
His Conscience	David Wayne	Waiter	Dayton Lummis
Julius	Lionel Monagas	Porter	Edward Broadley
Tommy Cobbe	Dwight Weist	Nurse	Elizabeth Dewing
Leonie Cobbe	Tamara Geva		

SYNOPSIS: Act I. Scene 1. *Jonathan Mallet's apartment. New York City.* Scene 2. *Le Coquille au Citron.* Act II. Scene 1. *The Treetop Inn.* Scene 2. *A room at St. Agatha's.* Scene 3. *Jonathan's apartment.* Act III. Scene 1. *Brixton's cellar.* Scene 2. *Jonathan's apartment.* Scene 3. *The same.*

The avidity with which Hollywood movie writers now and then seize upon playwriting as a furlough from the restrictions of the Hays office censorship and let themselves go in the direction of sex smut is again illustrated in this instance. The illustration, in point of fact, amounts to a three-sheet. Celebrated for his dirtiness in the years even before the suppressions of Hollywood contributed to its present accumulated bulk (*vide The Amorous Antic* and *The Marriage Bed* of fifteen seasons ago) , Pascal here discloses himself anew as one whose aforesaid celebrity was not unfounded.

As a springboard for his holiday, the film scenarist, who apparently recognizes originality as the only and cardinal sin, has had recourse to the conscience device offered in 1933 by Eugene O'Neill in *Days Without End,* in 1915 by Alice Gerstenberg in *Overtones,* in 1899 by Gunther Schwering in *Faust Up-to-Date* (in which, incidentally, Faust kicked out his Mephisto conscience just as Mallet kicks out his Faust ditto in *Peepshow*) , and a century or more before by the producers of stage paraphrases of the old Morality plays who had Good and Evil played by two actors made up much alike and with the former serving as the latter's shadow.

Taking over the device, Pascal has visited it upon what he very evidently and fondly imagines is a play in the manner of Schnitzler's *Anatol,* down even to the episodes of the farewell supper, the final battle royal with the mistress, and the ultimate vision of the marriage altar. All that he has managed to recapture, however, is the champagne bottle in the bucket of ice in the private supper booth. Beyond that, his play, which is overlaid with juvenile epigrammatic sex dirt, sounds as if it had been written in a Hollywood gents' room. The intention may have been the mood of Mahler's Fourth Symphony. The achievement is that of "Frankie and Johnny."

Pascal's efforts to be charmingly naughty in the Schnitzlerian tradition are strictly Alt Wienerwurst, resolving themselves into such smoking-car whimsicalities as the sex-satiated hero's observation, "I'd like to sit the next one out," and such titbits as the mistress' "A woman not in love can be cold in bed," with the Lothario's rejoinder, "And, I presume, vice versa." His amorous philosophy takes such vernal forms as "The trouble with you is that you've been a doormat and have let your wife walk over you; show her who is the master and you will see her change soon enough!" His general humor is reflected in such a passage as the Lothario's intended purchase of a Queen Anne room for his bride-to-be and, upon her discovery of his unfaithfulness, her suggestion that he make it a Henry the Eighth room. And his dramatic invention is to be appreciated in, among a dozen other things, the inevitable soft waltz played by the off-stage supper restaurant orchestra, the Lothario and the married woman dancing their farewell to its accompaniment, and the Lothario's inability to dismiss his partner's sex attraction once his arm now again encircles her waist.

The play, in short, suggests a woman's dainty negligée hanging from a hook in an outhouse.

Making matters worse, the acting in most cases — David Wayne, as the Lothario's Conscience, and Joan Tetzel, as

his fiancée, were exceptions — was more fruitfully suited
to a so-called problem play than to what was intended as
risqué comedy. John Emery, for example, played the Lothario as if he were Aubrey Tanqueray, and Tamara Geva
the mistress as if she were Mrs. Dane calling on Iris Bellamy.

TAKE IT AS IT COMES. February 10, 1944

A comedy by E. B. Morris. Produced and withdrawn after 16 performances by Armin L. Robinson in the 48th Street Theatre.

Program

Albert D. Bliven	*Frank Wilcox*	Stella	*Gloria Willis*
Cora	*Louise Lorimer*	Chief of Police	*Curtis Cooksey*
Elfreda	*Angela Jacobs*	Mayor Stone	*Arthur Griffin*
Tommy	*Jackie Ayers*	Mr. Plummitt	*John Souther*
Mary Sellers	*Marylyn Monk*	Dr. Witherspoon	*Harold Moulton*
Emma	*Sara Floyd*	Veronica	*Harriet White*
Kip	*Richard Basehart*	Wilbur Kenyon	*Robert West*
Anthony Pasquale	*Tito Vuolo*	Vincent Davis	*David Lewis*
Herb Jenkins	*Grover Burgess*	Radio Engineer	*James Rawls*
Andy Sellers	*Harry Pedersen*	Mrs. Pasquale	*Shaque Hampar*

SYNOPSIS: Act I. Scene 1. *Friday evening.* Scene 2. *Friday evening, a week later.* Act II. Scene 1. *The next morning.* Scene 2. *The following Friday evening.* Act III. *The next morning.*

Time. *The good old days — to be exact, the Spring of 1939.*

Place. *The living-room of the Blivens, in Wiltonwood, N. J.*

ONE MINUTE before the curtain went up I took my seat, noted in the program that line, *Time: The good old days — to be exact, the Spring of 1939,* and permitted myself the reflection that the play of any author guilty of any such prefatory cuteness could not possibly be other than pretty grim. Prejudice, however, being unbecoming to a salesman of the critical art, I cast it from me like the pox and politely composed myself for the embarrassing contrary proof that might eventuate.

The curtain lifted and disclosed a room in a small-town household with a radio giving its all. This hardly constituted a symptom of embarrassing contrary proof, since authors who lift their curtains on a radio giving its all, particularly if it be installed in a room in a small-town household, are almost uniformly discovered to get even mouldier as the evening goes on. The embarrassing con-

trary proof was further not forthcoming in the entrance of
the family's low-comedy Swedish servant girl, who, asked by
a spinster relative of the family if she was the new maid,
pointedly replied, "Yes, but I ain't no old maid." And when
the little son of the family, a Boy Scout, thereupon entered
with a lawn mower, followed shortly afterward by a volatile Italian male neighbor who impulsively sang snatches
from *Rigoletto* and transportedly blew a kiss after each, I
prepared myself for the worst. It didn't take much preparation.

What got into motion then was Plot No. 182 B, with very
slight variation, to wit, the indigent but peaceful and happy
family that finds itself suddenly and fortuitously the pos-
sessor, it imagines, of a large sum of money, the bickering
and acrimony that wealth inevitably brings with it (on the
stage), the vanishing of the golden mirage, and the return
to the happy and peaceful existence. The slight variation in
this case was that the money, instead of resulting from a hypothetical winning racehorse, sporty uncle from Brazil,
strange will, or alleged discovery of oil in the back-yard, belonged to a deceased gangster who had entrusted it to the
little Boy Scout son's care.

The fertility of the playwright in enriching the plot was
additionally vouchsafed in the introduction of the crooked
mayor of the small town, the genial cop ever on the look for
a free bottle of beer, the skinny spinster who imagined
she had a singing voice, the head of the local school board
who was indignant over the presence in the library of what
he denounced as a filthy book of verse and the disclosure
that it was the work of Walt Whitman, the up and coming
young lawyer husband of the daughter of the household,
the aforesaid Swedish servant girl who periodically and
drolly told this or that character to go to hell, the worm of
a paterfamilias who finally turned and told off those who
had long walked over him, the disclosure that the apparently kindly and upright neighbor was a notorious mobster,
and the scene in which the family celebrated its supposed
acquisition of wealth by getting joyously inebriated on two
ounces of champagne apiece.

The stage direction of Anthony Brown, hitherto competent enough, was once again based upon the familiar theory
that deficiency in action on the part of the script may
be concealed by visiting it upon the actors. The consequence was a stageful of characters who, by actual count,
sat still or stood still for but ten minutes out of the play's
whole two hour course. Surveying the stage, it further occurred to me that some young critic with nothing better to
do might start a crusade against the practice of actresses in
lining their eyes, above and below, with blue makeup. The
young critic will, of course, be firmly informed by the ladies
that the practice is necessary, since otherwise the stage lighting will make their eyes look a pallid blank. This, unless
the lighting is of the car-barn species, is pure superstition.
But, even if it were not, it is better to have the eyes fade a
bit from the physiognomy than to have them stick out of it
like a pair of indigo billiard balls. Not long ago I heard the
hero of a play, gazing rapturously into such a pair, breathe,
"Your eyes are like white swans dreaming on an azure lake."
I took one look at those white swans on that azure lake and
promptly got sick at my stomach.

GILBERT AND SULLIVAN REPERTOIRE
February 11, 1944

A road troupe formerly known as the Boston Comic Opera Company and now calling itself the Gilbert and Sullivan Opera Company, with R. H. Burnside as managing director, offered itself, with an assist by the Shuberts, for 54 performances in the Ambassador Theatre.

Principals

Florenz Ames, Robert Pitkin, Kathleen Roche, Bertram Peacock, Catherine Judah, James Gerard, Allen Stewart, Robert Eckles, Kathryn Reece, Roland Partridge, Marie Valdez, Mary Lundon, and Lewis Pierce.

Opening with *The Mikado*, the troupe proceeded seriatim to *H. M. S. Pinafore* and *Trial By Jury*, *The Pirates of Penzance* and *Cox And Box*, *The Gondoliers, Iolanthe, Patience, Ruddigore,* and *The Yeomen Of The Guard.* The presentations were unmistakably of the touring stock company table d'hôte species. Stage settings and costumes had the appearance of being the offspring of parents born in the beer garden operetta atmosphere of the 1890's, and most of the principals gave the impression that long road years in the employment of the Messrs. G. and S. had made continued service something of a chore. And the suggestion of a chore in connection with the whimsicalities of the precious twain is hardly conducive to any proper exposition of them.

As with one or two such troupes in the past, the lighting, always particularly valuable to the picture, was of the kind more aptly suited to the theatre's lobby than to its stage, which frequently took on the appearance, whatever the scene or hour of the day, of a Childs restaurant at lunch time. In this case, also, microphones and loud speakers were employed to amplify the voices of the singers, despite the facts that the latter sang loudly enough as it was to be heard as far south as Times Square and that the auditorium was one of moderate size. Further, Mr. Burnside, the director, saw fit to orchestrate the stage deportment of the players with, alternately, the stoic postures of so many Iokanaans and the pasture cavortings of Willie Howard. Even the Broadway Savoyards, those fowl who submit themselves to a spasm of indignation if, in another quarter, Portia's robe is so much as a shade off the familiar scarlet or Cyrano's nose an eighth of an inch too short and who generally revel in any presentations of their twin gods, however bad, couldn't quite digest these. Which is a record of sorts.

CAUKEY. February 7, 1944

A play by the Rev. Thomas McGlynn. Produced for 23 performances by the Blackfriars' Guild in the Blackfriars' Theatre.

Program

Ma	*Ruth P. White*	Miss Jenkins	*Claire R. Leyba*
Forrest	*John Tate*	Officer Larkin	*James Slater*
Mrs. Hatch	*Barbara Winchester*	Ed Barton	*Clarence O. Foster*
Emma	*Florence Fox*	Miss Stevens	*Geraldine Prillerman*
Henry	*Robert Lancet*	Gloria	*Betty E. Haynes*
Gas Man	*William Johnson*	Wentworth	*Vernon Chambers*
Lorraine	*Cathy Parsons*	Police Captain	*John J. McClain*
George	*Dennis McDonald*	Officer Thompson	*Charles Baker*

SYNOPSIS: *The action of the play takes place in autumn in one of our larger cities.* Act I. *A third floor rear apartment in a Caucasian ghetto. Late afternoon.* Act II. *Wentworth's office. The following day.* Act III. *The same as Act I. Three days later.*

T HE TRICK OF REVERSING the status of persons or classes, despite the reverend playwright's obvious belief that he had hit upon something new, has been familiar to the theatre for many years. Most often handled in terms of comedy, it has taken such forms as changing the position of the master of the house into that of his valet and vice versa (*Candlelight,* et al.) , the servant staff into lords of the manor and vice versa (Jerome K. Jerome's *Lady Bantock and the Servant Problem,* et al.) , the male sex into the feminine and vice versa (*The Warrior's Husband,* et al.) , etc. The present playwright, handling the notion in terms of drama, has reversed the status of the Negroes and whites. It is, aside from its lack of novelty, not a bad idea and one susceptible of stimulating dramatic treatment, but the Rev. McGlynn has managed to do little with it. Once his device is established, little ensues save the old-time conventional melodrama of the cruel, rich landlord and his helpless, about to be evicted tenants.

The aforesaid establishment of the device is likely enough. A Negro comes out upon the stage in a prologue and solicits the audience's interest in the white problem. What, he asks, can be done toward its solution, toward the improvement of the lot of these fellow men? Why can't these whites, these Caucasians, be raised in their estate to the level of the Negroes? There are objections from the audience. The Caucasians, shout various members of the latter, are naturally an inferior race, shiftless, untrustworthy, emotionally dubious. The wisest and safest course is to keep them just where they are, in their proper place, lest improvement of their condition lead to endless difficulties.

The play begins and we are presented with the reversed scheme. The Negroes are in a position of power; the whites in positions abject. One of the Negroes tries to help the ambitious son of the white family, living in a wretched tenement owned by the rich Negro landlord, but the son is humiliated by his vindictive brother who flouts him for accepting favors from a black. And so it proceeds with the stencils played upside down. There are a few amusing lines, as, for example, a Negro's observation that "A white baby is the cutest thing you ever saw"; and there are one or two fairish theatrical moments, as, for example, in the prologue noted. But the play in the aggregate, for all its honesty of purpose, takes on the fateful color of a stunt, and a stunt is hardly appropriate to the materials with which it seeks to deal, in this case solemnly. If Father McGlynn had had satirical comedy as his aim, the trick might have sufficed. Under the present circumstances it gets in the way of the theme, and is doubly assisted in its getting by feeble dramatic craftsmanship. One can hardly project any serious propaganda against bigotry through the musical comedy means of *By Jupiter*.

Deficient as the play is, it nevertheless provides something of relief, although hardly in its author's intention, from the numerous later-day plays which, under the new dispensation, view the Negro in so arbitrarily sympathetic a light that they impress any reflective Negro or white as ill-concealed and objectionable condescension. The Negro, for all the legitimacy of his complaint against the motion pictures, can surely have no slightest grievance as to the manner in which the drama of recent years has treated him. If there is any grievance as to treatment, it should come from the white man. It is a far cry from the dramatic day when a Negro was presented on the stage mainly either as a low comedian or a rapist pursued by the Ku Klux Klan, though even in that period and before he was occasionally beatified in rôles like Uncle Tom. The old order has changed. Today, he is treated with all the respect that the white man isn't. Only infrequently, as in some such play as *Native Son,* is there the slightest throwback to that old order, and even then he finally emerges as a helpless and very pitiable plaything of the fates, with the fates (white) in the role of the villain.

In the drama of the last years, the white man, on the contrary, has often been presented as a low, detestable, and ignominious creature. Take this present season alone up to the point of *Caukey. Those Endearing Young Charms* presented the white man as a contemptible lecher. *Try And Get It* ditto. *The Two Mrs. Carrolls* presented him as a miscellaneous poisoner and murderer, and a cheap seducer to boot. In *Murder Without Crime,* he was shown as a weakling, a cheat, a murderer, and a degenerate. In *Tobacco Road,* upon its return engagement, we saw him as an illiterate cousin to the pig, and in *A New Life* as an odious snob. *Land of Fame* displayed him, in at least half its characters, as a merciless brute, devoid of any semblance of decent instincts; and *Another Love Story* either as an empty-headed dolt or an unscrupulous gigolo. In *The Naked Genius* we were given him as a scabby gangster, and in *Slightly Married* as a consummate ass. *Manhattan Nocturne* pictured him as a sentimental fool, a crook, a shyster, and a pimp; *Outrageous Fortune* as a homosexual and a moral coward; and *I'll Take The High Road* as a complete moron, as did *Lady, Behave!* In the case of *Get Away, Old Man* he was shown as an abject money-grubber, a vain braggart, and a dipsomaniac; in the case of *Lovers And Friends* as an amorous imbecile; and in the case of *The World's Full of Girls*

as a seducer, Fascist underminer of the nation, man unable
to provide the necessities of life for his family, and general
shorthorn. *Pillar To Post* presented him as a moron twice
over; *The Voice of the Turtle* as a miscellaneous fornica-
tor; *Susan and God,* on its return, as a chronic drunkard;
and *Feathers In A Gale* as a bigot, lecher, and impenetrable
thick-skull. In *Listen, Professor!* we saw him as a seducer
and as a mind impressed by the babblings of children; in
Doctors Disagree as the inferior of the female sex; in *Over
21* ditto; in *Storm Operation* as a chalker on privy walls, or
as one given to an objectionable feeling of superiority; and
in *Peepshow* as a cheap philanderer. And in *Decision* and
Take It As It Comes, the last and directly preceding exhibits, he was presented, respectively, in substantial part either as already completely corrupt or potentially so.

What of the Negro in plays of the same period wherein
he at all figured, however slightly? In *Outrageous Fortune*
the black race was depicted in a faithful, loyal, tender, and
lovable light. In *Run, Little Chillun,* the Negro was shown
as a deeply religious and redeemed man. In *The Patriots,*
on its return, he was presented as the staunch friend of the
Democracy in its early and most trying hour. In *South Pacific* he was displayed as the superior of the white man. And
in *Decision* he was the one reason for the white man's fight
against prejudice and for freedom and justice. Even in
Othello he at last came into the immortal gallery of Shakespeare's magnificent, tragic heroes.

RIGHT NEXT TO BROADWAY
February 21, 1944

A comedy by Paul K. Paley. Produced as a bitter pill by the author in the Bijou Theatre.

PROGRAM

SAM	*Rubin Goldberg*	IRWIN COLE	*John Baragrey*
ADREY	*Gloria Mann*	GERTIE SMITH	*Cleo Mayfield*
MARIAN	*Dorothy Eaton*	DANNY	*Lee Bergere*
JERRY	*Roger Sullivan*	MR. LOUCHEIM	*Norman H. Miller*
DOTTY	*Frances Tannehill*	RAUBVOGEL	*Norman Rose*
"POPPA" WEINSTEIN		CHARLES BRADFORD RAMSEY 3RD	
	Leon Schachter		*Jack Bostick*
CHARLIE	*Joseph Leon*	HEINZ	*Otto Simetti*
LEE WINSTON	*Jeannette C. Chinley*	MOSKIN	*Jonathan Harris*
CARLO MARCHETTI	*James Russo*	BOSKIN	*Charles Cohan*
BEN	*Tom Daley*		

SYNOPSIS: Act I. *A spring morning.* Act II. Scene 1. *A week later.* Scene 2. *The following morning.* Act III. *A week later.*

Locale. *The entire action takes place in the office of Lee Winston on Seventh Avenue, New York City.*

SINCE THE AUTHOR was by profession a public accountant without experience in the theatre, since this was his first fling at playwriting, and since he found it necessary to produce his effort himself and at his own expense, the worst was to be expected. The effort duly took its place on the roost with such of the season's prime turkeys as *Victory Belles* and *Lady, Behave!*

What Mr. Paley attempted was a comedy about the garment industry. What he achieved was a humorless concoction involving the trials of a woman who seeks to revivify an old-fashioned dressmaking establishment with some modern ideas and the difficulties she encounters with the OPA, the unions, the models, et al. These difficulties assumed so comprehensive a bulk in the second act that it seemed all Mr. Paley had overlooked for his heroine was a sudden attack of smallpox.

When the first curtain rose, a dress model agitated her rear and sighed, "What I want is a man like Errol Flynn," whereupon another retorted, "Well, dearie, I guess you'll just have to close your eyes and be satisfied with the best you kin get!" The wit continued throughout the evening at that swift pace. The love interest got under way with the entrance of an actor with black, curly, greasy hair who, upon observing the heroine, exclaimed, "I know! We've met before! Don't you remember, it was in that little studio in the Rue de Potage in Paris? Let's go out to lunch." The sentiment continued throughout the evening at that delicate pace. The dramatic element was put into motion with the ringing of the telephone and the heroine's agony at the news, "If we don't get the 5,000 dollars you owe us right away, you won't get any more materials from us," and the heroine's lending, a moment later, of the last 250 in the shop to the gigolo who had captured her fancy. It continued throughout the evening at that rational and exhilarating pace. The sex element popped up with the entrance of a department store buyer who took a look at one of the models, propositioned her, and was apprised, "How many dresses are you buying? Only 500? You gotta buy 1,000 and sign here before I go out with you." It in turn continued throughout the evening at that saucy pace. And the stage direction by William B. Friedlander got off on the jump with all the actors behaving as if the cloak and suit emporium were a treadmill and continued throughout the evening at that race-track pace.

Less than two weeks' run and the author went back to the public accountant business, which pays.

NATHAN THE WISE. February 21, 1944

A revival of the play by Gotthold Ephraim Lessing, in the adaptation by Ferdinand Bruckner. Produced briefly by Erwin Piscator in the Studio Theatre.

Program

Nathan	Herbert Berghof	The Patriarch	Gregory Morton
Daja	Doris Winston	The Sultan Saladin	
Rahel	Elizabeth Lynn		Jay Williams
A Knight Templar		Monks {	Darren Dublyn
	Derrick Lynn-Thomas		Alan Shayne
A Lay Brother	Jack Bittner		

A REPRODUCTION OF Lessing's famous indictment of racial and religious intolerance and plea for humanitarianism and equality, the exhibit was, save for a diminution in ranting, practically the same as when shown two years before under the same auspices. The performance, now as then, took on largely the flavor of a sermon, and the staging remained still on the collateral pulpit side. Berghof's acting of the chief rôle periodically lent the drama some lift, but that drama with the passing of time seems more the property of the classroom and the library than the modern stage. On that stage, classic or not, it proves, I fear, something of a resounding opiate.

MRS. KIMBALL PRESENTS. February 29, 1944

A comedy by Alonzo Price. Produced as a miscomputation by the Messrs. Chandler and Gerken in the 48th Street Theatre.

Program

Harold L. Burton		Dick Hastings	*Michael Ames*
	Arthur Margetson	Cynthia Lane	*Elizabeth Inglise*
Ambrose J. Piel, Jr.	*Bruce Evans*	Babs Sloan	*Joan Cory*
Jim	*Hall Shelton*	Connie Kimball	*Vicki Cummings*
J. G. McGuire	*Jesse White*		

SYNOPSIS: Act I. Scene 1. *Dick Hastings' dressing room in a Broadway theatre. Eleven forty-five p.m.* Scene 2. *Dick's penthouse apartment in Sutton Place. One hour later.* Act II. *The penthouse. About noon the following day.* Act III. *The same one minute later.*

O NE MIGHT HAVE THOUGHT, if one were anesthetic to the eccentricities of the theatre, that the play about the man who pretends he is his friend's butler by way of a front to benefit their ends had been permanently laid to rest some time since. But one would have reckoned without Mr. Alonzo Price. Not only did Mr. Price again drag out the corpse but he strewed it with so many immortelles that the evening took on the aspect of an endless and rather handsome funeral cortège.

Mr. Price overlooked nothing in limbo. His two male characters were actors down on their luck trying to impress a wealthy and very silly woman backer of plays — just why, somewhat baffled the audience, as the woman was already so infatuated with the prettier of the two that she would doubtless have backed them in even something like *Mrs. Kimball Presents*. Having exercised his imagination thus far, Mr. Price didn't stop. Among other things, he introduced the character who is supposed to be a process server from whom one of the actors flees for two and one-half acts and who is finally revealed to be a movie agent with a fat contract for him. Also the pure young girl beloved of the prettier actor who, catching him in proximity to the woman play backer, suspects the worst and stamps haughtily from the room. Also the hard-boiled press-agent in the slouch hat who stands to one side throughout the evening making wry remarks. Also the property fried chicken which the two actor characters attempt to pass off on their rich woman guest as the imminent supper's pièce de résistance, and their dismay when she allows she is hungry and would relish some of it. (The joke about the champagne being ginger-ale is further introduced to inspirit the scene.) Also the homely actor's longing to play Cyrano de Bergerac and his subsequent recital of the lines to persuade the rich female that his friend, the pretty actor, reciprocates her affection.

The critical answer: Twaddle.

The public answer: Seven performances.

THANK YOU, SVOBODA. March 1, 1944

A comedy by H. S. Kraft, based on John Pen's novel, You Can't Do That To Svoboda. *Produced for prompt failure by Milton Baron in the Mansfield Theatre.*

Program

Colonel Fiala	Arnold Korff	Mr. Hanoi	Len Mence
Mr. Vesley	Francis Compton	Mary	Adrienne Gessner
Josef	Frank Conlan	The Padre	John Ravold
Doctor Burian	John McGovern	Hugo	Whitford Kane
The German Salesman		Sergeant Kurtz	Ronald Telfer
	William Malten	Private Recht	Louis Fabien
Svoboda	Sam Jaffe	Private Schmatz	Michael Strong
Mr. Novotny	Donald Keyes	Private Langheld	Dehl Berti

SYNOPSIS: *The action takes place in a village of Czechoslovakia, March 15 1939. Act I. A small inn. Act II. Scene 1. Mary's house. Scene 2. The inn. Scene 3. A cell in the police station. Act III. Scene 1. The inn. Scene 2. Mary's house.*

A FAMILIAR DEVICE of a certain type of play in the Teddy Roosevelt era was the half-witted man-of-all-work whom nobody about the place paid much attention to but who brought about the happy solution of the plot by ambling on at eleven o'clock, his mouth idiotically open, with the tin box containing the evidence against the villain for which everybody had been vainly searching and which he allowed he had found under the cow in the barn. "I wuz a-goin' t' throw it in th' garbage," he would drool, "but I thought mebbe it'd make fer a nice spittoon fer grandmaw." A familiar device of the directly succeeding Taft era was the conversion of the half-wit into a five-eighths-wit, the elevation of him into the principal character in the play, and the changing of the tin box into a sudden and unexpected accretion of an additional eighth of wit which similarly and somewhat miraculously brought about the happy solution of the plot. *Thank You, Svoboda* is largely a combination of the two. The half-wit is a Czechoslovakian peasant whom nobody pays much attention to, who is brow-beaten by the Nazi forces of occupation, and who accepts it all half-wittedly until the last moment, when his acquisition of the aforesaid extra eighth of wit causes him to find the tin box, in this instance containing dynamite, and to employ it to dismay the villains.

In the Taft era, the character was usually cast with some broken-English comedian like the late Louis Mann, and sitting before Mr. Kraft's exhibit I could not get out of mind that what I was looking at was Louie's ghost wandered into a play in which the villains of the older order were simply dressed up in Nazi uniforms and made to grunt more vociferously. Louie, you may relevantly recall, was in his day a flourishing card. Any play in which he condescended to appear had first to be completely rewritten so that he might have the stage for the greater part of the evening to himself. And when Louie had the stage to himself a monologue became the third act of *Ben Hur*. Louie's place in the offering under consideration was occupied by Sam Jaffe and about the only thing Sam didn't do in Louie's old spot was to convert sibilants into sprinkling cans. When Louie delivered any word with an *s* in it the audience down front had to reach for its raincoats, and if it contained two *s's* galoshes were in order. Aside from such Aquacade acting, however, Sam disclosed himself to be in the proud Louie manner, and his play was of the species that didn't in the least hinder him.

When the curtain went up and we first beheld Sam he was glued to stage center, with the dialect going full blast, slowly unwinding from his neck a ten-foot-long muffler. This was supposed to slay us. The muffler at length off, he proceeded to be dialectically lovable with a vengeance, his homely charm being so irresistible that the banker, lawyer, old colonel, innkeeper, and everyone else in the small Czechoslovakian town cottoned to him like a little brother. The bewitching qualities of Sam having been duly established over a period of what seemed sixteen hours, all was ready for the dramatic action, only there wasn't any. In its stead, what seemed another sixteen hours was devoted to a scene showing Sam preparing for a night's sleep on a humble window seat. First, Sam gradually divested himself of one coat after another, each one more grotesque than the other. This was supposed to slay us all over again. Then Sam took off his shoes and warmed his feet at the stove, revealing some funny socks. Thirdly, he painstakingly smoothed out and folded the ragged coats, placed them on the window seat in lieu of a pillow, affectionately patted them, and prepared to lie down. Suddenly a thought assailed him, his features negotiating a Russian ballet to get it over. Extracting his money from his pants pocket, he cautiously secreted it under the pillow. And Louie rolled over in his grave in acute envy.

The rest of the evening pursued the course, with Sam's homely lovableness increasing by the minute. And in the last act, just like Louie, he came on — after having appeared in the two preceding acts looking like a ragamuffin — dressed like a dude, feather in hat, cane and all, and put the Nazis who had done him dirt to rout. The only difference was that in Louie's time it was Otto Oberschlauser, the delicatessen dealer who had swindled him at pinochle, instead of Hitler.

Derived, as noted, from a novel by John Pen, Mr. Kraft's exhibit was less a play than a two and one-half hour induction to a play that never eventuated. A few amusing lines provided momentary relief, but the bulk of the exhibit, which expired after six showings, was constituted simply of Sam standing there, speaking pig-English, making baby-talk about a watch his sweetheart had given him, listening cutely to its ticking, and in the end being abruptly metamorphosed into a mastermind who got the Nazis by the tail.

Pen's novel was susceptible of better playwriting than Kraft was able to bring to it. A competent dramatist might not have been successful in fashioning a really good play out of it, but he would at least have been able to contrive a far better one than this, since Kraft apparently is an artisan to whom dramatic action is a deep mystery and dramatic speech something that may be given force only if on each and every occasion it be repeated three or four times.

The final effect was of having heard his play several times over on the same evening.

Since Pen demonstrated himself in his novel to be superior to his dramatist on these counts, among several others, it might have been wiser had he served as his own dramatist. But simply because many of our novelists and story writers have failed when they have tried their hands at playwriting, there has grown up among the genre, doubtless including Pen, a belief that the drama is not for them and that in the interests of self-esteem and peace of mind they had best lay off it. It is true that they have had bad luck and that for one who has succeeded in mastering the medium a half dozen have come croppers. But their acquired conviction that the technique is exceedingly mysterious and the private possession solely of born dramaturgical magicians is bosh and it would be well for the newer talents amongst them and for the theatre itself if they rid themselves of it.

Never has there been so eager a market for fresh dramatic talent, as is plainly evident in the famished theatre of the immediate day. Many of the established playwrights, it should be obliquely comforting to the novelists and story writers to note, have turned out to be incompetent in supplying the stage with what it wants and sorely needs, and the job they seem often unable longer to do might nicely be considered by the hitherto timid practitioners of other species of beautiful letters.

In other words, the novelists and story writers have not failed any worse than the playwrights themselves.

Consider the well-known playwrights who in the last four seasons have now and then come croppers: Odets, Connelly, Hecht, MacArthur, Anderson, Akins, Kaufman, Ferber, Owen Davis, Ervine, Carroll, Lonsdale, Patrick Hamilton, Bolton, Kennedy, Treadwell, Barry, Behrman, Rice, et al. Surely, the excursions into drama on the part of the novelists have not in comparison been so very disastrous. Moreover, when the latter have failed, it often has not been because of any considerable deficiency in the dramaturgical art. No novelist or short story writer who has had a play produced in the theatre in the period in question has shown, at his worst, any greater technical shortcoming than, for example, the experienced dramatist Marc Connelly indicated in his *The Flowers of Virtue,* or than the experienced Sophie Treadwell exposed in her *Hope For a Harvest,* or than the experienced Ben Hecht testified to in his *Lily Of the Valley.*

The novelist John Steinbeck, without previous dramatic experience, wrote *Of Mice And Men,* which achieved not only popular success but won the Drama Critics' Circle's award as the best American play of its year. The novelist Thornton Wilder won the Pulitzer prize, such as it is, with his plays, such as they are, *Our Town* and *The Skin Of Our Teeth.* William Saroyan, the short story writer, took the theatre by the ears with *My Heart's In The Highlands,* his first dramatic try, subsequently won both the Critics' Circle and Pulitzer prizes with his *The Time Of Your Life,* and ran a healthy second in the Critics' Circle's estimation with his following season's *The Beautiful People.*

All kinds of our novelists and story writers, in short, have proved that there is nothing particularly occult about the craft of playwriting. Tarkington proved it, and so did his collaborator Harry Leon Wilson, and so did Zona Gale and Jesse Lynch Williams and Arthur Kober and Clare Boothe and Rose Franken and Du Bose Heyward and various others. A sizeable proportion of the best plays collected annually by Burns Mantle are found, over the span of the years, to have been the work of novelists and story writers.

The difficulty that novelists often encounter with the dramatic medium is largely their own fault. Arnold Bennett once expressed the conviction that, compared with the writing of a novel, the writing of a play was as easy as rolling off a log. The poor plays that Bennett wrote offered testimony to the vacuity of his contention. Many of our novelists apparently suffer from Bennett's conviction. They look down upon the stage as something to be served with their left hands and consequently manufacture plays that are so bad the theatre will have none of them. The theatre is a demanding master. But it is also a generous one. The

novelist who approaches it seriously and with proper respect will, other things being equal, reap his reward from
it. The novelist who, on the other hand, views it primarily
as the potential source of easy money will end up in the
poorhouse, financially, dramatically, and critically.

I shall not be so unchivalrous as to mention names —
though they may be readily recognizable — but one of our
most important American novelists who several times has
tried to make the grade of the theatre has failed for the simple and signal reason that he looks upon drama with the
backstage eyes of an actor and with the mind of a confector
of machine-made plots. He would no more look upon the
novel, which he has served brilliantly, as anything other
than an art form than he would think of parading the boulevards with his trousers off. Yet, when he approaches playwriting, off come those trousers and the audience yells for
the police.

There are others in one way or another like him. One, of
the female gender, views the theatre as being nine-tenths
box-office, and tries assiduously to serve that nine-tenths
with no smallest regard for dramatic merit. Another, a
male, tries to shock the stage into accepting him as an independent and resolute artist, whereas all he discloses himself
to be is a dramatic hack with a loud tin gong. And still another, a woman, whose novels are on the circumspect side,
has woven artificial vine leaves in her hair when she has in-
vaded the theatre and peddled little more than pulp magazine sex.

It is novelists and story writers like these who, failing in
the theatre, have discouraged their brothers and sisters
from it. The latter, not stopping to discriminate and reason, have taken the failure of the former for something
more or less inevitable whereas it has been simply the result
of foolishness, blindness, avarice or mountebankery, or all
four in combination. The door is still wide open, however
and nevertheless, for any novelist or short story writer who
will expend upon the art of playwriting the pains he gladly
expends upon the art of the novel or short story. It is closed,
and tightly, only against those who deliberately cheapen

themselves, who regard the theatre in the light of a boozy holiday, who, like Bennett, look upon the drama as something slightly beneath their august talents, and who are merely out to rob what they think is the baby's bank.

BRIGHT BOY. March 2, 1944

*A comedy by John Boruff. Produced and withdrawn after
16 performances by Arthur J. Beckhard and David Merrick
in the Playhouse.*

Program

Tittman (Shakespeare)		Stevens (Steve)	John Cushman
	Carleton Carpenter	John Wallace (Specs)	
Willie Barnes	Beman Lord		Michael Dreyfuss
Si Williams	Frank Jacoby	Watts (Sleepy)	
Peterson (Pete)	Jeff Brown		William McGuire
Prof. McGiffin	Liam Dunn	Pinky Jenks	Eugene Ryan
David Bennett	Charles Bowlby	Dr. Sewell	Ivan Simpson
Allen Carpenter	Donald Buka	Margaret	Joyce Franklin

SYNOPSIS: Act I. Scene 1. *David's and Allen's room. Afternoon.*
Scene 2. *"Smoke Hill." A small hill off campus. An early evening. A few
weeks later.* Act II. Scene 1. *"Smoke Hill." Afternoon. A few weeks later.*
Scene 2. *David's and Allen's room. An evening two weeks later.* Act III.
"Smoke Hill." Ten days later.

Time. *Present.*

Place. *Brown Hall. A Boys' Prep School.*

MR. Boruff is by vocation an actor. His play, after an
encouraging start, slowly goes to pieces by virtue of his ingrained actor inability to restrain himself from theatrical-
izing his central character. The latter begins real enough,
but by the time the second act gets under way greasepaint
gradually overtakes him and in the end converts him into
a ham flirting, in this case unsuccessfully, with the plau-
dits of the box-office.

The character in point is a cynical student in a boys'
school who, taking a broad cue from his hero Machiavelli,
foregoes no evil means to gain his selfish ends. Proudly
aware of his superior intelligence and charm, he stops at
nothing, whether it be theft, blackmail, or what not. In a
word, a comprehensive scoundrel, but with the ingratiating
wile to make his victims swallow it and like it. Honestly developed, the character might have been a fascinating and

prehensile figure, but the actor-author's presumption that you inevitably have to reform such a character if your play is to be a success operates not only toward cheap sophistication but turns the play into an irritating failure. Mr. Boruff should know that scoundrels kept persistently immaculate as scoundrels have contributed to the box-office prosperity of any number of local plays, good and bad, from the days of *The Deep Purple* to those of *Craig's Wife* and on to those of *Guest In The House.*

Some of the playwright's reporting of life in a boys' school is accurately caught. The very fact that it is thus accurately caught unfortunately works for obviousness in a theatre which demands novelty at the expense of truth. The familiar business of boys riding one of their number triumphantly on their shoulders, the boy in love with the professor's young daughter, the boy who is learning to smoke, the boy who, indignant at another's anatomical reflection upon his girl, says, "Don't you talk that way about *her;* she's different!," and other such items, while fully recognizable to those who once attended such schools, have been repeated so often that audiences are tired of them and would prefer something fresher, however fraudulent, in their places. And the same in the case of the usual bursts into song, dormitory roughhouses, and the like.

By way of giving his generically incomplex play immediate impact, Boruff has made the further mistake of tacking on to its end an analogy between his central character and Fascism and between the school as a whole and tolerant Democracy, thus making it something like black and white Siamese twins by different fathers.

There is, however, no longer, it appears, much of a place in our theatre for plays of this general, fundamentally innocent species, be they meritorious or not. They are, in the Broadway phrase, "not exciting enough." And it is this arbitrary and often uncritical craving for excitement on the part of most present playgoers, both professional and lay, that frequently operates toward reducing the stage to the level of the screen Westerns, albeit comparatively epic. It is, further, this indiscriminate passion for high-pressure entertainment that places a premium on exhibits which, irrespective of honest merit, merchant it and that periodically brings into popular disrepute worthier exhibits which have only a calm gentility to recommend them.

The phenomenon is not difficult to comprehend. In the past, the stage afforded such a plenitude of melodrama that pure excitement-seekers could readily find all they wanted of it in such a wholesale dose of swords, pistols, sawmills, express trains and precipitous cliffs as would satisfy even the most bloodthirsty Nazi with a dozen beers under his belt. But, with the gradual disappearance of melodrama of the species, there has remained for those with an undying taste for it little to take its place. And the name of such persons, despite the high and lofty exercises of the critics, is still legion. While there has not been, I believe, a conscious effort on the part of most producers and playwrights to satisfy these insatiables, it is nevertheless, I suspect, a fact that they vaguely sense the public's basic appetite and have in one way or another been influenced to cater to it. The result has been a sensationalism of externals at the expense of internal dramatic and musical show values.

By and large, what the public lays out its money for these days is entertainment that provides something in the way of stimulation quite apart from the stimulation that may be a generic part of it. *Othello* thus becomes a great success not because of Shakespeare's play but because the public derives an added intoxication from observing in it a Negro actor making love to a white woman. The idea that the public flocks in turn to *The Voice of the Turtle* because it is an extremely skilful comedy is hard to believe. The public undoubtedly constitutes it a big success because, though under cover of deft writing, it purveys enough open-and-shut sex to satisfy a herd of Boccaccios, and not only purveys it but makes it so attractive and desirable that it brings the flush of youth back to the cheeks of even customers who haven't been in a theatre since E. S. Willard died. The trashy *The Two Mrs. Carrolls* contains sufficient prosciutto melodrama to crowd the box-office; and there is enough pseudo-paganism in the musical show ballet numbers

around town to galvanize those ticket-buyers who don't
know a ballet from a Virginia reel but who derive a kick
from the spectacle of a lot of scantily clad females being
chased around a stage by a posse of hypothetically lascivious
barbers.

I shall not extend the catalogue in further proof of the
general contention; it should be recognizable to anyone
who scrutinizes closely the present theatrical topography.
What I am directly thinking of is some such recent play as
Afinogenov's *Listen, Professor!* Here was a minor but pleasant little comedy that not only got poor notices from the
majority of the reviewers but also from most of that small
portion of the public that went to see it. Now, while I am
surely not going to argue that the play was any great shakes
— very far from it — it was nevertheless in its mild and
gentle way every bit as acceptable as any dozen comedies
that in other days proved appetizing to the public palate.
In this day, however, it missed what it takes to get people to
the box-office, which is to say that superimposed or extra
squirt of something or other, whether in the way of spectacular casting, internal faking or maybe sheer financial
outlay, which jounces the public like a shot of cocaine and
makes it superficially bounce. About the only means by
which it might possibly have been made into a commercial
success would have been to cast some popular movie mag-
nifico in the central rôle, incorporate a scene in which he
attempts a seduction of the young girl, bring down the second act curtain on a ringing tribute to the Army Air Forces,
and charge $8.80 for opening night seats.

If today your musical show costs less than $150,000 and
hasn't a bordello or boudoir scene, or at least a lot of jokes
about something of the kind, in it; if your farce, even one
about youngsters, doesn't deal with sex; if your play or
show, whatever it may be, doesn't have some pretty fancy
names on the marquee; if you don't add something else to
whatever you have in hand and see to it that that something
else is of a marijuana nature — if you don't do the one or
the other, the chances are that you will lose money. For one
exceptional *Life With Father* you will find a half dozen

plays that seem to have been rewritten in part by Maxie
Baer and Slapsy Rosenbloom. For one *Oklahoma!* you will
find two or three shows whose songs about the fragrant per-
fume of the west wind are interrupted by pool-room cracks
and a scene showing the leading lady battling weakly for
her honor on a chaise-longue.

A public that made a fortune for *Star and Garter,* that
turned the tide even for *The Naked Genius,* that has
packed into the 10-20-30 alarms of the Elisabeth Bergner
ruckus, that has kept the murder thrills of *Angel Street* in
operation for going on three solid years, that has turned a
comedy about a little girl who proclaims she is going to
have an impromptu baby into a veritable gold-mine, and
that has brought *Tobacco Road* back to town over a period of years is not a public willing to make any such
placid play as this *Bright Boy* a financial success, even were
it twenty times better than it is.

JACOBOWSKY AND THE COLONEL
MARCH 14, 1944

*A comedy by S. N. Behrman based on an original play by
Franz Werfel. Produced successfully by the Theatre Guild
in association with J. H. Skirball in the Martin Beck Theatre.*

PROGRAM

A YOUNG GIRL *Louise Dowdney*	MARIANNE *Annabella*
SLEEPING SHOPKEEPER	BRIGADIER *E. G. Marshall*
Harrison Winter	STREET SINGER *Joseph Kallini*
THE TRAGIC GENTLEMAN	CHILD *Jules Leni*
Herbert Yost	FIRST LIEUTENANT *Frank Overton*
OLD LADY FROM ARRAS	GESTAPO OFFICIAL
Jane Marbury	*Harold Vermilyea*
MADAME BOUFFIER *Hilda Vaughn*	FIRST GERMAN SOLDIER *Don Lee*
SALOMON *Harry Davis*	SECOND GERMAN SOLDIER
SZYCKE *Peter Kass*	*Bob Merritt*
SZABUNIEWICZ	PAPA CLARION *Harry Davis*
J. Edward Bromberg	THE DICE PLAYER *Philip Coolidge*
S. L. JACOBOWSKY *Oscar Karlweis*	SENATOR BRISSON *Donald Cameron*
AIR RAID WARDEN *Philip Collier*	THE COMMISSAIRE *William Sanders*
COLONEL TADEUSZ BOLESLAV	FIRST FRENCH SOLDIER
STJERBINSKY *Louis Calhern*	*Burton Tripp*
COSETTE *Kitty Mattern*	SECOND FRENCH SOLDIER
A CHAUFFEUR *Coby Ruskin*	*Edward Kreisler*
MONSIEUR SEROUILLE	
Donald Cameron	

SYNOPSIS: Act I. Scene 1. *The laundry of the Hotel Mon Repos
et de la Rose, serving as an air-raid shelter, Paris. Midnight, June 13.
Scene 2. In front of the hotel. Early morning. June 14. Act II. Scene 1.
A lonely road at St. Cyrille near Sables d'Ollones. June 16. Scene 2. An
open spot in the woods, near the city of Bayonne. June 16. Act III. Scene
1. The "Au Pere Clairon" waterfront cafe at St. Jean de Luz. Early evening. June 18. Scene 2. Mole at Hendaye, St. Jean de Luz. Night. June 18.*
*The action takes place from June 13th to June 18th, 1940, between
Paris and the Atlantic coast of France.*

IF ONE REMITS critical discomfort to the point of overlooking a periodic dramaturgical choppiness and an occasional too gusty dialogic wind, the play provides a pleasant

sail. The story is of two refugees from the Nazis seeking to escape from France before the latter close in on them. One is an aristocratic and aloof Polish officer, the other a humble Polish Jew. The action lies in the aristocrat's ingrained hesitation to avail himself of the Jew's aid, in the increased necessity of his reliance upon the Jew's inexhaustible shrewdness and cunning, and in his eventual reluctant conclusion that this is a funny world after all and that, whatever one's born beliefs, one had best emerge from one's traditional shell and welcome stern practicability where and when one can find it.

Although the scant outline may suggest just another of the long familiar stage testimonials to the Jews, this is hardly the case. The sentimental approach is present, but it is not pushed too far, as it most often has been in such exhibits in the past. The Jew comes in for his criticism and while that criticism is gentle it is nonetheless essentially forthright and unequivocal. In the original play Werfel carried sentimental approach much further than Behrman has permitted. The latter is responsible for converting what might have been merely another, if considerably better written, Jewish valentine into a play that wittily removes any such perfumed emphasis and is therefore much the better for it.

Although he wouldn't confess it even on his way to the electric chair, any reviewer who has been in operation for a considerable spell approaches certain plays violently prejudiced in their disfavor. Among them are these plays dealing in whole or in part with the Jews. When news reaches him that another such one is in the offing, he privileges himself an expansive grunt and on the night of duty hies himself painfully to the scene. The reasons are several, and not unintelligible.

In years long since gone by, it was the conviction of ten producers out of every ten that any play which depicted the Jews as a reservoir of all the godly virtues was good for all kinds of money. The conviction was based upon the argument that, whereas so large a portion of theatregoers were of that faith, the plays would prove irresistible to them. What is more, the conviction seemed to be perfectly sound, and season after season the money duly rolled in from an apparently endless succession of the greaseboxes, most of them unspeakable claptrap. For one honestly amusing play of the *Potash and Perlmutter* species there were half a dozen like *A Tailor-Made Man* and *Welcome Stranger* that were simply manufactured billets-doux. And for one somewhat more serious and entertaining exhibit like *The Five Frankfurters* there were a dozen like *As A Man Thinks, The House Next Door, Consequences,* and the Zangwill eli-elis that amounted solely to cheap pink colognes. The birth of critical prejudice against the species of drama in point proceeded from the con game thus set into motion.

The subsequent theatrical period did nothing to alleviate that prejudice, since whenever a play about the Jews showed up the generally safe advance betting was that it would disclose itself to be nothing more or less than a cagily contrived three-card-monte swindle with the playwright piously masquerading as a combination Broadway Spinoza and Mendelssohn. In both periods there were but two plays, Galsworthy's *Loyalties* and Wellman's *The Gentile Wife,* that offered anything at all worthy of the efforts of local criticism. And there was only one play in all of the European theatre, Schnitzler's *Professor Bernhardi,* that offered anything to that criticism on a touring holiday.

Nor did the passing of the years bring much to change matters. For one play like Behrman's *Rain From Heaven* the more recent stage unloaded a cargo of such josspots as *The Eternal Road, Good Neighbor, The Brown Danube,* and *Another Sun,* all as unstimulating as non-alcoholic slivovitz and all shamelessly concocted for the purpose of seducing the box-office. And for one play like Odets' *Awake And Sing* the unloading continued with a freight of such equally trashy stuff as *The Man With Blond Hair, Foreigners, Spring Song,* and *Professor Mamlock.* A mildly acceptable comedy like *Having Wonderful Time* or a valid biblical play like *Family Portrait* might come along once in a dog's age, but for the rest the fare was a table d'hôte of car-

amels of the quality of *Be So Kindly, Young Mr. Disraeli,
The Bride of Torozko,* et al.

Things thus came gradually to the pass where the Jewish
audiences themselves began to gag and to share the prejudice of professional criticism, and the consequence was that
most of these fraudulent pats on the back saw them staying
away from the theatres that showed them, and the plays'
subsequent failure. Like the loony Lionel Stander character in the old Hecht-MacArthur movie, *Soak The Rich,*
who, hearing a knock on the door of his mountain cabin
hideout, loudly demanded to know who was there, was informed that it was an agent of the League of Nations who
wished to present him with the whole world, doubtfully
and meditatively scratched his head, and foxily murmured
to himself, "There's something fishy about this," the audiences, meditating similarly if more intelligently, arrived at
the conclusion that they were being taken for suckers. And
it wasn't long before they said in so many words: Let up
on the marmalade, however sweet to the tooth it may be,
and be a little honest for a change, however bitter it may
be; otherwise, the curse of Cain and his storehouse upon
you!

For yet a while the con men didn't hear or listen, and
the old hokum periodically came, saw, and was duly conquered by the Cain janissaries. But common sense presently began at odd intervals to lift its head and to delineate
the Jews not as always unblemished little angels but much
as the rest of mankind, and with all of mankind's faults.
You can not, however, change a people overnight and despite their protestations for fair play, however much it
might hurt, the Jewish audiences didn't entirely cotton to
the new, or at least, rephrased more cognizable order. And
such a play as *Outrageous Fortune,* which looked things
pretty straight in the eye, found it could manage only a relatively short run to something of a financial loss.

The fate of *Jacobowsky And The Colonel* was therefore
interesting to observe. Although it is far from an unsenti-
mental approach to the Jews, it is equally far from the old
arbitrary depositing of laurel wreaths on their brows. Its

flattery is mixed with timeless truths and the inevitable and changeless trials that the race must bear. It is very indulgent but nevertheless discerning, and in its discernment the authors, or at least Behrman, have touched the vine leaves with stray little sprigs of poison ivy. It was accordingly up to the honesty of the Jewish audiences to accept or reject.

To work for such acceptance, the producers did not, of course, overlook any of the old, safe tricks. They cast in the leading Jewish rôle Oscar Karlweis, who is not only a winning actor but addedly a fellow of very great personal charm. They cast as the girl who affectionately takes his side no seedy Grand Street actress with wrinkled cotton stockings but the trim and pretty moving picture pin-up girl, Annabella. They directed, as the Jew's ultimate Pythias, Louis Calhern into a genial low-comedy performance. They did these and other things to cozen the trade. And it worked. The play succeeded.

For other than Jewish audiences the play, equally successful, surmounted the old critical prejudice by virtue of what was in the main intelligent observation embroidered with intelligent wit and humor. There may have been some rather too protracted stretches of talk, and some routine pistol melodrama exercised against the Nazis by way of making one oblivious of the long stretches, and — unbelievably enough from any such playwright as the usually circumspect Behrman — the stale ending business of "I will love you always; come back to me; I shall be waiting for you." But taken in its entirety the play was much more attractive than the majority of plays we had been getting and was to be commended to all those who, after years of often depressing experience, had sworn they wouldn't go again to one about the Jews even if all the rôles were played by Lillian Russell.

THE HOUSE IN PARIS. MARCH 20, 1944

A play by E. Mawby Green and Edward Allen Feilbert, based on the novel by Elizabeth Bowen. Produced to box-office groans by H. Clay Blaney in the Fulton Theatre.

PROGRAM

NAOMI FISHER	*Cavada Humphrey*	MADAME FISHER	*Ludmilla Pitoeff*
HENRIETTA	*Pauline Robinson*	MAX EBHART	*Michael Ingram*
LEOPOLD	*Alastair Boyd Kyle*	KAREN MICHAELS	*Lorraine Clewes*
TWO AMERI-CAN GIRLS	{ *Marguerite Lewis* { *Penelope Sack*	RAY FORRESTIER	*Isham Constable*

SYNOPSIS: Prologue. *The year: 1911. The lights will be turned on for a period of one minute between the Prologue and Act I. Act I. The past: April, 1900. Act II. The past.* Scene 1. *May, 1900.* Scene 2. *June, 1900.* Scene 3. *July, 1900.* Act III. *Continuation of the Prologue. The year: 1911.*

The entire action of the play takes place in the salon of Mme. Fisher's home in Paris.

IT WAS ONCE SAID by someone, apparently a complacent idiot, that the best way to dramatize a novel is to read it, throw it away, and proceed without further regard to it. The present dramatizers indubitably followed that course. That they read Miss Bowen's novel is at least superficially evident, at stray moments. That they then threw it away and proceeded independently is profoundly evident, at all other moments.

The novel is one of mood, suggestion, and overtones. The play that has been made from it is a very bad, exaggeratedly emotional melodrama that substitutes for the mood, suggestion and overtones facial contortions, silent spaces devoted to suggestion in the form of darksome stares at the audience, and overtones implied by a morbid wrinkling of brows.

It was quite obvious that Mr. Blaney is a producer who seldom, if ever, goes to the theatre. If he knew what has been going on in late years, it is extremely doubtful that

he would have put on any such play. He would have come
to learn, for example, that the play dealing with an evilly
selfish female who seeks to control and in the controlling
wrecks the lives of those about her is an all too familiar one
to audiences, and in its previous incarnations has been infinitely better on all counts than the play he had in hand.
He would have gathered that little is more disastrously
tedious and refractorily humorous to present day audiences
than pseudo-literary dialogue and too precise speech. He
would have known that long prologues are generally unwelcome; that dramatic misery, save it be handled by an expert playwright, is, unless here and there lightened, likely
to depress an audience to either yawns or nervous chuckles;
and that talk unrelieved by at least a semblance of action
is good for business only in the adjacent bars.

He would also have discovered from the performances in
English of such foreign actresses as Katina Paxinou and the
like that it is often box-office suicide to offer one of them
as a star before she has become at some ease with English
and has learned that what passes in the way of gestures, etc.,
on the European stage is hardly suitable to the American.
And he would accordingly have hesitated to introduce
Madame Pitoeff to local audiences without longer preparation. He would have found out all this and more. Furthermore, even had he insisted upon staying at home, he
would, if his fireside reading had been relevant, have come
to appreciate that one sure way to lose money is to put on
a Strindberg play, which *The House In Paris* in its essen-
tials is, that has had the misfortune not to have been written by Strindberg.

Madame Pitoeff, an actress of distinction in the theatre
of pre-war France, gave the appearance of regarding her
rôle as an exercise in the Berlitz method, and further indulged herself in such bizarre physical contortions, chief
among them an arch cocking of the head to one side and a
subsequent sudden propulsion of it at the character to
whom she was speaking, that the effect was of a self-admin-
istered course in chiropractic. Clarence Derwent's general
direction quite clearly had its genesis in one of the lesser

funeral parlors, the actors being made to comport themselves alternately like mourners and corpses. Stewart Chaney's setting alone indicated that anyone connected with
the exhibit had read the Bowen novel with any understanding.

The play closed after 16 performances.

MRS. JANUARY AND MR. EX. March 31, 1944

A comedy by Zoë Akins, originally called Plans For To-morrow. *Produced to small returns for 43 performances by Richard Myers in the Belasco Theatre.*

Program

Miss Belle	*Helen Carew*	2nd Expressman	*Robert F. Simon*
Charley Blaine		Germaine	*Mlle. Therese Quadri*
	Edward Nannary	Wilhelmina	*Barbara Bel Geddes*
Stevens	*Phil Sheridan*	Rolando	*Bobby Perez*
Mrs. January,		Carey	*Henry Barnard*
née January	*Billie Burke*	Burdette	*Henry Vincent*
Martin Luther Cooper		Clancy	*Dorothy Lambert*
	Frank Craven	John Deacon January	
1st Expressman			*Nicholas Joy*
	Roderick Winchell	Miss Peck	*Susana Garnett*

SYNOPSIS: Act I. *An afternoon in May.* Act II. Scene 1. *An evening in May.* Scene 2. *A morning in August.* Act III. *The same evening.*

The entire action is modern and transpires in the sitting-room of a small house in a New England town.

Observe the program and note the descriptive sentence: "The entire action is modern and transpires in the sitting-room of a small house in a New England town." Miss Akins is otherwise so literate a writer that she doubtless has used the word *transpires,* in place of *occurs* or *happens,* with critical deliberation. The dictionary defines *transpires,* as no one, surely including Miss Akins, need be told: "To emit or send off in the form of a vapor . . . to give off moisture, or perspire." Appreciating that her comedy's action is indeed decidedly vaporous and intermittently perspirational in its effort to sustain itself, she is accordingly less ungrammatical than might be supposed.

Slight and at times strainful though the exhibit may be, it is nevertheless a generally amusing and often drolly conceived little play. Its plot scheme is this. A butterfly-brained, enormously wealthy widow of three marriages given to an addled admiration of the Communist theory decides to prepare herself and her children for the world of tomorrow by adopting the simple life à toute outrance. To that end she instals herself, her offspring, her retinue of servants, and a wardrobe large enough to outfit the court of Louis XIV in a 40 dollar a month house in the upper New England countryside. Her landlord is an ex-President of the United States of the Coolidge type. The love affair that blooms grotesquely between them constitutes the body of the comedy.

Miss Akins has spun the story with the airy technique of knitting needles employed upon a candy spider web, sometimes with dialogue no better than the fluttery heroine's "I'm just a needle in a woodpile," more frequently with a nice, easy wit. The impression is of something like her very early and diverting comedy, *Papa,* written by the Clare Kummer of *Good Gracious, Annabelle.* That the script experienced a great deal of rewriting is obvious, and some of that rewriting, evidently designed to give it more solidity, has not been too fortunate. The business of the children, for example, is dull and might better have been left out, or at least approached with a nimbler touch. Yet the scenes between the rattle-pated widow and the dour ex-President, which constitute the anatomy of the evening, have enough humor and even charm to dissipate the interrupting elements and make the whole entertaining.

Viewing Billie Burke and Frank Craven in the rôles in question, one was again bemused by the reflection that year in and year out they invariably, save in the rarest of instances, give much the same performances. This is not to say that their performances may not on such an occasion as this be very good; it is rather to say that they seem to be essentially a one-rôle actress and a one-rôle actor and that they play that rôle, whatever its possibly divergent nature and the nature of their vehicles, irrespective of any other potential and conceivably more propitious interpretation of it.

I have now seen Miss Burke since, aeons ago in London, she made her first appearance as a dramatic actress with Charles Hawtrey in *Mr. George,* which antedated her first

local dramatic appearance in *My Wife* by a year. Although
the plays and rôles in which she has since offered herself
have intermittently varied, she is still giving almost exactly
the same performances in them that she gave shortly after
her emergence from musical comedy. Some of these, when
her rôles have not too rebelliously interposed themselves,
have been very attractive; some, when they have, have been
quite the opposite. For, regardless of her parts, she has always played Billie Burke In Person And In The Flesh with
a vengeance, much as if the parts were something on a
movie screen and she making a simultaneous stage personal
appearance before the audience.

Miss Burke has been so insistently Miss Burke and, aside
from any critical consideration of her acting, so impressive
in propria persona, that she has literally founded a Billie
Burke school. Time and again through the years we accordingly have observed junior actresses gurgling like soda
fountains, cocking their heads like effervescent canaries
and brushing around the stage like excited schoolgirls under the misapprehension that they were simply too darling
for words and that, if Charles Frohman were still alive, he
would promptly engage them as leading women to John
Drew. It threatened at one time, indeed, to get to the point
where one expected Flo Ziegfeld to hop out of his grave
and, momentarily confused, to propose marriage to the lot
of them. But any such confusion, whether on Flo's mori-
bund or our own more existent part, was evanescent, to put
it mildly. Billie Burke may be imitated as any one else may
be imitated yet, admire her or not, these others could and
can no more capture her essence than you can capture
Bobby Clark's by painting on eye-glasses, carrying a bamboo cane, sticking a cigar butt in your mouth, and dejecting yourself violently upon your seat. It would hurt you
more than it hurts Bobby, and in another direction it
doesn't hurt Billie who, whatever fault you may find with
her, at least started out being Billie on all cylinders, kept
up being Billie on all cylinders, and never once for a second tried, whether for good or ill, to be Duse, Mrs. Fiske
or Billy on even one cylinder.

Craven is a similar clinical exhibit, although it may hardly be said that he founded any school of imitators. Like Miss Burke, he has been playing the same rôle in every play he has ever appeared in, and I think I have seen them all. Take all the George Abbott detective characters with their dry voices and cool deliberation, send them out to pasture for a year on some New England farm, bring them back to the stage, and in combination you have Frank Craven. It matters not what he is playing, it's Frank rather than the rôle, and generally you like him, even when he is not so good. But, as in Miss Burke's case, when you get down to the foul business of criticism, you wonder if testimonials to his histrionic ability aren't much like testimonials to the genius of Edward Payson Weston who up to a ripe old age walked twenty miles a day, and always over the same route.

ONLY THE HEART. April 4, 1944

A play by Horton Foote, tested in December, 1942 by the same group in the Provincetown Playhouse. Produced to sparse audiences for a forced run of 47 performances by the American Actors' Theatre in the Bijou Theatre.

Program

India Hamilton	*Mildred Dunnock*	Albert Price	*Will Hare*
Julia Borden	*Eleanor Anton*	Mr. Borden	*Maurice Wells*
Mamie Borden	*June Walker*		

SYNOPSIS: Act I. *Living-room of Mamie Borden's house in a small town in Richmond, Texas. Early September of 1921.* Act II. Scene 1. *Afternoon. The following June.* Scene 2. *One week later.* Act III. *The next morning.*

CHARGE OFF THIS ERROR to some of the reviewers. When the play was originally put on down in environs of McDougal Alley they were apparently so overcome to find that, bad as it was, it was yet so superior to the many other bad plays they had encountered in the same environs that their bedazzlement got the better of them, with the result that they praised it out of all proportion, like a soldier tasting his first canned corned beef after a protracted diet of camel's knuckles. Reading their notices, the amateurs deliriously concluded that they had in their possession something of a dramatic gem, forthwith dreamed dreams of Broadway glory, and set about gathering the necessary funds to invade the precincts of the professional theatre. Among those in that theatre who had evidently taken the aforesaid notices as warmly to heart as the amateurs were Katharine Cornell, Margaret Webster, Howard Lindsay, Eva Le Gallienne, Hume Cronyn, Peggy Wood and Thornton Wilder, none of whom probably had seen the play or, if any of them had, were equally nousled by its purely relative status.

Came the great night of the exhibit's Broadway début, came then the dawn — and Cain rode again.

Even with some studious revisions of the original script, including the reduction of the characters from six to five, the transformation of the husband's mistress from a Negress to a Bohemian woman, and the changing of the period from 1935 to 1921, and with the further cautious recruiting of a largely professional acting company, the play proved again to be just about what it was in the earlier appraisal of the less inebrious reviewers. Which is to say a monotonous and painfully dull rehash of the theme of the domineering mother who brings unhappiness and worse to her family through her uncompromising selfishness. The author writes without imagination and with metronome insistence; he manages to bring to the old and stale materials no sense of dramatic life, no fresh observation; and his play, except for a single scene between the daughter and her young husband, plods its course with the heavy emotional repetition of a juke-box blues song. Nor did the acting company directed by Mary Hunter, the group's boss, do anything to relieve matters.

The occasion attested once again to the fact that these local experimental organizations seem for the major part in these later years to have gone to pot. About the only purpose they serve is wistfully to recall the far days when their counterparts really contributed something to the advancement of the theatre, those days when O'Neill was in the brilliant making, when Paul Green began to function, when Zoë Akins was writing in *The Magical City* the cue for such future drama as Maxwell Anderson's *Winterset,* and when other such green plants were beginning to promise flower.

Now and again, as in a play like *Career Angel,* one of the present-day groups may come forth with a relatively available idea, but even in such cases the playwrights display so great a dramaturgical infelicity that little comes to anything. The early experimental theatres, even at their weakest, often uncovered writers who knew something about the craft of playwriting. The current theatres, even at their best, seem to sponsor hopefuls who may occasionally hit upon such an available idea but who know so little about that craft that their plays are like sailboats without sails, and with leaky bottoms that quickly bring about their sinking.

Furthermore, even at such times as they manage to lay hold of plays by more experienced playwrights, the groups founder on their lack of purely theatrical skill. This was indicated when the group under immediate consideration in 1939 produced Lynn Riggs' *Sump'n Like Wings* and in the following year Paul Green's *Shroud My Body Down*. In this and in other respects, the organizations presently functioning in New York do not compare with similar bodies in many other sections of the country. These latter frequently prove themselves an added asset to the American theatre.

CHICKEN EVERY SUNDAY. APRIL 5, 1944

A farce-comedy by Julius J. and Philip G. Epstein, based on the book of the same title by Rosemary Taylor. Produced with fair results by Edward Gross in the Henry Miller Theatre.

PROGRAM

MRS. LAWSON	*Ethel Remey*	ROSEMARY BLACHMAN	
JEFFREY LAWSON	*Hugh Thomas*		*Jean Gillespie*
MISS GILLEY	*Diana Rivers*	CLEM	*Raymond Van Sickle*
MR. WILLARD	*Austin Coghlan*	MRS. LYNCH (MISS SALLY)	
EMILY BLACHMAN	*Mary Philips*		*Katherine Squire*
EVIE MAY	*Viola Dean*	JIM BLACHMAN	*Rhys Williams*
JAKE	*Roy Fant*	MR. ROBINSON	*Fleming Ward*
EAGLE	*Martin Skapik*	RITA KIRBY	*Ann Thomas*
OLIVER BLACHMAN	*Guy Stockwell*	GEORGE KIRBY	*Frank M. Thomas*
RUTHIE BLACHMAN		HAROLD	*David McKay*
	Carolyn Hummel	REV. WILSON	*Wyrley Birch*
CARLOS	*Tino Valenti*	MILLY MOON	*Hope Emerson*

SYNOPSIS: Act I. Evening. Act II. A week later, in the late afternoon. Act III. A few days later. Afternoon. During this act the curtain will be lowered a moment to denote the passing of a few hours.

The entire action of the play takes place in the living-room of the Blachman home in Tucson, Arizona. Time. 1916.

PLAYS ABOUT BOARDING-HOUSES offer an understandable temptation not only to novice playwrights but to the lazier species of experienced. The nature of the setting makes it possible to introduce a quota of varied types and characters without the usual dramaturgical difficulties. With a boarding-house, the necessity for rational and ingenious explanations for such introductions disappears; the playwright can bring on, without apology, any shape or form of human flesh, however anomalous and grotesque.

The present playwrights, Hollywood movie scenario writers by profession, have outdone in this respect those playwrights in the past who have peopled their boarding-houses with everything from an embodiment of the Saviour (*The*

Passing of The Third Floor Back) to Jack-the-Ripper (*The Lodger*) and from hypothetical Bluebeards and thieves (*At Mrs. Beam's*) to snake lovers and home manufacturers of fireworks (*You Can't Take It With You*). Their roster includes, among others, the combination president of a bank, street-car line and laundry who hasn't a sou, an idiotic boy poet, a nymphomaniac, an old frontier trader with a filthy mind, a woman who spends all her time in the bathroom, a pair of grafting children, a street-car conductor, an Indian, a Negress, a female vaudeville yodeler six and one-half feet tall, the widow of a wholesale grocer who imagines that she is being lasciviously pursued by Indians, a supposed German spy, a socially conscious young man from Boston, a seller of can-openers, a male boarder who has a penchant for sneaking up the back stairs into women's rooms, a business tycoon from Perth Amboy, New Jersey, a woman over-conscious of her Dixie ancestry, a clergyman, a Mexican raiser of poultry, and a schoolmarm. Only missing are Leopold and Loeb.

Exercising the liberty with Miss Taylor's book which as film writers they have exercised with the literary purchases of Hollywood, the playwrights have contrived an exhibit that bears the same close resemblance to the essence of the book that the usual motion picture bears to the work from which it was derived. The liberty on this occasion is, however, of a markedly different nature than that indulged in in screen quarters.

It becomes increasingly evident that the average Hollywood movie scenario writer views the theatre much in the same light that a gob who has been at sea for a protracted period views port. It represents to him, as hereinbefore noted, the opportunity for the fling that has long been denied him by official discipline in the form of Hays office censorship and, at last given the chance, he jumps at it like a sailor at the first blonde.

The season has provided us with some touching pictures of the boys on the loose. Edward Chodorov, executing an Houdini escape from the Hollywood straitjacket, had the time of his life cutting up sex capers in *Those Endearing*

Young Charms. Another film literatus, Sheldon Davis, made Chodorov's holiday look like Blue Monday in Erie, Pa., with the anatomical celebration called *Try And Get It.* Nunnally Johnson, one of the illustrious yeomen on the Hollywood lots, had himself such a biological spree in *The World's Full Of Girls* that he has since been under strict doctors' orders to rest up. Ernest Pascal pleasured himself a picnic in *Peepshow* of such sexy proportions as must have made his colleagues at home boil with envy. And here we have the brothers Epstein gayly privileging themselves a long-distance nose-thumbing at Mr. Hays which must give that circumspect gentleman the creeps.

The boys have overlooked nothing to make their call in port self-exciting. They have grabbed at every chance to be naughty like starved mice at cheese. Where a writer with no Hollywood suppressions to get rid of might have foregone the temptation to be bawdy, they have taken off their Vine street coats (the ones with the eight-inch checks and pearl buttons) and have pitched in with the abandon of a couple of tars on a bender. That they have enjoyed their vacation enormously was evident on the opening night when, I was informed by persons who observed them, they warmly embraced each other and danced a little congratulatory jig at every line that would have made someone like S. N. Behrman punctiliously blush in embarrassment.

The worst of it is that I seem to have had almost as good a time as they did. I say almost because they pile on the indelicacies so unremittingly that one suffers a periodic surfeit. But the indelicacies are for the most part so funny and so forthright and unmincing that they are irresistible, even to one who is inclined to look askance at a smoking-car masquerading as a theatre stage.

The play they have built around the saucy gags isn't much in the eyes of criticism. It simply introduces a lot of eccentrics into the Arizona boarding-house of a quarter-century or so ago and causes them to put the gags into motion. It also rather strainfully seeks to pass itself off for a play by including for moral respite a straight young love story and by desperately dragging in some spy business and an impromptu financial windfall to achieve an ending to what has no dramaturgical beginning or middle. It further violates good dramaturgy by losing all sight of certain of its most interesting characters — the nymphomaniac for one — in its later passages, has intermittent recourse to such established humor as the single bathroom in an eleven-room house, and engages in such equally established stage business as the man making to embrace a woman and accidentally embracing another man instead. But small matter. One doesn't think too much of such things when one is in the clutch of laughter, any more than one thinks of Aristotle at a gay minstrel show, of Schlegel at a comical burlesque show, or of William Archer at an hilarious farce like this.

The company, headed by Rhys Williams and Mary Philips, was tip-top; the setting by Howard Bay humorously correct; and the direction by Lester Vail first-rate.

BOBINO. April 6, 1944

A play with music, designed for children, by Stanley Kauff-
mann and Leonard Marker. Produced for a series of mati-
nees by the American Theatre For Young Folks, organized
by Henri Leiser, in the Adelphi Theatre.

PRINCIPALS

Alfred L. Linder, Jack Bittner, Mae Cooper, Bernard Kay, Ronnie Jacoby,
Priscilla Draghi, Peggy Ribble, Mary Ellen Glass, Herbert Kenwith,
George Bloostein, Margaret Coates, and the four Paulette sisters.

SHOWN ORIGINALLY some time before in the little downtown Studio Theatre, the entertainment is apparently,
judging from their reaction, well suited to the tastes of
youngsters, although the management's firmly expressed
belief that it is equally suited to the tastes of adults is open
to considerable doubt. It hasn't quite enough fresh imagination and humor for that. Composed in the once-upon-a-
time form, the versified fable dealing with a boy who understands the language of the birds and beasts involves
King Pompo, the descendant of a long line of rulers defec-
tive in mental gifts; Celestina and Fontanell, the customary princess and prince; Bulzaboo, the ubiquitous giant;
Cupid, with bow and arrow; and the not unfamiliar quota
of animals — lion, tiger, horse, monkey, et al. — impersonated by humans. In sum, a vaudeville with a thread of
fairy-tale running through it, with humor derived largely
from the antics of the impersonated animals, and with sentiment extracted largely from the emotions implicit in the
more innocent popular ballads.

PUBLIC RELATIONS. April 6, 1944

A comedy by Dale Eunson. Produced for 29 performances by Robert Blake in the Mansfield Theatre.

Program

Martin	*Owen Coll*	Dolores Maxwell	
Sophie Sawyer	*Suzanne Jackson*		*Yolanda Ugarte*
Nancy Mason	*Frances Henderson*	Girl Reporter	*Joan Beard*
David Robinson	*Bradford Hunt*	Madge Torrance	*Betty Blythe*
Mr. Bartlett	*James Russo*	Eleanor Hollis	*Virginia Sherry*
Maurice Maxwell	*Michael Ames*	Frank Hollis	*Mason Adams*
Anita Sawyer	*Ann Andrews*	Bubbles	*Lynette Browne*
Wallace Maxwell			
	Philip Merivale		

SYNOPSIS: Act I. *Early afternoon.* Act II. Scene 1. *Sunday afternoon.* Scene 2. *About 9 o'clock Sunday night.* Act III. *Monday afternoon.*

The action, throughout, takes place over a weekend in the living-room of "The White House," Beverly Hills, California, in the summer of 1942.

Mr. Eunson is a denizen of the Hollywood studios, although not regularly in the capacity of a scenario writer. His exhibit is a Hollywood play and, like most Hollywood plays written by such denizens, a very bad one. Not being a scenario writer, the author's emphasis is not primarily on sex but on what he apparently believes is a rapt theatrical interest in the personalities of well-known screen figures. Like others who have suffered a similar delusion, he very quickly discovered that the theatre is not in the least concerned with such fowl. The consequence was his play's prompt failure.

But even were the aforesaid interest existent, Mr. Eunson's ability whether as a student of human eccentricities or as a playwright would be clearly insufficient to take advantage of it. His humor is of the species that beseeches response from such hoary facetiæ as a woman's indignant objection to being addressed as Madam; his dialogic delicacy

embraces such fragrances as allusions to sweat and depila-
tories; his dramaturgy is of the sort that causes a number
of his chief episodes to occur off-stage; and his conception
of dramatic comedy is to bring on a lot of ill-assorted couples, have them elaborately sneer at one another, and ring
down his act-curtains when they momentarily run out of
sarcasm.

The characters set against one another are a renowned
screen pair of the silent picture days who have been di-
vorced and who have remarried, the man a hard-boiled
young show-girl, the woman, a young dolt connected with
the industry; the son of the couple, a follower in his father's screen footsteps, and his young wife, a movie actress;
and an assortment of screen hussies, young and old, snide
third generation offspring, shabby in-laws, and the indige-
nous like.

Although, as observed, the sex note is not the evening's
main vibration, it is by no means entirely silent. One of
the female characters has the man-itch; one of the male
characters in the early stages of his marriage is already carrying on with a movie wench; and another tries to recapture his youth by physical contacts with eighteen-year-old
pushovers. Mr. Eunson is not dirty in the sense that many
of the ̇Hollywood writers are when they essay compositions
for the stage; he is rather dirty by indirection, like a wolf
avoiding in conversation with a feminine vis-à-vis any suggestion of four-letter words and what they stand for but
slyly insinuating his purpose in metaphorical synonyms.

The only really acceptable play thus far written about
Hollywood remains *Once In A Lifetime,* whose authors,
the Messrs. Kaufman and Hart, were of that world quite
apart. It was a good play because it was written by men expert in the craft of playwriting. It was also a good play because its authors were not part and parcel of their subject
matter and hence so deeply a part of it that they were either
overly taken in by its direct dramatic possibilities or overly
rebellious at its cheap pretensions. Mr. Eunson offers himself as a combination of the two points of view. But, as
might perhaps be expected, he hasn't the gift to realize the

first or to conceal the fundamental stridor of the second in the persuasions of satire.

The acting company wandered around the stage as if browsing in a second-hand book store. And the direction of Edward Childs Carpenter, which was responsible, was further of the kind which caused the characters, when spoken to, to adjust themselves either upstage or ten feet removed from the speaker, giving the whole the aspect of questions fired at so many lecturers by members of the audience.

In sum, an all-around botch.

FOLLOW THE GIRLS. APRIL 8, 1944

A musical show, with book by Guy Bolton, Eddie Davis and Fred Thompson, music and lyrics by Dan Shapiro, Milton Pascal and Phil Charig. Produced with success by Dave Wolper in the New Century Theatre.

PROGRAM

YOKEL SAILOR	*Bill Tabbert*	MARINE	*Charles Conaway, Jr.*
DOORMAN	*Ernest Goodhart*	BUBBLES LAMARR	*Gertrude Niesen*
FIRST GIRL FAN	*Terry Kelly*	SPUD DOOLITTLE	*Tim Herbert*
SECOND GIRL FAN	*Rae Macgregor*	DINKY RILEY	*Buster West*
BOB MONROE	*Frank Parker*	PHYLLIS BRENT	*Toni Gilman*
ANNA VISKINOVA	*Irina Baronova*	DAN DALEY	*Robert Tower*
GOOFY GALE	*Jackie Gleason*	PETTY OFFICER BANNER	*Lee Davis*
SEAMAN PENNYWHISTLE		CAPTAIN HAWKINS	*Walter Long*
	Frank Kreig	FELIX CHARREL	*Val Valentinoff*
CATHERINE PEPBURN		OFFICER FLANAGAN	
	Geraldine Stroock		*George Spaulding*
PEGGY BAKER	*Dorothy Keller*	DANCE TEAM	*The Di Gitanos*
SAILOR VAL	*Val Valentinoff*		

SYNOPSIS: Act I. Scene 1. *Outside Spotlight Canteen — evening in August, 1943.* Scene 2. *Inside Spotlight Canteen — same evening.* Scene 3. *Outside Naval Training Station, Great Neck, L. I. — next day.* Scene 4. *Trophy room, Great Neck estate.* Act II. Scene 1. *Flower garden, Great Neck estate.* Scene 2. *Room in house — midnight.* Scene 3. *Navy Park, Great Neck, L. I. — next day.* Scene 4. *Good ship Lady Luck — four weeks later.* Scene 5. *Inside Spotlight Canteen — next night.*

M R. WOLPER, who here bowed himself in as a theatrical impresario, is a Broadway night club operator blandly indifferent to the fact that the faculties of customers when not impaired by alcoholic liquor and distracted by night club osphresiology are likely to tend toward some discrimination. In testimony whereto, I offer a chronological outline of this, his maiden effort.

8:40 p.m. — Opening: The chorus boys dressed as soldiers, sailors and marines singing the stock introductory number whose lyric consists largely of popular names in

the news: Katharine Cornell, Lunt and Fontanne, Frank
Sinatra, Walter Winchell, et al. Enter the fat comedian in
civilian clothes who wants to enter the canteen to see the
strip-teaser whom he loves. He is refused admission and is
informed that only soldiers and sailors may enter. A sailor
approaches and tells him that his uniform has a zipper at-
tachment. After cavorting about the stage for several minutes, indicating pleased meditation, the fat comic rips off
the sailor's uniform. Blackout.

9 p.m. — Inside the canteen, with the girls dressed in
enough spangles to outfit a circus. The tenor sings a song,
"The grass is always green where you are, the sky is always
blue where you are." The fat comic reappears, curves his
right hand over his head and ejaculates, "What the hell!"
Follow two hoofers who negotiate a fast dance, the woman
partner singing a ditty called "You Don't Dance" and the
male partner, at the conclusion of the hoofing, drolly kicking her in the seat.

9:15 p.m. — The chorus reappears in more spangles and
is followed by the entrance of Bubbles, the strip-teaser,
who delivers a number called "Strip Flips Hip," duly accompanied by the hip flips. The fat comic curves his right
hand over his head and ejaculates, "What the hell!" Enter
a regal brunette. The strip-teaser tells her to go about her
business. "I am my own mistress!" haughtily retorts the regal one. "That must be wonderful for you for a change!"
snaps back the stripper.

9:25 p.m. — Two male and one female hoofer perform
a hard-shoe number, the meanwhile delivering a ditty,
"Thanks For a Lousy Evening." Re-enter Bubbles, the
stripper, backed by the chorus in still more spangles, and
followed by the fat comic, who curves his hand over his
head and ejaculates, "What the hell!" "When I was in burlesque," observes Bubbles, "they yelled 'Lights off' and I
thought they said 'Tights off'." Then a song by the fat
comic to Bubbles: "You're perf, you're magnif, you're won-
derf, you're grand."

9:32 p.m. — "Here comes Anna Viskinova, the greatest
ballet dancer in the world!" "She's beautiful!" "She's the

toast of the town!" "You'll all adore her!" Enter Irina Baronova, of the Russian ballet, who is made to execute, of all things, a stock Marche Militaire.

9:42 p.m. — The girls come on in five times the number of spangles they have worn before, parade around, and exit. Bubbles reappears in a purple light and moans a paraphrase of "Body and Soul" called "Twelve O'clock and All's Well."

9:48 p.m. — A hoofer shuffles before a curtain while the scene is being shifted. The fat comic appears, curves his hand over his head and ejaculates, "What the hell!" Blackout.

9:50 p.m. — Scene: the trophy room. The chorus girls come on in even more spangles. The fat comic mentions the Virgin Islands. The tenor in love with the ballet dancer says wittily, "I have an idea that the virginity of the natives is somewhat overestimated." He follows with a reprise, "The grass is always green where you are, the sky is always blue where you are." At its conclusion, he observes that he thinks the regal brunette is a suspicious character. "She is a witch," he allows. "You mean bitch," exclaims the ballet dancer.

10 p.m. — The ballet dancer does another turn in a red dress, the number naturally being called "Flamingo Dance."

10:10 p.m. — Bubbles and the entire company, in spangles, appear after the three hoofers before noted have negotiated another dance, ending with one male kicking the other in the seat. The fat comic curves his hand over his head and ejaculates, "What the hell!" "Follow the Girls," loudly sings the ensemble. Curtain.

Act II. 10:20 p.m. — The girls enter clad in enough spangles to outfit ten circuses. The scene being a flower garden, the tenor, backed by the sailors, sings a song about John Paul Jones. Another dance by the hoofers, at the conclusion of which the female member for a change kicks one of the males in the seat. The fat comic curves his hand over his head and ejaculates, "What the hell!" The tenor and ballet dancer come on arm in arm. The tenor reprises, "The grass is always green where you are, the sky is always blue where you are."

10:35 p.m. — A room in a house. In order to keep his rival from marrying the strip-teaser, the fat comic gives him a Mickey Finn and tells him he is on a boat and that the sea is very rough. Convincing himself, the fat comic rushes to the bathroom to vomit. On come the two hoofers who squirt seltzer bottles at the rival to persuade him that he is drowning. Blackout.

10:45 p.m. — The show-girls, spangled to the ears, walk on in the rôles of bridesmaids. Bubbles (Gertrude Niesen) sings a saucy number, "I Wanna Get Married," which, humorously delivered, provides some surcease, even though one verse has to do with the singer's purchase of a bureau and the wish that some man may share her drawers.

10:50 p.m. — Another dance by the ballet dancer, followed by a couple of ballroom dancers with the male partner swinging the female around on his shoulders (the ballroom they come from must be peculiar). The regal brunette then reappears. The fat comic learns that she is a German spy, thus freeing from suspicion the ballet dancer. Several plants in the audience hiss the brunette, whereupon she walks to the footlights and drolly hisses the audience. The fat comic curves his hand over his head and ejaculates, "What the hell!" (He has previously donned a WAVE's blue skirt, leading an elderly officer to mistake him for a woman and to make a date with him.)

11 p.m. — The chorus now again issues forth in more spangles than have been seen on the stage in the last fifty years combined. The fat comic and Bubbles, aided by two of the comedy hoofers, sing a song, "A Tree That Grows in Brooklyn," which scintillatingly includes allusions to Flatbush, Jamaica and Canarsie. The hoofers go into another dance, terminating with one kicking another in the seat.

11:10 p.m. — The entire bespangled company gathers at the footlights and lifts its voices, "The grass is always green where you are, the sky is always blue where you are." The fat comic puts his arms around Bubbles; the tenor puts

his arm around the ballet dancer; the hoofers again kick
one another in the seats; and the fat comic curves his hand
over his head and ejaculates, "What the hell!" Curtain.

The public, albeit sober, thought it was swell.

"— BUT NOT GOODBYE." April 11, 1944

A fantasy originally known as I'll Be Seein' You, *by George Seaton. Produced with bad luck, resulting in only 23 performances, by John Golden, in association with Harry Joe Brown, in the 48th Street Theatre.*

PROGRAM

Sam Griggs	Harry Carey	Ralph Humphrey	Hal K. Dawson
Howard Baker	Wendell Corey	Jimmie Griggs	John Conway
Amy Griggs	Elizabeth Patterson	Dr. Wilson	Raymond Largay
Jennifer Griggs	Sylvia Field	Benjamin Griggs	J. Pat O'Malley
Tom Carter	Frank Wilcox	Rev. Pritchard	Harold McGee

SYNOPSIS: Act I. *Early evening.* Act II. Scene 1. *A few minutes later.* Scene 2. *Two hours later.* Act III. *Immediately afterward.*

The action takes place in the home of the Griggs family, somewhere along the coast of New England, in the summer of 1910.

THE EXCEPTIONAL Hollywood scenario writer who does not view the stage as the opportunity for Hays circumscribed sex jinks seems to view it as the opportunity for his hidden talents in fantasy. We thus periodically get a Ben Hecht soaring into the theatre with a *Lily Of The Valley,* a Ketti Frings with a *Mr. Sycamore,* and a George Seaton with an exhibit like that under consideration. Mr. Seaton has been no more auspicious in his flight than any of the others.

Death and the hereafter are apparently favorite topics of some of the Hollywood refugees, and in Mr. Seaton's case they are again on tap. A paterfamilias dies of a heart ailment and, since he has gambled with monies vital to his family's future, reappears as a spirit intent upon retrieving the funds. In the quest, he is aided by the spirit of his father, who successfully calls upon the invisible powers when crises present themselves. Under Mr. Seaton's Hollywood wand, the fantasy takes on all the rich delicacy of an old Palace vaudeville act, suitably festooned with such gags as the paterfamilias ghost's, "I'm so scared I'll probably get

heart failure," with his father's ghost's rejoinder, "It's a little late for that," and with such others as one spook's indignant observation to another, "I wouldn't be seen dead with
you!" Nor is the delicacy of the fabric diminished in its
concluding moments, which show the villain converted into
a ghost by a divine stroke of lightning, turning his back to
the audience at the final curtain, and disclosing his bare
backside through a rent in his lightning-struck trousers.

Since the action of the play is laid in 1910 and since most
of the dreadful jocosities are placed in the mouth of the
ghost of a man then already long dead, the playwright
might contend in extenuation that their lack of humorous
juice is apposite. But it is contrarily plain that he esteems
himself something of a contemporary wit, which is an over-
estimation equal to his regard for himself as a hand at fanciful caprice.

The play which assures audiences that there is a life after
death is, if its other elements are half-way acceptable, likely
to find a hospitable reception. In time of war that reception naturally becomes even warmer. So great in such periods is people's wish to believe that, far from being the end
of things, death is really the beginning of an everlasting
Stork Club, that any exhibit which can faintly convince
them of the fact is in line to get the money.

Memory seems to indicate that it takes an exceptionally
bad such ghost play to fail. In the general run, show an
audience David Warfield returning from the grave to look
sagaciously after a mistreated little boy whom he has loved
on earth or Leonora Corbett returning gayly from the beyond from what apparently has been a semester with Della
Fox and the audience doesn't care a hoot whether or not it
is run over by a taxi and killed on its way home. Show it
Jane Cowl coming back after death in the latest creations
by Mildred Manning and looking better than ever or
Martha Scott emerging from the cemetery looking like the
candy bride on a wedding-cake and telling everyone that
death is more enjoyable than the *Follies* and existence
thereafter akin to life in pre-war Paree, and you have to
hire an extra man in the box-office to count up.

It has been that way for more than three decades now. Only when a play is otherwise so poor or, like *Bury The Dead* or *Miracle At Verdun,* definitely less sentimental in its approach to the funeral parlor, may that extra man be dispensed with. It is thus that the plays in both categories which have brought back the deceased in soldiers' uniforms and made them comport themselves more like George Sokolsky than like Faust and Rip Van Winkle at a college reunion alone have failed to qualify with the trade.

Other things being equal, however, the customers — save maybe the younger ones at the matinees — experience a genial comfort in any workmanlike stage demonstration of the theory that Kaufman and Hart were talking through their hats when they said that you can't take it with you. For that, not only in this but in other directions, is the way of a theatre whose mission in the popular estimation is the business of reassurance. If, for example, it can sufficiently reassure the ladies that a woman of fifty-five may, if she desires, merely by putting on a young girl's dress handily win away her daughter's twenty-year-old beau or the men that any fellow so creaky he can barely stand up may capture his beautiful stenographer from the Yale football hero simply through a wistful confession to the beauty that he is old enough to be her father — if it can do that, two extra men are needed to handle the tickets.

Since death is presently uppermost in many persons' minds and sorrowfully deep in their hearts, the appearance sooner or later of some such play as this " — But Not Goodbye" was therefore to be expected. It was a pity, with all the easy money aching to be spent, that it wasn't a better and more persuasive play than it was, but even so it seemed for the time being — until its star actor fell ill, had to leave the cast, and thus threw a wrench into the box-office — to serve the thirst for reassurance in the case of that share of the public which isn't particularly discriminating as to its eschatological booze. To the other share it was merely another defeated attempt on the part of a Hollywood movie writer to negotiate sound fantasy.

Mr. Seaton, I fear, lacks the gift to make any excursion

into metaphysics more than a vaudeville ferry ride. After all, if I, for one, am to be persuaded that the after-life is something of a fact, the job will have to be done by a playwright with more convincing materials in hand than old Lew Morrison lightning and thunder tricks, jokes about living in California being just the same as being dead, spirits who have apparently been spending all their time in Heaven with Winchell Smith, Thurston, and Block and Sully, and mundane villains made up to look like a cross between Mephisto and Frank Harris.

The acting in the main was a derivative of the old Seth Prouty and Marcus Loew schools, as was Richard Whorf's stage direction equally of the Denman Thompson and E. F. Albee.

THE SEARCHING WIND. April 12, 1944

A drama by Lillian Hellman. Produced with large success by Herman Shumlin in the Fulton Theatre.

Program

Moses Taney	*Dudley Digges*	Ponette	*Alfred Hesse*
Emily Hazen		1st Italian Waiter	
	Cornelia Otis Skinner		*Edgar Andrews*
Alexander Hazen	*Dennis King*	Hotel Manager	*Walter Kohler*
Catherine Bowman		Eppler	*William F. Schoeller*
	Barbara O'Neil	Capt. Heydebreck	*John Cole*
2nd Italian Waiter		Edward Halsey	*Eric Latham*
	Joseph de Santis	James Sears	*Eugene Earl*
Samuel Hazen	*Montgomery Clift*	Count Max Von Stammer	
Sophronia	*Mercedes Gilbert*		*Arnold Korff*

SYNOPSIS: Act I. Scene 1. *The drawing-room of the Hazen home, Washington, D. C., 7:30 of a spring evening, 1944.* Scene 2. *A room in the Grand Hotel, Rome, October, 1922.* Scene 3. *Same as Scene 1. Two hours later.* Act II. Scene 1. *A corner of a restaurant in Berlin, autumn, 1923.* Scene 2. *A room in Hotel Meurice, Paris, September, 1938.* Scene 3. *The drawing-room of the Hazen home, about 10:30, same evening as Act I, Scene 1.*

S︎UCH CRITICS as are given to estimating the importance of a play, whatever its quality, in proportion to the importance of its subject matter have proclaimed Miss Hellman's exhibit a masterpiece of dramaturgy. A philippic against compromise and appeasement, it is in the view of less journalistic appraisers rather simply an overwrought, often muddled and generally subordinate example of pamphleturgy.

Miss Hellman, who began as a dramatic artist, shows steadily increasing signs of having converted herself into a crusader, with the stage and occasionally the films called upon to serve as her soap-box. The odiousness of the Nazi doctrine, the plight of the Jews, the holiness of the Soviet ideal, the danger of pacifism and appeasement — these and other such topics disturb her pristine artistic calm and goad

her to battle. Even in her extra-theatrical life she no longer
knows peace of soul. It is a rare committee formed to improve the accommodations of the Negroes at the Ritz-Plaza,
or to make Palestine a future Newport for the Jews, or to
improve the quality of impoverished Chinese peasants'
chow mein, or to instruct Tom Lamont in the underesti-
mated virtues of the Stalin economy, or to guarantee the
right of free speech to Morris Ernst that does not find her
name high up on its stationery. That all this is maybe here
and there commendable enough and that it redounds to
the estimability of Miss Hellman as a public-spirited woman
is obvious. But one fears that it has taken its toll of her as
a dramatist of any critical merit.

Her present and latest play clearly indicates the damage
done by the infections. It is not, of course, that a dramatist may not choose any subject he or she elects. That surely
needs no restatement. It is rather that chronic indignation,
which seems to have become an attribute of Miss Hellman,
has a way of invalidating dramaturgically the most important of subjects. Hot wrath is the province of cheap melodrama. Worthy drama calls for at least a portion of equa-
nimity, cool reflection, and philosophical poise.

In *The Searching Wind,* the author presents us with an
American diplomat and his family in the Washington of
the present year and, by means of flashbacks, the Grand Hotel in Rome at the time of Mussolini's rise to power, a Berlin restaurant (evidently Horcher's) at the time of the up-
rising against the Jews, and the Hotel Meurice in Paris on
the eve of Munich. The progress of political laissez-faire
and appeasement is depicted in counterpoint to her three
central characters, the diplomat, his wife and his mistress,
whose personal conduct parallels that of those responsible,
in the author's opinion, for the eventual mess of world
war. The net effect is of a more or less stock triangle play
acted in front of a series of news reels.

In neither of the two stories, the political nor the love,
which are dovetailed only with transparent strain, is Miss
Hellman's thinking very clear or her direction firmly in
hand. Her diplomat protagonist, though he eventually is

brought to see appeasement in its true light, is essentially so puny a figure that employing him as a pivotal argument in the crisis suggests a William Steig drawing of a small boy dreaming of cornering Hitler at the point of a wooden bayonet. Her elderly liberal publisher who wearily retires from the fight and is cynically willing to let things take their course is weakened as a character of any retrospective consequence by being provided with a mind that indulges in stock jokes about Harvard and, generally, the conversational virtuosity of a retired banker out of the old Charles Klein drama. Her woman character beloved of the diplomat, a teacher of English in a women's college, is embellished with a persistent Ibsen expression and the unrelieved emotions of a persecuted Hal Reid heroine, making not only the admiration of her by the protagonist the mark of a sentimental half-wit but herself a waywardly comic figure. And so with some of the others.

The dramaturgy, besides suffering from the handicap usually imposed by flashbacks, resorts, among other things, to the scene that involves the butler and maidservant in a discussion of the family's affairs and the scene between the two hostile women taking stock of each other across a table, in more than one way reminiscent of Strindberg's *The Stronger*. The dialogue, when it essays wit, regales itself with such paste as "I often wonder if people drink to talk or talk to drink." The technique of dialogic economy resorts to such familiar subterfuges as "I know what you are thinking," "I know what you are going to say; don't say it," and the like. And the intrinsic philosophy is no more vernal than charging the older generation with all the mistakes that have led to the present catastrophe and placing the hope for the future in the hands of theoretically all-sapient youth.

The play throughout has the air of being about to say something of enormous weight and consequence and never saying it. The impression is of a relay race that starts off under bright and promising skies and that, no sooner the first runner hands the second the object to carry on with, is drenched with wet, delaying the latter in his delivery of the object to the third runner all too long, and causing the third then not only to drop it but to slip and fall sprawling on the track.

The conclusion of the play rests in nothing more original than the sharp telling off of those members of the family hypothetically responsible for the present state of affairs by the young soldier son who has been wounded in Italy. If in no other way Miss Hellman therein indicates her dramatic poverty. Not only is the business stale and of easy hokum all compact, but no modern dramatist of consequence would argue his or her point to a finish by recourse to any such facile and highly sentimental device. One can not convincingly counter what is implicitly adult by youthful emotionalism. The sound dramatist pursues logic, and particularly if it be concerned with any such theme as Miss Hellman's, through the reflections of maturity; he does not end the chase in the mind of a juvenile actor, however personable, sympathetic and eloquent. That is for matinee audiences, or the films.

I have told before of Eugene O'Neill's remark to me in connection with his projected cycle of plays dealing in a sense with personalized American history. "American history?" I asked him. "Yes," he smiled; "but you can be damned sure not the kind of dramatic writing that has an actor rush in shouting, 'Andrew Jackson has just been elected President!'" *The Searching Wind* is the kind of dramatic writing that figuratively has someone periodically rushing in and shouting that Mussolini is marching on Rome, that Chamberlain is on his way to Munich, and that Hitler is about to march against France.

Miss Hellman's play, in short, while it has several moments in her valid older style — those involving the very ably drawn character of the German diplomat among them — is supremely unworthy of the expectations which she herself through some of her earlier performances has induced in us. The acting varied from first-rate in the instance of Arnold Korff and pleasantly competent in the instances of Cornelia Otis Skinner, Dudley Digges and Montgomery Clift to indifferent and worse in the cases of Barbara O'Neil and some other members of the company. Herman Shumlin's direction, while expert in its details, was in its overtones so grimly pretentious that it emphasized doubly the pretensions of the script.

PRETTY LITTLE PARLOR. April 17, 1944

A tragi-drama by Claiborne Foster. Produced and withdrawn after 8 performances by John Moses and Ralph Bellamy in the National Theatre.

Program

Jefferson Hilyard		Clotilde	*Stella Adler*
	Sidney Blackmer	Mr. Kennedy	*Paul Parks*
Anastasia	*Marilyn Erskine*	Dennis Baldwin	*Kip Good*
Dora	*Joan Tetzel*	Mr. Jonas	*Edward Begley*
Henry	*Mel Roberts*		

SYNOPSIS: Act I. *Afternoon.* Act II. *About six months later.* Scene 1. *Before dinner.* Scene 2. *After dinner.* Act III. *Afternoon. Three days later.*

Time. *1905.*

The entire action of the play takes place in the Hilyards' parlor of a moderately priced family hotel in a small city in the United States.

THE AUTHOR is a retired actress who has evidently spent the larger part of her retirement in reading popular plays of the Nineties and in attending many of those of more recent vintage. It is a pity that she did not exercise greater discrimination in both directions, since in both cases she has clearly absorbed the worst elements. The plays which she has read have infected her with such dialogue as, "I knew nothing of the great, outside world; I was like a child, innocent in the ways of men, to whom all was wonder; I did not mean to do wrong; I was a plaything of the fates." And the plays which she has seen have left their mark in such situations out of *Bought And Paid For* as the man-of-affairs' blunt sexual proposal to the woman who would help her weakling husband; such scenes out of a dozen problem dramas as that wherein the husband sodden with drink implores his wife to resume marital relations and is imperiously sent reeling back to his drunken couch; and such a central character as the uncompromisingly rapacious and evil woman who will do anything to gain her selfish ends.

Wielding a brush dipped solely into either black or white, Miss Foster paints her characters in billboard style, and with all the subtlety implicit in that art. And writing with a pen dipped similarly into either snake-poison or peach jelly, she causes them to speak like either movie villains or movie ingénues.

In the picture of her central figure, the author has outdone all her Broadway competitors. She has rolled into one the combined attributes of all the season's vulgar tarts, domineering witches, married cheats, calculating prostitutes, shrewish money-grubbers, and other such odoriferæ. In the hands of a competent playwright such a character may, of course, take on a genuine depth, psychological profundity, and dramatic value. But Miss Foster, being no Strindberg or Wedekind or, for that matter, even George Broadhurst, projects merely an emetic who suggests Pinero at the age of seven writing blackmail letters to Lucretia Borgia, on toilet paper.

Miss Adler, who pleasured herself in the rôle, brought to its portrayal all the tricks of the species of Middle Western stock company actress of the Nineties who used to receive the women customers on the stage after the matinees and autograph her photographs for them, including the business of tapping fingers on a table to indicate meditation, indecision, impatience, sly cunning, dawning resolution, acute nervousness, and everything else save alone good acting. The direction by Ralph Bellamy heightened the unintentional parody of the whole.

SHEPPEY. April 18, 1944

A "portrait" by W. Somerset Maugham. Produced to mi-nor box-office returns for 23 performances by Jacques Chambrun in the Playhouse.

Program

Albert	Harry Sothern	Miss James	Vera Fuller Mellish
First Customer		Bessie Legros	Doris Patston
	Wallace Widdecombe	A Strange Woman	
Miss Grange	Cathleen Cordell		Catherine Anderson
Sheppey	Edmund Gwenn	Mrs. Miller	Barbara Everest
Second Customer		Florrie	Frances Heflin
	Oswald Marshall	Ernest Turner	
Mr. Bolton	Alexander Clark		Anthony Kemble-Cooper
Bradley	Gerald Savory	Dr. Jervis	Horace Cooper
A Reporter	Cledge Roberts	Cooper	Victor Beecroft

SYNOPSIS: Act I. *Bradley's barber shop in Bond Street, London.* Act II. Scene 1. *The living-room of Sheppey's house at Camberwell, London. A week later.* Scene 2. *Same, three days later.*

THIS IS ONE of its talented author's distinctly inferior performances. It amounts to what is basically so obvious a kleptomania in appropriating the standard ingredients of popular drama of the last fifty years as to be almost impertinent. Yet Maugham's irrepressible sardonicism and winking worldly humor contrive to make a share of the supine ingredients lively and acceptable. It is critically a poor play — it changes moods with little preparation and its middle section repetitively talks itself into desuetude — but it somehow persists in being often entertaining in spite of itself, like certain other critically poor plays.

It suggests internally a revue of sections of half a hundred plays. The protagonist who tries to practise the doctrines of Christ in the present world and who is crucified for his pains is out of Channing Pollock's *The Fool* and other such exhibits. The prostitute and thief who are taken into the benefactor's household and who, despite his kindness and generosity, yearn to go back to their old way of life are out of Haddon Chambers' *Passers-by* and plays of a kidney. The derision of the medical profession is out of Shaw's *The Doctor's Dilemma,* as the figure of Death with its gentle philosophy is out of Casella's *Death Takes A Holiday* and Osborn's *On Borrowed Time.* The sudden fortune through a winning sweepstakes ticket has figured, in one way or another, in scores of plays. And that is but part of the story.

If the characters are familiar, the humor machinery is hardly less so: the saucy manicurist who shows her legs on all occasions; the comical business incidental to shaving a man; the gags implicit in hair tonic; the posing for a newspaper photographer, with the unwelcome intruder horning into the picture; the pompous young ass with Parliament aspirations; the jokes involving kippers, Democracy, and Paris; the married man afraid of his wife; etc.

Nevertheless, with what seems to be in the nature of a sly challenge Maugham has taken over these dramatic and humorous remnants and constituted them very fair pastime. Laying hold of the stalest dramatic materials he has partly revivified them, and laying hold of the old humorous materials he has frequently squirted enough wit into them to make them bounce. That he has at least in a measure rewritten the play since it was originally shown in London and on the Continent more than a decade ago seems likely.

In that excellent book, *The Summing Up,* Maugham has written, "The public would be surprised if they knew how often an author's purport is misrepresented by the director's stupid obstinacy and how much vulgarity and silliness for which they blame him are due to the director. The director is a man of ideas, but of few, and that is a disastrous thing . . . A director who thinks of a scrap of dialogue, a bit of business or a scenic effect will attach so much importance to it that he will cheerfully hang up the action of the play or distort its meaning in order to introduce it. Too often the director is vain, self-opinionated and unimaginative; he is sometimes so autocratic that he will force the

cast to reproduce his own intonations and his own man-
nerisms; the actors, dependent on his good word to get
parts and on their docility to gain his favor, can but slav-
ishly do as they are told; thus taking all spontaneity from
their performance. The best director is the one who does
least."

Mr. Maugham, on this occasion at least, had to eat his
words. Cedric Hardwicke directed his play not only for everything there was in it, but for some valuable things that
weren't in it.

ALLAH BE PRAISED! April 19, 1944

*A signal musical comedy failure, book and lyrics by George
Marion, Jr.; music by Don Walker and Baldwin Bergersen.
Produced for 20 performances at a loss of $160,000 by Al-
fred Bloomingdale in the Adelphi Theatre.*

PROGRAM

CASWELL	Jack Albertson	TUBAGA	Anita Alvarez
RECEPTIONIST	Helen Bennett	EMIR	John Hoysradt
TEX O'CARROLL	Edward Roecker	ZARAH	Milada Mladova
CLERK	Sheila Bond	YOUSSOUF	Joey Faye
CITIZEN	Joey Faye	NIJ O'CARROLL	Pittman Corry
ABDUL	Sid Stone	MARCIA MASON MOORE	
BULBUL	Jack Albertson		Patricia Morison
CAROL O'CARROLL		MIMI McSLUMP	Jayne Manners
	Mary Jane Walsh	MERCHANT	Tom Powers
ROBERTA	Marge Ellis	McGRAB	Natalie Wynn
PAULA	Lee Joyce	GIRL ABOUT TEHERAN	
DORIS	Mary McDonnell		Eleanor Hall

The scenes are laid in New York, Persia, and Hollywood.
The time. *February 20 and 29, 1948.*

WHEN THE SHOW was tried out on the road and found to
be sorely wanting, Mr. Bloomingdale, the producer, who is
a member of the well-known New York department store
family, called in Cy Howard, a show fixer, and asked his
opinion as to what could be done to salvage the investment.
Howard took one look and, according to report, advised,
"Throw it away, and keep the store open nights." Mr.
Bloomingdale saw fit not to follow the counsel, brought the
show into New York, and the first-night audience instantaneously acclaimed Mr. Howard's acumen.

Handsomely set and costumed by the proficient George
Jenkins and Miles White, the exhibit offered nothing to
warrant the expensive background. The book was less a
book than a mere book jacket, and a flimsy jacket at that:
the skeleton sketch of a Dartmouth graduate who goes to

Persia and winds up, in a manner inscrutable to the closest
ear in the audience, with a harem of American women. The
bare bones clacked under a film of humor of the appended
nature:

1. "What is a eunuch?" — "A man about whom it is two bad."
2. "How many wives have you got?" — "365, one for each day
   in the year, and oh boy, this is Leap Year!"
3. "Speaking of mathematics, how did you get such a figure?"
   — "I eat too much."
4. "Is it a boy elephant or a girl elephant?" — "What difference can that possibly make?"
5. "You are inarticulated." — "Maybe, but I'm not incapaci-
   tated."
6. "I got my D at Dartmouth." — "You're sure it wasn't at
   Dannemora?"
7. "She's got a big asset." — "Her face is all right, too."

The highest inventiveness in the lyrics, in turn, was a
song called "What's New In New York," with the prescriptive catalogue of allusions to Lindy's and the local like.

Other items: a series of imitations of the radio broad-
casters Kaltenborn, Swing and Heatter by a night club performer who had been doing the same act around the cafés
for several years; three or four chorus dances in Oriental
rhythm, with the girls thrusting forth their right legs, as-
suming a half-sitting posture, and suddenly cocking their
heads to one side, as if to relieve a crick in the neck; the
scene in which a diminutive comedian made up to a six-
foot Amazon; the business in which two girls who looked
alike confused the comedian and made him believe he was
seeing things; the female vocalist who tried to get her song
numbers over by punctuating the lyrics with thrusts of her
fists at the audience; the uniform pronunciation of February as Febyouary; and the characters wittily named Bul-
bul, Tubaga, and Mimi McSlump.

The show with scenes in a harem seems to have had a peculiar fascination for novice producers ever since the day,
33 years ago, when one called *The Harem Doctor,* by T. E.
Murray and Eustace Baynes, showed up briefly in London.

Their notion probably is that it provides a facile opportunity for introducing the chorus girls in gauzy habiliments and for merchanting a sufficient number of risqué jests about eunuchs. Save for the omnipresent corpulent eunuch called Phatfellah and the ancient harem houri called Hasbeena, the novice producer of the present show has hewn generally to the familiar line. The one relieving feature of the evening was the appearance, among the stageful of robot dress models with plastered, upswung hair, wax features and pink-pomaded legs showing from their slit skirts, of the naturally attractive and accomplished Milada Mladova, even though I, for one, have now seen enough toe pirouettes to last me for life.

WAR PRESIDENT. April 24, 1944

A play by Nat Sherman. Produced by The Escholiers under the auspices of the Experimental Theatre, Inc., for two matinee performances in the Shubert Theatre.

Program

John Hay	*Philip Sand*
Joel Starbuck	*Kenneth Dana*
Mrs. Lincoln	*Joanna Roos*
Abraham Lincoln	*Joel Ashley*
Tad Lincoln	*Donald Rose*
Willie Lincoln	*Teddy Rose*
Bob Lincoln	*Harvey Marlowe*
Edwin M. Stanton	
	William Marceau
Gen. George B. McClellan	
	Alexander Scourby
Senator Benjamin Franklin	
Wade	*Russell Collins*
Senator Zachariah Chandler	
	Paul Ford
Mrs. Ellen McClellan	
	Barbara Pond
Gen. William F. Smith	
	Morton DaCosta
Fernando Wood	*Gregory Morton*
Horatio Seymour	*Peter Gregg*
Gen. Philip Kearny	
	Kenneth Dana
Gen. Joe Hooker	*Joseph Leon*
Horace Greeley	*Graham Velsey*
Congressman Kelly	*Bruce Halsey*

THE Experimental Theatre, Inc., seems to be acutely Lincoln-conscious. Last year it busied itself with *Yours, A. Lincoln,* a play based upon Otto Eisenschiml's book, *Why Was Lincoln Murdered?* It was a bad play. This year it has busied itself with a play showing Lincoln's relations with General McClellan, who was later to oppose him for the Presidency. It is a somewhat better play, but still a bad one.

In three acts, with scenes shifting from Lincoln's office in the White House to McClellan's headquarters in Washington and before Richmond, and covering the years 1861–1865, the action, euphemistically speaking, details the difficulties of the President with his dawdling and vainglorious General and subscribes to the theory that the latter was willing not to shatter Lee but to be satisfied with a military stalemate if guaranteed the Democratic nomination for the Presidency. The earlier portions of the play have a

measure of dramatic lift, but the later portions dawdle off
into a McClellan-like sluggishness. The whole has an air
of wide and intelligent reading and research ineffectually
cast into the mold of active drama.

HELEN GOES TO TROY. April 24, 1944

A new version of La Belle Hélène, *book by Gottfried Rein-hardt and John Meehan, Jr., lyrics by Herbert Baker, and musical arrangements of the Jacques Offenbach score and interpolations by Erich Wolfgang Korngold. Produced un-successfully by Yolanda Mero-Irion for the New Opera Company in the Alvin Theatre.*

PROGRAM

PHILOCOMUS	*George Rasely*	AJAX 1ST, KING OF SMALL	
CALCHAS	*Ralph Dumke*	NATION	*Jesse White*
HELEN, QUEEN OF SPARTA		AJAX 2ND	*Alfred Porter*
	Jarmila Novotna	MENELAUS, KING OF SPARTA	
ORESTES	*Donald Buka*		*Ernest Truex*
PARTHENIS	*Doris Blake*	AGAMEMNON	*Gordon Dilworth*
LEILA	*Phyllis Hill*	ACHILLES	*Hugh Johnson*
PARIS, PRINCE OF TROY		LADY-IN-WAITING	*Jane Kiser*
	William Horne	PREMIERE	*Katia Geleznova*
DISCORDIA	*Rose Inghram*	DANSEUSES	*Kathryn Lee*
MINERVA	*Doris Blake*		*Nancy Mann*
JUNO	*Rosalind Nadell*	PREMIER	*Michael Mann*
VENUS	*Peggy Corday*	DANCERS	*John Guelis*
POLICEMAN	*Michael Mann*		*George Chaffee*
WHITE WING	*John Guelis*		

SYNOPSIS: Act I. Scene 1. *The Temple of Jupiter in Sparta.* Scene 2. *Mount Ida.* Scene 3. *The Temple of Jupiter in Sparta.* Scene 4. *A street in Sparta.* Scene 5. *The Temple of Jupiter in Sparta.* Act II. Scene 1. *Helen's bath in the palace.* Scene 2. *King's private banquet hall.* Scene 3. *A road near Sparta.* Scene 4. *Helen's boudoir.* Scene 5. *Outside palace door.* Scene 6. *Helen's boudoir.* Scene 7. *Corridor in the palace.* Scene 8. *Main banquet hall.*

THE PRODUCTION bears approximately the same relation to the original *La Belle Hélène* that Stanislaus Stange's *Cashel Byron* bears to the novel of Bernard Shaw. The original Offenbach score, when it has not been cut outright, has been rearranged and reorchestrated; fourteen newly adapted numbers from the composer's *Périchole, Doctor Ox, Genevieve, Roi Carotte* and *Robinson Crusoe* have been interpolated; a 6/8 serenade from *The Bridge Of Sighs* has been changed into the modern fox trot tempo and further incorporated; the "Barcarolle" from *The Rhine Nymphs* and later *The Tales Of Hoffman* has been brought in as a so-called theme song; the book has been embellished with feeble topical allusions and such humor as dubbing Menelaus a louse, with his retort, "Yes, I am Menelouse"; the scene from the old burlesque shows wherein a husband suddenly counts the feet in his and his wife's bed and is dumfounded to find six instead of the expected four has been lugged in; Menelaus sings a snatch of Jerome Kern's "The Last Time I Saw Paris"; there is a number parodying grand opera; a can-can dance is introduced into the second act; and Helen appears at one point in a Cecil B. DeMille bathtub.

Patterned basically after the Max Reinhardt pre-war Berlin production, the exhibit additionally confounds the *La Belle Hélène* alumnus with goddesses who pronounce such a word as *exactly* as if its first syllable had been laid by several indignant hens; a drop curtain decorated with Neville Chamberlain's umbrella; a lyric about newsboys selling extras; a "Dance of Procreation" in which the participants comport themselves in terms of immaculate conception; a "Grecian Frieze" number that more closely suggests Broadway night club wallpaper; a Paris who looks disconcertingly like David O. Selznick; and a Calchas, the able prognosticator, who thoughtlessly resembles Wendell Willkie.

There is something yet more disturbing in the looks department. Jarmila Novotna has a singing voice beside which the legendary Helen's would unquestionably have sounded like Tom Dewey's. She also has other obvious and applaudable gifts. But, when the management requests that one imagine her to be such a beauty as the world never before or since has heard of, one finds oneself helpless to oblige. The order, of course, is a pretty large one in the case of any actress who appears in the rôle. Nevertheless, the imagination was sufficiently satisfied when Lillian Russell appeared in it, and equally so when Evelyn Laye played it in London twelve years ago. On the other hand, one has engaged the spectacle of various German and French ladies who, if they were instrumental in launching so much as a single ship, would doubtless experience the same tragic result that was the portion of Buster Keaton in one of the old silent movie comedies.

It is nothing personally against the talented and gracious Jarmila that she is unable to suggest, even in so fancy-free an exhibit, the ravishingly lovely heroine. I do not, indeed, know of any actress operating in the local theatre who could, though there are amongst the lot some fair creatures. But even the fairest of them could not, I fear, manipulate me into the persuasion that she was of such lulu aspect that all Greece would swoon at the mere sight of her and that the very topless towers of Ilium would wobble at her approach.

There are those who magnanimously insist that the business of any theatregoer in such a juncture is to remit judgment and to accept as a heaven-shaking beauty any actress so designated by the producer. They point out, generous souls that they are, that, unless one was willing to do it in the past and in other directions, fully half the actress heroines of romantic drama would have made the plays take on the complexion of *Krausmeyer's Alley*. And they are eminently right, at least so far as a few of those plays have been concerned. *The Far-Away Princess,* for one, in its local productions demanded either that one accept the actress in the name rôle as an overpowering vision or put on one's coat and go home. But the average actress romantic heroine is less hard to swallow, since she is not presented as any such acme of men's dreams but more often only as the figment of a brief siesta. Anthony Hope's Flavia is not urged upon us as the most gorgeous creature who ever lived, nor is Justin McCarthy's Katherine de Vaucelles, nor is Daudet's and Fitch's Fannie Legrand, nor are any of those other memorable girls. But, all libretto or book joking aside, Helen is; and that is the way we willy-nilly have been born to regard her; and the request in the present instance is thus a bit too much.

Nor do the settings of Robert Edmond Jones contribute any more greatly to visual satisfaction. They miss the desired invention and whimsical loveliness; they are largely the sort of thing, somewhat simplified, that decorated the operetta stage in the far days of *The Sorcerer* and *The Princess of Trebizonde;* they have nothing of the delicacy and humor and charm of, say, Oliver Messel's for the London production hereinbefore mentioned. The costumes by Ladislas Czettel, furthermore, while attractive in color are minus any style, and the ballet slippers look as if they had seen long service in a track meet. And the ballet numbers, finally, are repetitious and, when not repetitious, silly, as in the case of the drunken debauch number which pictures less a pagan alcoholic spree than a lot of females sick at the stomach from too much oversweet circus pop.

La Belle Hélène, one of the theatre's most lingering and affectionate memories, was never like this.

EARTH JOURNEY. April 27, 1944

A fantastic comedy by Sheldon Davis. Produced to small attendance for a short engagement by the Blackfriars' Guild in the Blackfriars' Theatre.

Program

The Property Man		A Messenger	Jack Sherry
	Alexander Cooper	The Executioner	Leo Herbert
Chorus	Ian Maclaren	First Bearer	James Alexander
Shao Kung	Edward Steinmetz	Second Bearer	Hugh Thomas, Jr.
Cheng Wu Ti	Robert Hayward	Third Bearer	Howard Berland
Tai Wan	Christina Soulias	Fourth Bearer	Dennis McDonald
Tchang Lo	William Monsees	Assistant Property Man	
Tchi Fah	Carol Dunning		Michael Blair
Loy Din	Bernice Grant	Attendant Emperor	
Su Tong Po	John Rosene		John E. Montgomery
Li Chien	Elizabeth Hunt	Ladies of ⎧	Margaret McKenna
See Nan	Ann Donaldson	the Court ⎩	Catherine Campbell
Mei Fah Ling	Irene Parker		

SYNOPSIS: *First episode, the temple; second episode, the highway; third episode, the palace; fourth episode, the dawn.*

SINCE THE AUTHOR's previous contribution to the season was *Try And Get It* (*q. v.*) , one was to be pardoned for approaching this, his second, in a cold sweat. As it was sponsored by a Catholic organization, any fears that it might be as mucky as the earlier play were, of course, unwarranted. The quivers were reserved rather for its quality, and they were duly found to be not unwarranted.

On this occasion Mr. Davis has for a change bestirred himself in fantasy which is as clean as a whistle, but the whistle is unfortunately of a peanut-stand mellifluence. His story, based upon an old Chinese legend, concerns the stone idol of a prince brought to life by a wicked priest on condition that he murder the emperor and the crown princess whom the priest despises. The resuscitated prince, upon beholding the princess, falls in love with her and, after a series of adventures involving, among other things, lessons in benevolence to the hitherto selfish emperor, is again returned to stone by the priest for refusing to live up to the terms of his bargain. The staging follows the Chinese pattern: the hypothetically invisible property man and his assistants, the chorus who explains what is what about the action and the equally non-existent scenery, etc. The whole amounts generally to little more than a poor imitation of *The Yellow Jacket* and indicates once again that fantasy remains the privilege of dramatic poets and not the diversion of playwrights whose apparent forte consists in evolving lines like "Drag your fanny outa bed, Miss Vivienne; it's ten o'clock!"

A HIGHLAND FLING. April 28, 1944

A comedy fantasy by Margaret Curtis. Produced for early failure and withdrawn after 4 weeks by George Abbott in the Plymouth Theatre.

Program

Charlie MacKenzie, Former Laird of Cairn McGorum, a Ghost *Ralph Forbes*	Lila Graham *Marjorie Davies*
	Hamish Hamilton *John Robb*
Jeannie MacKenzie, Formerly His Wife, an Angel *Frances Reid*	Alicetrina MacLean *Gloria Hallward*
	Jamie MacTavish *John McQuade*
Sir Archibald MacKenzie *John Ireland*	Sandy MacGill *Nicholas Saunders*
The Lady of Shalott *Margaret Curtis*	The Reverend Douglas Stuart *St. Clair Bayfield*
Rabbie MacGregor *Karl Swenson*	Mrs. MacGill *Margaret Morrissey*
Lizzie MacGregor *Marguerite Clifton*	Mora MacTavish *Pax Walker*
	Ian *James McFadden*
Bessie MacGregor *Patti Brady*	Mrs. Ferguson *Margaret Thomas*
Malcolm Graham *Ivan Miller*	Mr. MacDonald *James Lane*

SYNOPSIS: Act I. Scene 1. *Outside the castle walls, a midsummer night.* Scene 2. *The next morning, Sunday.* Act II. Scene 1. *The bar at the "Rose and Thistle," early the same afternoon.* Scene 2. *Outside the castle walls, later the same day.* Act III. Scene 1. *The "Rose and Thistle," an hour or so later.* Scene 2. *Outside the castle walls, that night.*

The action of the play takes place some years ago in a remote little village nestling near the foot of Cairn McGorum in the mountains of Scotland.

W RITTEN by Miss Curtis as a vehicle for her sufficient acting talents and eventually securing the leading rôle for herself only, as she expressed it in a newspaper interview, at the point of a gun, this is an exceptional play from the hands of a novice. Combining originality, imagination and humor, it amounts in the aggregate to a refreshingly witty and winsome fantastic conceit. The staging by Mr. Abbott, adroit in its rough tavern comedy scenes, was, however, so like a tank assault in the matter of its moonlit mood in the scenes outside the walls of the ruined castle that it was small wonder the less deliberative reviewers were confused into attributing to the author the heaviness of treatment for which he was largely responsible. Mr. Abbott is clearly no man for cobwebs.

Although a ghost play, Miss Curtis' is far from being one of the conventional reassurance machines described in an earlier section. Its basic tone is rather that of something like Noel Coward's *Blithe Spirit* embroidered with flights in a J. M. Barrie direction. The hereafter is not depicted as a Methodist's dream of a million dollar production of the Grand Transformation scene in *Uncle Tom's Cabin* nor yet as a J. Hartley Manners version of the Heaven of Molnar's *Liliom* but, for any man given to a persistent admiration of earth's rare beauties and galvanizing pleasures, as not entirely desirable. One such man that was is the quondam Laird of Cairn McGorum, Miss Curtis' central character. Fond of the fleshpots in life, his ghost is barred from Heaven until he shall redeem his sins on earth by the conversion of a mortal as sinful as he. Full of hesitations and misgivings, since he has become smitten with a fair, if balmy, young girl whose childish faith makes him visible to her, but egged on by his still possessive wife, now an angel, with crafty hints that the girls Up There are very delectable creatures and lonesome, the ghost sets about reforming the countryside's worst libertine. And is at last duly on his way to the celestial kingdom.

Once there, however, he finds that things are not what they have been cracked up to be, and that existence does not even remotely compare with gala existence on earth. Glum and disconsolate, he is about to resign himself to his miserable lot when he is apprised that he is to be barred again, this time on a technicality, the technicality being the redeemed sinner's last moment irresistible pinching of a pretty barmaid's bottom. Relievedly returning to earth, the Laird's ghost again makes up to the fair young daftie but finds that a young man's warm kisses as against his cold own have alienated her love. Yet still he would remain in the beautiful and exciting thisness of this side of Paradise.

His wife, however, continues to dog him; and as the play
ends she swoops down from above and totes him, yelling
and protesting, up to the Heaven to which he doesn't want
to go.

The incidental byplay is often drolly delightful, and the
general imagination seldom falters. The weaknesses of the
play lie in the author's periodic lapses into such substitutes
for poetic expression as the routine allusions to moonlight,
purple mists, distant hills, and fragrant flowers; in an induction which is now and then labored; and in her intermittently obvious consciousness of the tenor of such plays
as are associated with the name of Barrie. But she has contrived nevertheless a quite remarkable play for a beginner:
one owning to an infinitely greater measure of genuine
fancy than we encounter in many plays by considerably
more experienced dramatists; one that gathers both Heaven
and Earth into a smiling intelligence; and one that, though
it may miss here and there and miss signally, is on the whole
much too valuable to a prosaic and needy theatre to have
been contemptuously dismissed by all save one of the reviewers theoretically entrusted with that theatre's finer
future.

PICK–UP GIRL. MAY 3, 1944

A play by Elsa Shelley. Produced to modest business by Michael Todd and members of his office staff in the 48th Street Theatre.

PROGRAM

JUDGE BENTLEY	William Harrigan	MR. BRILL	Bigelow Sayre
MISS PORTER	Doro Merande	POLICEMAN OWENS	Morty Martell
MRS. BUSCH	Edmonia Nolley	ELIZABETH COLLINS	Pamela Rivers
COURT CLERK	Douglas Keaton	JACKIE POLUMBO	Joe Johnson
DOOR ATTENDANT	William Foran	MISS RUSSELL	Dorothy Blackburn
MRS. COLLINS	Kathryn Grill	MR. COLLINS	Frank Tweddell
LARRY WEBSTER		RUBY LOCKWOOD	Toni Favor
	Zachary A. Charles	PETER MARTI	Marvin Forde
MRS. MARTI	Lili Valenty	JOAN	Lois Wheeler
ALEXANDER ELLIOTT		JEAN	Rosemary Rice
	Arthur Mayberry		

SYNOPSIS: *The action of the play takes place in a juvenile court. The time is late afternoon of a day in June.*

THE TITLE brings up memories of the old Al Woods artworks, and the play itself substantiates their accuracy. Harking back to the court-room melodramas of the period which were mainly devoted to the trials, for one reason or another, of fallen women, Miss Shelley has exercised herself to bring one such journalistically up-to-date by converting the ci-devant adult prostitute into a war-time juvenile delinquent. But, for all her recourse to the current newspaper headlines and excursions into the question of immediate social responsibility, her exhibit remains in critical essence little more than the time-honored stage machinery. Since it concerns itself with a subject close to the moment — the juvenile delinquency aforesaid — it has a deceptive surface air of vitality, yet it persists basically in being a feeble Living Tabloid version of the late Federal Theatre's Living Newspaper species of alarm, with the tabloid in question printed largely in Old Gothic, tinted.

The notion that the playwright deserves praise for not having sensationalized her materials, sponsored by many of the reviewers, is a bit difficult of assimilation. She pretends, true enough, to avoid any such sensationalism but it is there nonetheless, and with the port guns booming. If she avoids direct articulation of the four-letter words, she leads up to and away from them with such elaborate intimations and pseudo-hesitant and abashed precautions that they take on twice the suggestiveness and jolt. After a considerable mock show of reserve she drags, as theoretically painful to her sensitiveness, literal statements from witnesses on the stand as to the obscene scrawlings on her wayward heroine's apartment doors, and further is not averse to getting fornicators into bed together under alleviating cover of the judge's gentle interrogations. And when it is disclosed that her young delinquent has contracted syphilis, she resorts to the old dodge of moral indignation to extenuate such a sensationalism as Brieux himself in his *Damaged Goods* hardly exceeded, and incidentally becomes somewhat ridiculous in merchanting a melodramatic four-alarm fire that might quickly have been extinguished with a squirt of knowledge of the latterly discovered penicillin treatment.

As is more or less inevitable with such plays culled from the headlines, an intermittent force, despite the quality of the dramaturgy, oozes into the audience. But that dramaturgy in this instance is so lacking in skill that the spaces between lift and decline give to the whole the feel of a court-room reporter who has covered the story largely from the saloon next door. Nor are the author's efforts to relieve the grimness of her composition with touches of humor and sentiment any too fortunate. In the first case, the efforts take such shapes as the observation on the part of a court-room attendant devoted to the racing forms that a certain horse has been scratched, followed by an inquiry on the part of a female comic as to who scratched it. And in the second case, the injection of wistful love scenes between the little heroine and her loyal boy friend have the aspect of an arbitrary attempt to pretty up the otherwise sordid proceedings akin to incorporating a zither into "Frankie and Johnny." Finally, even if the body of her dramatic action were handled with thrice the present dexterity, her play would still be a poor one on the grounds of her extensive and prolonged moralizings from the bench, which provide the stubborn impression of a colored professor in a sporting house playing "Onward, Christian Soldiers," and which Ben Lindsey enunciated much more eloquently in much the same terms all of thirty years ago.

HICKORY STICK. May 8, 1944

A play by Frederick Stephani and Murray Burnett. Produced and withdrawn in the same week by Marjorie Ewing and Marie Louise Elkins in the Mansfield Theatre.

Program

Mary Donlan *Sarah Floyd*	Steven Ames *Richard Basehart*
Miss Jastrombowski	Samuel Berg *Ray Fry*
Wanda Sponder	Lionel Warner *Albert Popwell*
Peter Jastrombowski *Bill Hunt*	Calliope Oliver
Eugene Walsh *Lawrence Fletcher*	*Violet J. Kennedy*
Rita Pessolano *Adrienne Bayan*	George Uhorchak *Johnny Croce*
John MacLemore *Jeff Brown*	Paula Taliaferro
Tony Pessolano *Vito Christi*	*Lorraine Pressler*
Mrs. Bettina Pessolano	Grace Umbdenstock *Janet Dowd*
Frieda Altman	Gladys Steele *Frances Thaddeus*
Karen Lorimer *Adrienne Marden*	Elizabeth O'Hare *Peggy Wynne*
Patrick MacLemore, Sr.	Sophie Novak *Marjorie Milliard*
Farrell Pelly	Helen Orth *Celia Babcock*
James Kirkland *Steve Cochran*	Lewis Rainey *Ross Matthew*
Frank Antonucci *Danny Leone*	Joe Pessolano *Dehl Berti*

SYNOPSIS: Act I. Scene 1. *Guidance office.* Scene 2. *Kirkland's classroom. A few minutes later.* Act II. Scene 1. *Guidance office. Three months later.* Scene 2. *Kirkland's classroom. The next day.* Act III. *Kirkland's classroom. Five minutes later.*

THE CURTAIN DESCENDED upon the year with what is known in theatrical parlance as a school play. The list of these plays of adolescent school life is a long one, and ranges all the way from such fair specimens as *Young Woodley* and *Little Ol' Boy* to such lesser ones as *Remember the Day* and *Honor Bright* and still lesser ones as *Bright Boy, What a Life!,* and *Brother Rat.* The appeal which they have to playwrights is understandable, since it is an uncommon practitioner of belles lettres who doesn't esteem himself as being especially gifted by nature in the delineation of the young of the species, among which he himself as an erstwhile child figures with an enormous recollective cunning.

The majority of the plays fall roughly into three grooves. The first contains the plays of an auld-lang-syne flavor which in a mixture of sentiment and humor retail in terms of the present the remembered idiosyncrasies of the youthful classroom and its mentors. The second contains the plays of an outright farcical nature which are generally built around an athletic contest, a school show, or something of the sort and which are in essence little more than old-time George V. Hobart musical farces minus the music and with boys and girls cast in the adult rôles. The third contains the plays of more serious intent which are laid in reform schools, military schools, preparatory schools, or more or less eccentric public schools and which go in for sociological implications and other such more recherché thematic exercises. *Hickory Stick* falls into the last-named catalogue.

The idea of the play, though it has already in one form or another seen doughty service, still retains some theatrical validity. The rehabilitation of maladjusted youth is a theme that can stand an amount of repetition, if the playwrights are of any ability. It is, however, the misfortune of the present twain that they are not. They may know the superficials of the theme from a measure of observational experience but they reveal themselves otherwise as just a pair of goldfish swimming aimlessly around on top of the sociological bowl. What is more, they are such extremely poor playwrights that their poverty in that direction emphasizes doubly the indigence of their general appreciation of the subject.

In the first place, their exhibit is not one play but two plays, each quite different from the other and both bad. On the one hand, there is the play about the vocational school itself and the problem, largely physical, of handling its ruffian pupils. On the other, there is the play about a psychopathic case involving a youth tragically bedevilled by the philosophies of Schopenhauer and Nietzsche and the effort to handle it psychologically and with purely mental discipline. The conflict between the two is completely ruinous to whatever it was that the playwrights had mainly in purpose and suggests that one of them, a Hollywood movie scenario writer, had his mind set upon a play patterned after one of the *Big House* and reform school screen epics while the other, a comparative illuminatus, had his in turn set upon a play patterned after Wedekind's *Awakening of Spring.*

As an inkling of their combined talents, consider their introductory scene laid in the guidance office of the school. This scene, which runs for twenty-two minutes and which is supposed to serve as an induction to their profound thesis, consists largely of an oafish, burlesque flirtation between a male teacher in the school and a fluttery old maid worker in the office. The flirtation business is intermittently interrupted by the entrance of an assortment of hoodlum pupils, all of them furiously chewing gum. The male pupils comport themselves in the accepted tough-mug manner, throwing out their sweatered chests, talking out of the corners of their mouths, and whenever referring to themselves pointing at themselves with in-turned thumbs. Their characterization is completed by vocabularies that consist almost entirely of such words as *crap, guts, can, goose, hell,* and *bastard.* The distaff pupils, represented by a swaggering, leggy, brunette symbol, are characterized with equal brilliance by a vocabulary confined for the most part to *yeah, Jeez, stinks,* and *lousy.* The hard-boiled literary air is subsequently furthered in a general direction by sundry allusions on the part of various characters to the bladder and kidneys, to biological functions and to that room in the schoolhouse where they may be relieved. The curtain to the scene comes down, after a brief colloquy between a newly arrived teacher and an older one, on the fluttery old maid's pronouncement that the main thing in life is "always to maintain your dignity" and the coincidental old vaudeville comic business of being poked in the rear by a passing boy toting a window-stick.

What follows is no noticeable improvement and offers, among other choice flora, some highly exotic blooms. The class in English instruction, for example, seems to be chiefly concerned with the identification of O. Henry's real name.

The pupil who prefers to read Schopenhauer and Nietzsche to joining in any such kindergarten quiz is viewed by the teacher as a dubious fellow, and as something of an outcast. The class throughout the forty minute act occupies itself mostly in staging a schoolroom version of Olsen and Johnson's *Hellzapoppin* with an obbligato of *Sons O' Fun,* and the humor throughout is derived from its numerous excursions to the toilet, followed on its return by facetiæ connected with the visit. A gangster fugitive from the police is further introduced, with something of the dramaturgical reasonableness of introducing Dutch Schultz into *Othello,* merely to plant a revolver with which one pupil may later shoot another. The heroic teacher whose mission is to save and redeem the ill-adjusted adolescents is caused meekly to resign from his crusade at the first sign of trouble. There is miscellaneous talk of "good lays" and the like. There is a long, moist passage in which a pupil reads the last letter of his brother who has been killed in battle at Guadalcanal, and the consoling bequest to him on the part of his brother's buddy of the deceased's campaign ribbon. There is the episode in which the comic Irish father berates his son for using profanity and in the process himself resorts to it. There is, in conclusion, the faint suggestion of the theme of *Tomorrow The World* multiplied by twenty and written by the author of *Pick-Up Girl* on one of her off days.

* * *

And then came the interregnum, and the summer shows.

Especially Interesting Performances

THE STUDENT PRINCE
Barbara Scully

THOSE ENDEARING
YOUNG CHARMS
Virginia Gilmore

THE MERRY WIDOW
Marta Eggerth
Milada Mladova

MURDER WITHOUT
CRIME
Henry Daniell

PORGY AND BESS
Todd Duncan

A NEW LIFE
Betty Field

ONE TOUCH OF VENUS
Mary Martin

ANOTHER LOVE
STORY
Arthur Margetson

OTHELLO
José Ferrer

MANHATTAN
NOCTURNE
Terry Holmes
Eddie Dowling

OUTRAGEOUS
FORTUNE
Elsie Ferguson
Frederic Tozere
Brent Sargent

THE INNOCENT
VOYAGE
Oscar Homolka
Herbert Berghof

A CONNECTICUT
YANKEE
Vera-Ellen

LOVERS AND FRIENDS
Katharine Cornell (albeit largely standardized)

CARMEN JONES
Muriel Smith
Carlotta Franzell
Luther Saxon

THE VOICE OF THE
TURTLE
Margaret Sullavan
Elliott Nugent
Audrey Christie

THE PATRIOTS
Cecil Humphreys
Julie Haydon

LISTEN, PROFESSOR!
Susan Robinson

SOUTH PACIFIC
Wini Johnson

STORM OPERATION
Cy Howard

SUDS IN YOUR EYE
Jane Darwell
Kasia Orzazewski
Brenda Forbes

328

MEXICAN HAYRIDE
Bobby Clark
June Havoc

DECISION
Raymond Greenleaf
Howard Smith

THANK YOU, SVOBODA
Adrienne Gessner

BRIGHT BOY
Donald Buka
Charles Bowlby

JACOBOWSKY AND
THE COLONEL
Oscar Karlweis
Louis Calhern

CHICKEN EVERY
SUNDAY
Rhys Williams
Mary Philips
Katherine Squire

FOLLOW THE GIRLS
Gertrude Niesen

THE SEARCHING
WIND
Arnold Korff

SHEPPEY
Edmund Gwenn
Barbara Everest
Doris Patston

ALLAH BE PRAISED!
Milada Mladova

HELEN GOES TO TROY
Ernest Truex

A HIGHLAND FLING
Margaret Curtis
Patti Brady

PICK–UP GIRL
Kathryn Grill
Pamela Rivers
Marvin Forde

Index of Plays

All For All, 73
Allah Be Praised!, 305
Another Love Story, 83
Army Play-By-Play, The, 18
Arsenic and Old Lace, 169
Artists and Models, 119

Blossom Time, 50
Bobino, 282
Bright Boy, 258
Bright Lights of 1944, 67
" — But Not Goodbye," 291

Career, 110
Career Angel, 136
Carmen Jones, 150
Caukey, 242
Chauve-Souris 1943, 37
Cherry Orchard, The, 221
Chicken Every Sunday, 278
Connecticut Yankee, A, 133
Cox and Box, 240

Decision, 232
Doctors Disagree, 185
Duke in Darkness, The, 218

Early To Bed, 7
Earth Journey, 314

Familiar Pattern, 48
Family Carnovsky, The, 88
Feathers in a Gale, 176
Follow the Girls, 286

Get Away, Old Man, 143
Golden Land, The, 89
Gondoliers, The, 240
Goodbye Again, 114

Hairpin Harmony, 75
Helen Goes To Troy, 310
Hickory Stick, 322
Highland Fling, A, 316
House In Paris, The, 268

I'll Take the High Road, 122
Innocent Voyage, The, 128
Iolanthe, 240

Jackpot, 216
Jacobowsky and the Colonel, 263

Lady, Behave!, 131
Land of Fame, 70
Laugh Time, 53
Listen, Professor!, 179
Lovers and Friends, 147
Lucky Days, 89

Manhattan Nocturne, 100
Merry Widow, The, 29
Mexican Hayride, 228
Mikado, The, 240
Mrs. January and Mr. Ex, 271
Mrs. Kimball Presents, 249
Murder Without Crime, 41
My Dear Public, 55

Naked Genius, The, 94
Nathan the Wise, 248
New Life, A, 63

One Touch of Venus, 77
Only the Heart, 275
Othello, 90
Our Town, 205
Outrageous Fortune, 115
Over 21, 193

Patience, 240
Patriots, The, 174
Peepshow, 234
Petrified Forest, The, 112
Pick-Up Girl, 319
Pillar to Post, 167
Pinafore, H. M. S., 240
Pirates of Penzance, The, 240
Porgy and Bess, 61
Pretty Little Parlor, 300
Public Relations, 283

Ramshackle Inn, 197
Right Next to Broadway, 246
Ruddigore, 240
Run, Little Chillun, 39

Searching Wind, The, 295
Sheppey, 302

Slightly Married, 97
Snark was a Boojum, The, 44
South Pacific, 189
Stars on Ice, 15
Storm Operation, 207
Student Prince, The, 3
Suds in Your Eye, 213
Susan and God, 171

Take It As It Comes, 237
Thank You, Svoboda, 251
Those Endearing Young Charms, 5
Tobacco Road, 52
Trial By Jury, 240
Try And Get It, 21
Two Mrs. Carrolls, The, 24

Vagabond King, The, 16
Victory Belles, 102
Voice of the Turtle, The, 158

Wallflower, 226
War President, 308
What's Up, 124
Winged Victory, 138
World's Full of Girls, The, 155

Yeomen of the Guard, The, 240

Index of Authors and Composers

Afinogenov, Alexander, 179
Akins, Zoë, 271
Anderson, Maxwell, 207
Anstey, F., 78
Anthony, Norman, 67

Baker, Herbert, 310
Batson, George, 197
Behrman, S. N., 263
Bein, Albert, 70
Bein, Mary, 70
Bell, Thomas, 155
Bennett, Robert Russell, 150
Bergersen, Baldwin, 305
Berns, Julie, 89
Bizet, Georges, 150
Bolton, Guy, 216, 286
Boruff, John, 258
Bowen, Elizabeth, 268
Bruce, Norman, 73
Bruckner, Ferdinand, 248
Burnett, Murray, 322

Caesar, Irving, 55
Caldwell, Erskine, 52
Charig, Phil, 119, 286
Chekhov, Anton, 221
Chodorov, Edward, 5, 232
Crothers, Rachel, 171
Curtis, Margaret, 316

David, Mack, 67
Davis, Eddie, 286
Davis, Owen, 44

Davis, Sheldon, 21, 314
Denham, Reginald, 226
Dietz, Howard, 216
Donnelly, Dorothy, 3, 50
Duke, Vernon, 216

Epstein, Philip G., 278
Epstein, Julius J., 278
Eunson, Dale, 283

Feilbert, Edward Allen, 268
Fields, Dorothy, 228
Fields, Herbert, 133, 228
Foote, Horton, 275
Förster-Meyer, 3
Foster, Claiborne, 300
Franken, Rose, 115, 185
Friml, Rudolf, 16

Gershwin, George, 61
Gershwin, Ira, 61
Gerstenberg, Alice, 102
Geto, Alfred D., 18
Gilbert, W. S., 240
Golden, Alfred L., 131
Gordon, Ruth, 193
Gottesfeld, Charles, 55
Green, E. Mawby, 268

Haight, George, 114
Halévy, Ludovic, 150
Hamilton, Patrick, 218
Hammerstein, Oscar II, 150

Hart, Lorenz, 133
Hart, Moss, 138
Hellman, Lillian, 295
Heyward, Dorothy, 189
Heyward, Du Bose, 61
Hoffman, Aaron, 73
Hooker, Brian, 16
Hughes, Richard, 128

Jamerson, Pauline, 176
Janney, Russell, 16
Johnson, Hall, 39
Johnson, Nunnally, 155

Kasznar, Kurt S., 18
Kauffman, Stanley, 282
Kesselring, Joseph, 169
Kingsley, Sidney, 174
Kirby, Nan, 110
Kirkland, Jack, 52, 213
Kohn, Rose Simon, 167
Korngold, Erich Wolfgang, 310
Kraft, H. S., 251

Lasswell, Mary, 213
Laurence, Reginald, 176
Lee, Gypsy Rose, 94
Lehar, Franz, 29
Leon, Victor, 29
Lerner, Alan J., 124
Lerner, Sam, 55
Leslie, Aleen, 97
Lessing, Gotthold Ephraim, 248
Lipson, David S., 48
Livingston, Jerry, 67
Loewe, Frederick, 124
Lonsdale, Frederick, 83
Luther, Frank, 119

Marion, George, Jr., 7, 305
Marker, Leonard, 282
Marks, Gerald, 55
Maugham, W. Somerset, 302
McGlynn, Thomas, 242
Meehan, John, Jr., 310
Meilhac, Henri, 150
Mérimée, Prosper, 150

Morris, E. B., 237
Murray, Gerard M., 136

Nash, Ogden, 77
Neiman, Irving G., 18
Nelson, Ralph, 18

O'Dea, John B., 18
Offenbach, Jacques, 310
Orlob, Harold, 75
Orr, Mary, 226
Osborn, Paul, 128

Paley, Paul K., 246
Pascal, Ernest, 234
Pascal, Milton, 119, 286
Paver, Charles, 70
Pen, John, 251
Perelman, S. J., 77
Phillips, Peggy, 179
Pierson, Arthur, 124
Porter, Cole, 228
Price, Alonzo, 249
Prumbs, Lucille S., 122

Reichert, H., 50
Reinhardt, Gottfried, 310
Rice, Elmer, 63
Rigsby, Howard, 189
Roberts, Ben, 29, 216
Rodgers, Richard, 133
Romberg, Sigmund, 3, 50
Ross, Don, 119

Saroyan, William, 143
Schubert, Franz, 50
Scott, Allan, 114
Seaton, George, 291
Secunda, Sholem, 89
Shakespeare, William, 90
Shapiro, Dan, 119, 286
Shattuck, Mrs. Richard, 44
Sheldon, Sidney, 29, 216
Shelley, Elsa, 319

Sherman, Charles, 67
Sherman, Nat, 308
Sherwood, Robert E., 112
Siegel, William, 89
Singer, I. J., 88
Smith, Dodie, 147
Stein, Leo, 29
Stephani, Frederick, 322
Sullivan, Arthur, 240

Taylor, Rosemary, 278
Thompson, Fred, 286
Thompson, J. Lee, 41
Twain, Mark, 133

Vale, Martin, 24
Van Druten, John, 158

Walker, Don, 305
Waller, Thomas, 7
Walling, Roy, 100
Walters, Lou, 119
Weill, Kurt, 77
Werfel, Franz, 263
Wilder, Thornton, 205
Willner, A. M., 50
Witty, Don, 75

Yellin, Gleb, 37

A NOTE ON THE TYPE USED IN THIS BOOK

The text of this book has been set on the Linotype in a type-face called "Baskerville." The face is a facsimile reproduction of types cast from molds made for John Baskerville (1706–1775) from his designs. The punches for the revived Linotype Baskerville were cut under the supervision of the English printer George W. Jones.

John Baskerville's original face was one of the forerunners of the type-style known as "modern face" to printers: a "modern" of the period A.D. 1800.

The typographic scheme and the binding design are by W. A. Dwiggins. The book was composed, printed, and bound by The Plimpton Press, Norwood, Massachusetts.